The Duty to Secure

T0386564

States have social contractual duties to provide security for their people, but just what measures are morally required? Should states be obligated to address real/objective existential threats via securitization (i.e., threat-specific, often liberty defying, rigorously enforced, and sometimes forcible emergency measures)? Do non-state actors or international organizations also have a moral duty to securitize, and if so, why, when, and to whom? Would such duties pertain only to populations in one's own state or also to people in other states? *The Duty to Secure* offers answers to these and other questions, setting out a rigorous theory of morally mandatory securitization that examines the duties of actors at all levels of analysis. Morally mandatory securitization has practical implications, including for NATO's Article 5 and the responsibility to protect norm, both of which currently take account of only a narrow range of threats.

RITA FLOYD is Associate Professor of Conflict and Security in the Department of Political Science and International Studies at the University of Birmingham. This is her third monograph, following on from *Security and the Environment: Securitisation Theory and US Environmental Security Policy* (Cambridge University Press, 2010) and *The Morality of Security: A Theory of Just Securitization* (Cambridge University Press, 2019).

The Duty to Secure

From Just to Mandatory Securitization

RITA FLOYD

University of Birmingham

CAMBRIDGE
UNIVERSITY PRESS

Shaftesbury Road, Cambridge CB2 8EA, United Kingdom

One Liberty Plaza, 20th Floor, New York, NY 10006, USA

477 Williamstown Road, Port Melbourne, VIC 3207, Australia

314–321, 3rd Floor, Plot 3, Splendor Forum, Jasola District Centre,
New Delhi – 110025, India

103 Penang Road, #05–06/07, Visioncrest Commercial, Singapore 238467

Cambridge University Press is part of Cambridge University Press & Assessment,
a department of the University of Cambridge.

We share the University's mission to contribute to society through the pursuit of
education, learning and research at the highest international levels of excellence.

www.cambridge.org
Information on this title: www.cambridge.org/9781009468954

DOI: 10.1017/9781009468947

First published 2024

A catalogue record for this publication is available from the British Library

A Cataloging-in-Publication data record for this book is available from the
Library of Congress

ISBN 978-1-009-46895-4 Hardback
ISBN 978-1-009-46893-0 Paperback

Cambridge University Press & Assessment has no responsibility for the persistence
or accuracy of URLs for external or third-party internet websites referred to in this
publication and does not guarantee that any content on such websites is, or will
remain, accurate or appropriate.

To ARF, CSF, and the HB; *family and my best friends*

Contents

Acknowledgements

The bulk of this book was written during 2019 when I was in the extremely privileged position of being an Independent Social Research Foundation (ISRF) mid-career fellow, with my project Emergency Politics: Security, Threats, and the Duties of States. This afforded me the time to think and write entirely freed from all teaching and administrative duties. I can't thank the ISRF enough for this support. I would also like to thank the research support team at the University of Birmingham (UoB) who had input into the grant application, especially Alana Tomlin.

This book was written in my home office and in the Costa Coffee shop in Bishop's Cleeve, usually sitting opposite my political theory husband, Jonathan Floyd, who was working on his own projects but who was mostly (yes, I admit I can be like a dog with a bone) happy to have his brains picked on issues concerning this book. Turns out, it is so much easier to straddle the divide between International Relations and political theory when one is married to a political theorist. Thank you, HB; so glad you're on my team! Also, thanks for taking care of the home schooling during COVID.

I am grateful to John Haslam for giving me a chance to rewrite parts of the book following a first round of reviews. I am thankful to the reviewers for pressing me hard on all the right points. This book is much better for it!

Many people have helped me with parts of this project, but my single biggest gratitude goes to Jonathan Parry, formerly of UoB but now based in the Department of Philosophy, Logic, and Scientific Method at the London School of Economics and Political Science. Time and again Jonathan has pointed me to relevant literature, discussed key points, and alleviated my worries that things don't hang together. I owe him big time!

Several friends, colleagues, and peers have read parts or all the book, at various stages. I should say that I did not know many of the people listed below prior to asking them to read parts of this book, and I was amazed for the generosity with their time. I am grateful to Chris Brown, Tony Lang, and James Pattison for reading all the manuscript, and for their comments and encouragement, and to Ian Paterson, Matt McDonald, and Cian O'Driscoll for reading Introduction and Chapter 1. I am indebted to Jeff McMahan for reading a draft of Chapter 1 and putting me on the more logical path on one or two key issues. Thanks to David Miller for reading and commenting on Chapter 2 and subsequently discussing the book with me in person. I am grateful to Aiden Hehir for reading and commenting in detail on Chapter 5 and a previous Chapter 6 (that did not make it into the final book). I am tremendously grateful to Tom Peak for his help and advice on the rewritten (following an R&R (revise and resubmit)) Chapter 5.

My thanks to Nora Grigore and Danny Frederick for discussing various tedious aspects of moral philosophy with me via email. Huge thanks to Stuart Croft for his unwavering support and especially for helping me brainstorm responses to reviewers' comments. Finally, my thanks to Barry Buzan for moral support.

At Birmingham I am indebted to my colleague Mark Webber, who is always happy to talk about my work and who helped me with all things NATO. I am also grateful to Adam Quinn, Asaf Siniver, Marco Viera, Stefan Wolff, and Patrick Porter for their comments at the internal Security Studies Brown Bag and/or on other occasions. A big shout out also to my Muirhead Tower third-floor east-wing gang Sotirios Zartaloudis, Peter Kerr, and Emma Foster for always having a laugh.

I'd like to thank my postgraduate students on G22 Security Studies and select undergraduate students for discussing just and mandatory securitization with me. I am especially grateful to my former student Daniel Jensen, who talked about his experiences as a solider on NATO-led missions.

I am grateful to my mother-in-law, Ann Floyd, for her interest and support of my work (including looking after the kids in the holidays) and who has an uncanny knack for asking hard questions.

Parts of this work have been presented at various forums over the past few years. I am grateful to audiences for their comments and suggestions during the following talks: 'Why mandatory securitization can save R2P', paper presented at the ISA 2023 Annual Convention, Montreal, Canada; 'Morally mandatory securitization: Implications for the responsibility to protect', MOMO Philosophischer Arbeitskreis,

Berlin, 18 July 2022 (here especially to Wolfgang Sohst); 'Just securitization, what is it? And why does it matter?', Central European University, Vienna, 22 April 2022 (here especially to Thomas Fetzer); 'The morality of security', invited talk at Virtual CASIS West Coast Security Conference: Critical Security, Vancouver, Canada, 22–26 November 2021; 'Securitization and just securitization', invited talk at Rethinking European Security, Chatham House, 24 November 2021; 'Just securitization and migration', invited talk at roundtable discussion The Securitization of Migrants and Ethnic Minorities: Current Issues and Debates for the SECUREU, University of Barcelona, 25 November 2021; 'The ethics of security: Reflections on just and mandatory securitization', University of Glasgow, 31 October 2019; 'A duty to be violent, or to violate', ISRF Annual Workshop, St Hugh's College, University of Oxford, October 2019; and, last but not least, 'Mandatory securitization, outcome responsibility and victimhood', paper presented at British International Studies Association Annual Conference, London, June 2019 (here especially to Karin Fierke).

Finally, I would like to thank my wonderful children, Arwen and Corin, for their unconditional love, for forcing me into a non-work headspace, and for all the fun and cuddles. My books are great (I hope), but you two are the best things I've ever done.

Glossary

This book establishes and works with a specific terminology. Some of this terminology was developed in my 2019 book, and some of it is new to this book. Terms are explained when first encountered; however, I think this one-stop shop is useful to the reader.

Agent-benefitting securitization refers to a securitization where the primary beneficiary of securitization is the securitizing actor.

Agent-caused threats refers to a threat that is a consequence of an agent's behaviour but is not intended by that agent. I differentiate between two sub-types of agent-caused threats: (1) by obliviousness, that is, when people do not realize that their (combined) actions are potentially threatening to other entities; and (2) by harmful neglect, that is, when relevant agents fail to protect against foreseeable harmful events/consequences.

Agent-intended threats refers to a threat that is intentionally levelled at another actor, order, or entity.

Agent-lacking threats refers to a threat that does not originate from human agents (e.g., a truly natural disaster, a vector-borne disease).

Ameliorated moderate last resort an interpretation of last resort, whereby last resort is satisfied when plausible and less harmful options have been tried at least once and failed to satisfy just cause.

Audiences refers to the addressee of the securitizing move; ergo the referent object in need of protection and/or the agent and source of the threat being warned off.

Executor of securitization refers to security professionals, for example, police, border guards, and employees of private security firms enforcing security policy. In non-state securitization, divisions are less applicable and executors are (likely to be) the same as securitizing actors.

Functional actors refers to individuals and groups who veto/endorse securitizations in which they are not the referent object of securitization or the threatener. In short, these actors contest/sanction securitization on behalf of others. As such they are functionally distinct from audiences-as-addressees of securitizing speech acts.

Just reason prescribes the reason when securitization is morally permissible; in Just Securitization Theory, this is the presence of an objective existential threat.

Just referent object designates that a referent object (i.e., the entity in need of protection) is entitled to self-defence or eligible to defensive assistance only if it is morally justifiable and specifies that moral justifiability is tied to the satisfaction of basic human needs.

Just securitization refers to a securitization that is morally permissible (justified) but not morally obligatory.

Mandatory other-securitization by consent refers to situations when just referent objects have either requested help, or acquiesced to the offer of rescue, including, when necessary, via securitization.

Mandatory other-securitization without consent can take one of two forms: (1) would-be securitizing actors do not have the consent of the host state for the rescue/intervention; (2) the host state (i.e., the government) has consented to other-securitization but (part of) the beneficiary (the population) has not.

Mandatory securitization refers to the moral duty or obligation to use exceptional measures in self- and other-defence from intended and intent-lacking threats. In this book, I also use the term 'mandatory securitization' as a shorthand to refer to the – here developed – wider theory of mandatory securitization.

Must cause is the point when securitization is morally obligatory as opposed to morally permissible and hence optional.

Primary-duty bearer is the actor with the primary moral obligation to other-securitize.

Referent object benefitting securitization refers to a securitization where the primary beneficiary is the referent object identified as existentially threatened by the securitizing actor.

Securitization refers to the use of issue-dependent extraordinary emergency measures, usually coupled with a threat articulation. Parallel to self- and other-defence, I differentiate between self-securitization and other-securitization.

Securitization against refers to defence via extraordinary security measures short of war against a threat (verb form: e.g., *securitize against* terrorism).

Securitization of refers to the defence of a referent object via extraordinary security measures short of war (verb form: e.g., *securitize* outsiders).

Securitization pre-emptor an actor who seeks to pre-empt securitization by discouraging would-be securitizing actors from initiating securitization.

Securitization requester an actor who seeks to convince more powerful/ strategically positioned actors of the need to securitize.

Securitizing actor the agent whose relevant behavioural change constitutes securitization or who is in a position of power over other agents who can execute relevant measures.

Securitizing move generally speaking, the identification of an existential threat; in Just Securitization Theory, relevant securitizing moves are those by securitizing actors, which amount to either a warning to agents at the source of the threat and/or promises of protection to referent objects.

Abbreviations

AIDS	Autoimmune Deficiency Syndrome
ASEAN	Association of Southeast Asian Nations
AU	African Union
AWACS	Airborne Warning and Control System
BBC	British Broadcasting Service
EU	European Union
GDP	Gross Domestic Product
HIV	Human Immunodeficiency Virus
ICISS	International Commission on Intervention and State Sovereignty
INGO	International Non-governmental Organization
IPCC	Intergovernmental Panel on Climate Change
IR	International Relations
JST	Just Securitization Theory
MERCOSUR	Southern Common Market
NATO	North Atlantic Treaty Organization
NGO	Non-governmental Organization
OSCE	Organization for Security and Co-operation in Europe
PESCO	Permanent Structured Cooperation
PMSC	Private Military Security Company
RtoP or R2P	Responsibility to protect
SANFFA	Security: A New Framework for Analysis
TPIM	Terrorism Prevention and Investigation Measures
UK	United Kingdom
UN	United Nations
UNFCC	United Nations Framework Convention on Climate Change
UNSC	United Nations Security Council
USA	United States of America
WHO	World Health Organization

Introduction

I.1 Purpose of This Book

Terrorism, climate change, organized crime, immigration, state failure, fake news, nuclear proliferation, infectious diseases, natural disasters, anti-microbial resistance, cyber threats, the list of real or perceived security threats, are seemingly endless. Rhetorically at least all these issues (and many others besides) have – at one point in time – been elevated to security threat status to all manner of 'referent objects', including states, regions, group identity, individuals, and even non-human entities (e.g., the biosphere, different animals, and plant species) (Buzan et al., 1998). The rationale for the increase in security language is usually the hope that security threat status will translate into an issue that is addressed quickly and efficiently by relevant power holders. After all, security pertains to survival and as such it commands more urgent action than other negative states of being (notably, inequality, injustice) (Buzan et al., 1998: 39).

The hope that the link to security will deliver the desired result is not unfounded; after all, states are *obligated* to provide security for people living within that state (cf. Chapter 2, Section 2.2; Chapter 5, Section 5.4). But are states and other actors morally obligated to address real/objective security threats via *securitization*? which is to say by using threat-specific, often liberty defying, rigorously enforced, and sometimes forcible emergency measures to address a threat, for example, mass surveillance, limited military action, and forced restrictions on freedom of movement. The answer to this question is not straightforward. Thus, we know that securitization does not necessarily lead to greater security as a state of being,[1] and that security interests' conflict. During the writing of this section (April 2020) for example, I – along with millions of other Britons – am in lockdown because of the

---

[1] The term is Herington's 2015: 29–32.

UK government's response to the coronavirus crisis – a clear example of securitization. While this measure appears to ensure health security (directly by slowing down infections and indirectly by not overburdening the National Health Service), the economy is in freefall, with businesses big and small faced with great economic insecurity.

By contrast, we also know that provided several stringent criteria (including just cause, right intention, and proportionality) are satisfied, securitization can be morally permissible (just) (Floyd, 2019a; Wolfendale, 2022; Polko and Ratajczak, 2021; Makahamadze and Sibanda, 2021; Dimari and Pakadakis, 2022, Thumfart, 2022). And from just securitization it is but a small step to contemplate whether sometimes securitization is not merely morally permissible and hence optional, but morally required, or else mandatory.[2] Further impetus is given to this when we consider that some threats (at a minimum, an incurable and deadly infectious disease affecting *all* people equally) seem to be so significant that they *require* nothing short of a securitizing response because the alternative of not acting in this way has more harmful consequences.

Moreover, states already have a social contractual duty to ensure citizens' security (e.g., Sorell, 2013, N. Lazar, 2009). What is more, the condition of morally mandatory securitization already extends beyond the borders of nation-states also to outsiders, albeit on a very limited number of issues. Notably, as part of the responsibility to protect (RtoP), unaddressed atrocity crimes within sovereign states already require the international community to protect affected individuals from genocide, crimes against humanity, war crimes, or ethnic cleansing everywhere (cf. Chapter 5; see also Glanville, 2021: 7), where necessary with a range of securitizing measures and, in some cases, even with war.[3] Unlike with states, where there is a contractual requirement to secure people within the state (albeit not via securitization), here the

---

[2] I use the word mandatory not in a legal sense, but rather in the way Cécile Fabre does in her work on mandatory rescue killings, where she considers the existence of 'a moral duty to kill in defence of another' (Fabre, 2007: 363).

[3] I am not suggesting that these crimes *require* that the international community takes military intervention; instead – in accordance with paragraph 139 of the 2005 World Summit outcome document – they require the UNSC to act using means at its disposal, some of these are exceptional in the relevant sense. The wording of ¶139 is as follows: 'The international community, through the United Nations, also has the responsibility to use appropriate diplomatic, humanitarian and other peaceful means, in accordance with Chapters VI and VIII of the Charter, to help protect populations from genocide, war crimes,

moral duty to intervene rests on 'the fundamental moral premise that human suffering ought to be tackled' (Pattison, 2010: 19), which is based on the principle of the moral equality of people.

Just Securitization Theory (JST), which, in this capitalized form refers to my version of a theory of just securitization as developed in my 2019 book *The Morality of Security: A Theory of just securitization*, rests like practically all secular, moral theories on the moral equality of people. Beyond 'a requirement of equal treatment' the moral equality of people also includes – at a minimum – a general, but not an assigned, duty to enable people to live minimally decent lives (Miller, 2007: 28).[4] Taken together, we can say that there exists a prima facie case for a theory of morally mandatory securitization to complement a theory of morally permissible securitization. The development of such a theory is the objective of this book. As part of this, I will trace existing commitments that are in line with morally mandatory securitization; nevertheless, the theory here developed is overtly normative. It is 'a theory that states standards, values, or concrete proposals that involve criticism of present arrangements and thus calls for change in order to create a better future' (Castree et al., 2013: 349).

Three interrelated principal research questions inform the analysis:

(1) In what circumstances is securitization morally required?
(2) Who, or what kinds of actor, are morally required to securitize, and to what referent objects?
(3) On what grounds are different types of actors required to undertake self- or other-securitization?

Several secondary research questions are also important, including: Can unjust actors be morally required to securitize or is this the prerogative and responsibility of just actors only? Is there a pro tanto[5]

---

ethnic cleansing and crimes against humanity'. To be sure the duty entailed in RtoP is not a legal duty, but a moral duty. Jennifer Welsh explains: 'The text agreed to in 2005 does not, in itself, establish any new legal obligations, but rather authoritatively interprets states' *existing obligations* to prevent and respond to atrocity crimes and adds a political injunction for them to implement what they have already agreed to (Welsh, 2019: 56, emphasis added; see also Glanville, 2021: 7).

[4] This is the moral minimum; cosmopolitan scholars believe that more is owed (see below).

[5] In contrast to an overriding obligation, a *pro tanto* duty is a duty that can be overridden by other moral considerations.

obligation to securitize simply when securitization is morally permissible? What, if any, factors, or concerns can override the pro tanto obligation to securitize? In cases where several actors have a pro tanto obligation to securitize, who is the primary duty-bearer, and why? And who must act when designated primary duty-bearers fail?

I.2 Place in the Literature and Value Added

My interest in mandatory securitization grows out of my previous work on morally permissible securitization. It is my ambition to build up a subfield of 'just securitization studies', where scholars develop, refine, and challenge principles of just securitization with a view to positively influence security practice. Put differently, JST offers emancipation from 'poor security practice towards a more just and enlightened security practice' (Floyd, 2022: 279).[6]

Just securitization studies are ultimately incomplete without a corresponding theory of the moral obligation to securitize (Floyd, 2019a: 210–211; 2016b). Notably while my JST aims to enable scholars and the public to hold practitioners accountable for how they practise securitization (justly or unjustly), the here-proposed theory goes further. The theory of morally mandatory securitization enables users to hold 'should-be' securitizing actors accountable for *not* securitizing, after all duties enable actors to demand relevant action and to place blame for inaction' (cf. D. Owens, 2015). This is important. Thus, while state actors tend to overzealously securitize against all manner of things as matters of national security, after all securitization has well-recognized benefits for the security industry, indeed for all 'security-Fuckers', as Mark Neocleous (2008: 5) albeit citing James Kelman so crassly puts it, states are less eager to securitize when people in other states are

---

[6] Some might object that JST does not have emancipatory potential. Ian Loader, for example, has argued that JST offers 'a politics of radical limitation, not a politics of transformation' (2022: 172). Indeed, many consider securitization and emancipation incompatible. Claudia Aradau (2004), for example, seeks emancipation away from security, and Ken Booth seeks emancipation away from securitization. By contrast, I hold that whether the two or compatible depends on what one means by emancipation. 'If Emancipation means freedom from legal, political, or social controls it is quite possibly incompatible with securitisation, however, if emancipation means freeing people from poor security practice towards a more just and enlightened security practice it is compatible. Clearly, I mean emancipation, not Emancipation' (Floyd, 2022: 279).

threatened. Moreover, state actors are often blinded by ideological commitments and beliefs. For example, left-leaning governments are unlikely to securitize against immigration and are thus unlikely to act on a corresponding duty, while right-leaning governments are likely to securitize against immigration when it is morally impermissible, for example, because there is no real threat.

The theory of morally mandatory securitization can also guide policymakers and security practitioners on their duties to secure and to securitize, respectively. As such, the theory has the potential to make a positive difference in the world. Notably, the theory gives way to a revision of North Atlantic Treaty Organization's (NATO) Article 5 and to a refocusing of RtoP away from humanitarian war and on a broader range of issues. Moreover, if adapted it would ensure that relevant insecurities (i.e., those that affect just referents and that are sufficiently harmful) are addressed – including, when necessary, via securitization – *before* they get even worse, including *before* they can turn into war. As such, the theory of morally mandatory securitization is closer to the work of Burke et al. (2014), who, with their theory of cosmopolitan security, seek to increase every person and other sentient beings' condition of being secure, than my previous book, which some saw as simply focusing on managing or limiting insecurity caused by securitization (cf. Burke et al., 2014: 8; Loader, 2022).[7] Unlike some of these writers, however, I acutely distinguish between security as a condition (being secure) and security as a special kind of social and political practice (securitization) (see Herington, 2015: 29–32, for these distinctions). This means that I do not start from the assumption that the right kind of 'securitization' is a desirable solution, let alone a panacea to the world ills. Instead, *I consider the need for securitization ultimately a failure of politics and decision-makers to prevent insecurity.* While not all forms of insecurity are preventable (the realist in me ultimately believes that humans are prone to tribalism and hence conflict[8]), many – given

---

[7] I have rebutted this interpretation elsewhere (Floyd, 2022: 279). For our purposes here it is enough to note that a world in which unjust securitization is reduced or avoided altogether is more secure than one where no such regulation exists.

[8] Although tribalism does not necessarily lead to violent conflict (it can be expressed through sport for example), it relies on 'us-versus-them thinking' and thus has the potential to spill into violence as in the case of rampant identity politics on US campuses (Lukianoff and Haidt, 2019, Fukuyama, 2018).

the right political institutions, behaviour, and fair distribution of resources – are preventable (cf. J. Floyd, 2017a). This is a point I will return to in the conclusion to this book; for now what matters is that because the prevention of insecurity is not widely practised or successful, insecurity remains very much part of the human condition. If this is so, then we need a theory that tells us when exceptional emergency measures may be used, and how such policies ought to be carried out. This was delivered by JST. Beyond that, however, we are also in need of a theory that enables 'us' to demand securitization effectively. In short, we need a theory that tells us *when* reluctant relevant actors *must* securitize to address insecurity. In other words, we need a theory of morally mandatory securitization.

To achieve my wider goals, my theory of morally mandatory securitization must be fair, relevant, and able to guide action in the real world. In short, I agree with James Pattison's (2018) view that moral theorizing for international politics must be pragmatic. Any such theory should be, first, 'determinate'. This is, it should 'offer clear normative prescriptions that can be used to advise policymakers, and [...] to hold them to account for their selection of measures [and be able to] guide the public debate' on the relevant issue (Pattison, 2018: 19). Second, a theory needs to be 'relevant' and concern the here and now. Third, it needs to be intuitively 'plausible'. And fourth, it needs to have 'wide appeal', by which he means that 'the approach could be endorsed by those who have differing but reasonable underlying world views' (Pattison, 2018: 20).

In my view, an important contributing factor towards determinacy is that my theory must recognize that there are limits to what morality can demand (this also falls into plausibility) that need to be built into the theory itself. For example, it is important that states are awarded enough self-determination in matters of (national) security. Moreover, it is crucial that principles of fairness govern burden sharing for other-securitization. In more detail, I hold that moral responsibility for an agent-caused but not intended threat obligates – in the first instance – threateners to react and not more capable states or even the international community in form of the United Nations (UN). Evidently, where threateners will not act, 'remedial responsibility' (Miller, 2007) must pass to other actors, including to the United Nations Security Council (UNSC).

While the ethics of security/securitization is slowly gaining in importance (see, e.g., Nyman, 2018, and Burke et al., 2014; Browning and McDonald, 2013) the policy-relevant question, whether states and other actors have a moral duty to securitize is widely neglected. The reasons for this are different for distinct theoretical approaches to security. Traditional scholars in security studies, which is to say realists and liberals, believe that states need to deal with threats when they (have the potential to) lead to violent conflict. In other words, there is no question to be answered. Copenhagen School scholars and other constructivists ignore the question because they consider securitization a securitizing actor's political choice, and usually the wrong one, as all securitizations have adverse consequences. Critical theorists such as Ken Booth are generally pro-security, but often so opposed to the state that they consider states as counterproductive to achieving security. Moreover, Booth (2007) – and ultimately also Burke and other 'security cosmopolitans' – believes that true security (as a state of being) is best achieved if the means match the ends, ergo that non-violent means are used, a position that does not sit easily with morally mandatory securitization, which includes the use of violent means.

Although steeped in security studies, the here-proposed approach sits perhaps most comfortably with the emerging work on the ethics of 'soft war' (Gross and Meisels, 2017), 'alternatives to war' (Pattison, 2018, also Dill 2016), or the *jus ad vim* (force short of war) (Walzer, 2006 [1977]: xv, Brunstetter, 2021). This is so for two reasons. First, like me this emerging literature draws heavily on the just war tradition. Second, many of the measures discussed as part of this nascent literature are expressions of securitization. Soft war or 'forcible alternatives to war' (Dill, 2016), for example, refer to types of war that do not involve armed conflict or kinetic force. A narrower reading is the *jus ad vim*, which considers the use of military force short of war (Brunstetter and Braun, 2013). In its broadest reading, 'alternatives to war' (Pattison, 2018) comprise a range of activities including economic sanctions, dialogue, mediation, arms embargoes but also positive incentives. In short, Pattison's alternatives to war refer to a mix of politicization and securitization. While this literature is thus relevant to what is proposed here, none of these scholars offer a comprehensive ethics of securitization.[9] Most notably, all such work focuses

---

[9] Pattison's book on the alternatives to war is ultimately concerned with justifiably of war (2018: 214).

on agent-intended threats only (notably Pattison, 2018, focuses on atrocity crimes and aggression), and it is limited to conflicts between groups that are so intense that the state can no longer protect civilians and vital infrastructure.[10] By contrast, my framework includes besides agent-intended also agent-caused and agent-lacking threats of lesser intensity. Indeed, the defensive measures that comprise securitization – in relevant cases – precede war. Moreover, as far as I can see, the literature on broadly 'soft war' is largely about the moral permissibility of war-like responses, not moral obligation. The reason for this is simple: it is generally believed that war-like responses in self-defence are an actor's prerogative (cf. Chapter 1, Section 1.2). As we shall see in Chapter 1, however, this changes were other-defence, most notably armed humanitarian intervention is concerned.

As this shows, the theory of morally mandatory securitization as developed in this book does not exist in a vacuum. Indeed, many of the themes discussed in this book have been explored by others in extensive detail. Notably, social contract theorists discuss the duties of states towards their citizens (Hobbes, 2002; Gauthier, 1969, Sorel, 2013; N.C. Lazar, 2009, Glanville, 2013). Scholars concerned with humanitarian intervention or RtoP discuss the duty to intervene militarily to save strangers (e.g., Glanville, 2021; Pattison, 2010; Tesón, 2014). Global justice scholars examine more broadly the duties the better off have to the least well off and why they have such duties (e.g., Miller, 2007; Risse, 2012; Pogge, 2001; Caney, 2005; Brock, 2009). Just war scholars have examined the relationship between unjust regimes, rights, and obligations (e.g., Rodin, 2002; McMahan, 2005). Given this, the sceptical reader may ask what is the added value

---

[10] Jessica Wolfendale (2017) provides an illuminating definition of the meaning of war that can account for soft wars. Given that there may be no casualties in soft war (note a standard definition of war is 1,000 battle deaths during one calendar year), a key feature of this account must rest with the intensity of the conflict. Wolfendale focuses on what she calls the intensity of hostilities. She argues: '[...] a conflict meets the criterion of intensity [of war] when it becomes so disruptive that the ability of civilians to meet their basic needs is seriously threatened, and the local authorities are unable to effectively control the conflict and protect civilians and civilian infrastructure from harm' (Wolfendale, 2017: 21). Although Wolfendale does not quantify how many civilians must be affected her phrasing suggests that she means only those kinds of conflicts that – like kinetic – war has serious effects on the civilian population at large.

of the theory of morally mandatory securitization? I would like to start by saying that practically all new and innovative scientific contributions are only ever newish; inevitably we all work with what has gone before. Not doing this would be both ignorant and unscientific. Inevitably, this means that oftentimes, newness lies more in making new links between existing literatures or findings, rather than truly novel approaches to either method, theory, or an empirical question. From this baseline then, what is it about the theory of mandatory securitization[11] that makes it worthwhile?

Two things in particular stand out. First, uniquely, the theory of mandatory securitization offers a *big picture* approach on who has a duty to securitize, when and under what circumstances. Unlike more direct theories, for example, on armed humanitarian intervention, it is not tied to specific actors or acts but rather it considers the duties to secure and securitize by any actor on any issue.[12] This ability stems from the theory's rootedness in securitization theory, which, as we shall see, is very much an open-ended framework that allows us to understand a hugely complex area of issues by separating the security landscape into different sectors of security (environmental, military, and so on), different referent objects (states, orders, identities, etc.), and providers of security (states, regional bodies, and so on) (Buzan et al., 1998). Moreover, although not knowing a priori what form securitization will take (beyond it being a deviation from normal conduct) is a considerable challenge for the just securitization theorist, this also has vast benefits. Most notably, our understanding and theorizing are not limited to what we already know. As such, the theory leaves open room for things we have not yet experienced. It is thus securitization theory that can theoretically grasp COVID-19's novel social distancing best.

Second, the theory of mandatory securitization offers a comparatively rare non-cosmopolitan perspective on issues of global justice. While statist, communitarian, and other non-cosmopolitan accounts of global justice exist (most notably Miller, 2007; Walzer, 1990 but also Nagel, 2005), they are in the minority. The reason for this is that

---

[11] Henceforth, I use morally mandatory securitization and simply mandatory securitization interchangeably, as I have made it clear how mandatory is understood in this book.

[12] RtoP, for instance, is inapplicable to many of the most pressing security threats (including climate change, infectious disease, or cyberattack), diminishing its ability to deliver greater overall security.

most people interested in global justice are interested in the subject because they are concerned with achieving equality or with ending poverty. In other words, they are committed to achieving global justice (cf. Nagel, 2005: 119). By contrast, non-cosmopolitans generally hold that we do not have a duty of justice to the less well off, but simply a humanitarian duty to alleviate suffering. Although the theory of mandatory securitization builds on top of a theory of just securitization (namely JST), it is important to recognize that JST is not a theory of justice. It is a theory of justified action; it does not advance a theory of distributive or global justice. The normative grounds JST and mandatory securitization appeal to are facts about human well-being, moral equality, and a corresponding humanitarian duty. As such my theory offers a much less demanding contribution to the global justice literature than most. Indeed, by focusing on a duty to securitize, the theory of mandatory securitization makes the topic of moral duties more manageable, perhaps even more palatable, than general theories of global distributive justice, which focus on global inequality. To be sure, I am not claiming that the duty to securitize is necessarily the only duty actors have; my claim is rather that by thinking of the duty to securitize, the general subject of moral duties is rendered accessible to reluctant practitioners, policymakers, and the public. This is even more the case because the word securitization is increasingly used outside of academia in the think tank community, including in dialogue with policymakers (see, e.g., NATO, 2021a, 2021b, Amnesty International, 2017, 2018).

I.3 The Meaning of Securitization

Securitization theory was initially developed by Ole Wæver in the late 1980s and the 1990s and developed further in collaboration with inter alia Barry Buzan (collectively called the Copenhagen School) in the late 1990s and the 2000s. In the school's 1998 seminal *Security: A New Framework for Analysis*, securitization theory is described as a third way between realists' narrow and Critical Theorists' excessively wide take on the meaning and nature of security (Buzan et al., 1998: 203–207). Rather than focusing on the objective existence of threats, the novel contribution offered by Wæver and his colleagues was to view the practice of security as an illocutionary speech act. To wit, an issue becomes a security threat when it is socially and politically constructed as such, notably in language. While language thus plays a major role in securitization, the Copenhagen School also argued that *successful* securitization involves the use of extraordinary measures (Buzan et al., 1998: 25–26). The inclusion of extraordinary measures served to sort important securitization from less important ones and was thus in line with the claim that the theory simultaneously opens and yet limits the meaning of security. Due to some inconsistences across and within Wæver's individual and the Copenhagen School's joint writings, however, not everyone accepts that successful securitization involves actual policy change (i.e., the adoption of extraordinary measures), and indeed multiple interpretations of securitization exist (see, e.g., Huysmans, 2011; Neal, 2019; Corry, 2012).

More postmodern scholars, for instance, are fixed on the role of language in securitization (e.g., Philipsen, 2020). For these scholars, securitization succeeds when a relevant audience accepts the existential threat articulation contained in the securitizing move. The audience begins to feature in Wæver et al.'s, writings from 1998, however, without sufficient explanation of who or what this is (Stritzel, 2007). I have argued elsewhere (Floyd, 2019a, 2016a) that the term audience makes sense only when audiences are treated coterminous with the addressees of securitization. And that if securitizing moves are either warnings or promises (as once suggested by Wæver 1989, 42), then audiences are either threateners or referent objects of securitization (Floyd, 2016a).[13] I have shown that the actors' acceptance of the warning or the promise entailed in the securitizing move can but may not affect the trajectory of securitization (Floyd, 2019a: 55–58). Consequently, in the absence of a conclusive relationship between audience acceptance and securitization's success (in a sense of completeness), the audience ought not to play a decisive role in the process of securitization. In JST it is bracketed from the process of securitization (for more detail see Chapter 3, Section 3.3.1).

---

[13] Interesting about all this for the purposes of this book is that promises – at least between those who share the ordinary meaning of promise – entail obligations (see, Pritchard, 2002: 257–265). Even so, my point is that a promise for protection does not obligate a would-be securitizing actor to securitize; it merely obligates them to act on the insecurity. But this need not be through securitization, unless – as I argue in Chapter 1 – securitization is a last resort.

Moreover, for the purposes of studying the ethics of securitization, securitization involves the use of threat-dependent extraordinary measures to combat the danger.[14] Considering that threats are different, this can take a myriad of forms. The securitization of terrorism is likely to involve an increase of powers of a state's executive, including the home secretary (or equivalent), while the police force may be awarded controversial coercive powers to fight terrorism (including detention without trial or extensive powers of surveillance and one-off military strikes[15]). By contrast, in cases of currency collapse in a liberal market economy, securitization might take the form of capital controls on private money to stop the outflow of funds, while private money may forcibly be used to keep the national economy afloat or to fund bail-outs of specific sectors of the economy (cf. Floyd, 2019d). In cases of the securitization of the environment or the climate (droughts, etc.), securitization might involve the passing of emergency laws that forbid citizens to conduct hitherto ordinary activities (involving the use of water), as well as an increase in police powers to enforce these new laws. In case of military threats – for example, the nuclear threat from North Korea – securitization often refers to a range of punitive economic sanctions against the aggressor state. Finally, in the case of COVID-19 in many states, securitization took the form of nationwide lockdown, increased police powers to enforce the lockdown through

---

[14] Elsewhere (Floyd, 2016a) I have argued that if securitization is a social and political construction decided by practitioners, it follows that securitization succeeds when practitioners consider their response a security response. In other words, I have allowed for emergency measures that are not exceptional but rather routine procedure. While such an approach is valuable in so far as it allows a comprehensive picture of security practice in the world, in my work on ethics and security I work with the exception only. After all, the fact that the measures are exceptional raises concrete ethical questions most acutely (see also Floyd, 2021).

[15] This follows Daniel Brunstetter (2021) who sets out the *jus ad vim* in considerable detail. He recognizes that the use of kinetic force constitutes war, but also that to count as a war enough force must be used. Limited strikes are not war; they are used for the purpose of deterrence or with a view to destroying military capabilities (2021: 10). He argues: 'The decision to go to war has often been seen as akin to "crossing the Rubicon" – that is, accepting the responsibility, the costs, and the risks of going all in, but also with an eye to the potential benefits to be gained. The turn to limited force expresses a preference *not* to cross the Rubicon, as it were – to eschew the responsibility, the costs, and risks of going all in [...]' (2021: 6).

steep fines, the closing/reinstatement of borders, tracing apps, and much else besides.

These examples do not exhaust the concept of securitization, but they merely demonstrate that the descriptive words *exceptional* or *extraordinary* designate that whatever is done to address a given threat is at odds with 'whatever passed as normal until an exception was installed' (Wæver and Buzan, 2020: 6). Given that in autocratic states what passes as normal is often far removed from the normal in free societies (for instance, the now lifted restriction on women driving in Saudi Arabia), a more accurate definition of exceptional politics might be that the exception entails measures and conduct that most reasonable persons[16] would ordinarily (i.e., in times when there is no relevant threat) consider unacceptable largely because of the harm or the violence they risk or entail.[17]

Another way to think of securitization is as the breaking of established rules (Buzan et al., 1998: 26).[18] The notion of rules aids our understanding of this multifaceted concept further. Depending on the threat, the rules that are broken may be rules within states or societies (e.g., when free societies expand surveillance and curtail freedom of movement) but also to the myriad of informal and formal rules that regulate, indeed co-constitute global international society in times of peace. While rules and practices are not distributed evenly throughout all sub-global international societies (Buzan, 2004), some rules

---

[16] For more on the reasonable person standard, see below. Note that invoking this standard enables one to avoid the issue whether unacceptability is culturally specific.

[17] Much has been written about the process how exceptional powers are awarded. In liberal democracies, the old Schmittian idea that securitizing actors can break rules simply in virtue of the threat alone has been modified. Many scholars hold that in liberal democracies securitizing actors (e.g., the state's executive and other branches of the wider executive (i.e., police)) are awarded special powers by parliament (i.e., legislators) often through new emergency legislation (a process that is often checked by the judiciary) (see, e.g., Sarat, 2010: 7; Dyzenhaus, 2010; Zedner, 2009, Neal, 2013). In other words, in liberal democracies, the other branches of government are *not* necessarily excluded from securitization, even though when an issue is securitized the executive is often left abnormally empowered.

[18] The reference to rule-breaking can be misleading. Thus, for some emergencies specific rules exist, meaning that in times of emergency rules are to be followed not broken (e.g., International Health Regulations). However, emergency rules are different from normal rules and justified only by the presence of the emergency.

and practices are accepted by all. For example, all states use channels of diplomacy to interact with one another; they tend to abide by existing trade agreements; they are sovereign over their territory and people and much besides. Punitive economic sanctions, unexpected and/or harsh trade tariffs, the cutting of diplomatic ties, other forms of coercion (e.g., the threat of expulsion from specific regional bodies, etc.) that break these practices and rules are thus expressions of securitization.

Securitization is not the prerogative only of individual state actors; collectives of states (e.g., the European Union (EU) or NATO) and other actors also can use exceptional emergency measures to deal with a perceived threat. Moreover, NATO, the EU, and individual states can not only securitize against threats to their members, or to the organization at large (i.e., self-securitization); instead, these actors can also use extraordinary emergency measures with the aim to save *outsiders* from suffering great harm. Let us call this other-securitization.

As we shall see in the next subsection, in line with my JST, not only people qualify for the status of just referent object (the thing or entity in danger). Some ecosystems and non-human species (both plant and animal) as well as more abstract things such as political and social orders can be just referent objects for securitization. This means that just other-securitization could quite legitimately focus on threats to these kinds of just referents. Given, however, that (in line with criterion 2 of JST below) the justness of referent objects depends on the referent object's contribution to human well-being, relevant threats to things and orders are always also indirect threats to people (cf. Chapter 1, Section 1.3). Hence, I think it is legitimate to speak of outsiders as the ultimate referents of other-securitization in the way I do.

Other-securitization may – on occasion – see an actor (for instance, a state or NATO) act on the territory of another sovereign state (e.g., aid the host state with enforcing curfews or border controls during a pandemic). Often, however, other-securitization will be restricted to measures that are launched remotely, such as sanctions, expulsion, and one-off military strikes. To be sure, however, not all securitizing action taken to coerce other states is necessarily primarily a case of other-securitization. For example, securitizing action by non-rainforest states that aim to compel states with rainforests to stop deforestation of the same might be driven by the urge to save local peoples, but it could be one of self-securitization against climate change.[19] As ever in securitization studies, it is therefore important to be clear on who securitizes, what entity, and by what means (cf. Buzan et al., 1998: 27).

On the issue of clarity, it is important to take note of another thing. In securitization studies, it is common to use the expression 'the securitization of X' and to refer by X to the threat. For example, the securitization of climate change designates that actors have constructed climate change as a threat. The preposition 'of' here likely results from the fact that securitization is concerned with the social and political construction *of* security threats. Certainly, a more adequate formulation would be to speak of the securitization *against* climate change. Especially also because at times, by the X in the 'securitization of X', scholars mean not the threat, but the referent object instead (this is also sometimes expressed as securitizing X), for example, when they speak of the securitization of identity, health, the environment, or women's rights. The securitization of health, for example, does not mean a defence against health, but rather a defence against disease to ensure health. Given the customs described, my term 'other-securitization' could potentially be interpreted to mean 'the securitization of another to protect the self' or even 'securitization against another'. Nothing could be further from the truth. I use the terms self-securitization and other-securitization as analogous with self-defence and other-defence both of which we can find in just war theory (cf. McMahan, 2005: 1). I do this because securitization is of course a specific form of defence (i.e., the use of exceptional countermeasures short of war to combat a threat), and self-securitization thus simply refers to the defence of the self by means of securitization, while other-securitization refers to the defence of outsiders/others/third parties by means of securitization. To make this clear to the reader, in this book I differentiate between the securitization *of* X, whereby X refers to the referent object, and the securitization *against* X, in cases where X is the threat. When used as a verb, this leads to the hard-to-get-used to phrase 'securitize against, for example, climate change'.

---

[19] I use this example purely to showcase that action to compel others to do something locally is not necessarily one of other-securitization. In other words, I am aware that much deforestation is driven by rich states' demand for palm oil, soya, and beef.

I.4 Synopsis: Just Securitization Theory

While the present book is free-standing and complete, my theory of the obligation to securitize builds on my existing work on the moral permissibility to securitize (Floyd, 2019a). Just Securitization Theory is relevant for this project because obligation entails permissibility; after all *no one can have a duty to do something unless that something is also morally permitted.* Importantly, however, this does not mean that readers of this book must agree with the specifics of JST, but it simply means that readers must understand that a general theory of morally mandatory securitization is based on the finding that securitization can be morally justified. Given that in my case this takes the form of JST, it is necessary to explain this theory in some detail.

Just Securitization Theory sets out universal moral principles designating when states and other actors are *permitted* – from an ethical point of view – to use exceptional emergency measures. The moral principles advanced fall into three different groups:

1) Just initiation of securitization (specifying when the move from politicization to securitization is morally permissible),
2) Just conduct in securitization (specifying what practitioners of security need to consider when they carry out securitization), and
3) Just termination of securitization (specifying when and how securitization must be unmade).

Just Securitization Theory combines insights from moral philosophy's just war tradition with insights from security studies' securitization theory. This is an unusual marriage to say the least. Ole Wæver, the originator of securitization theory, has strong postmodernist leanings (see Floyd, 2010: 23–31). As such, he does not engage in differentiating perceived from real threats and indeed his version of securitization theory is concerned mainly with how issues become security threats through threat construction in language. Neither does he believe in the desirability, nor in the possibility, of universal truth claims regarding morality (Wæver, 2011). The just war tradition by contrast sits firmly in analytical political and moral philosophy with proponents subscribing to universalism and reason, taking manifest aggression as a just cause for war. So why then combine these two theories? The advantage of Wæver's securitization theory vis-à-vis all other existing theories of security is that the theory has no fixed view on who securitizes, the origin of threats, or the objects in need of being saved (referent objects). As such, the theory is uniquely able to capture different actors at all levels of analysis[20] and manifold threats to all manner of referent objects. That – for me – is *the* unique 'selling point' of securitization theory. It is the reason for why I have spent so many years engaging with this theory, and why I commence from securitization regarding the morality of security.

So far so good, but can an ethical approach that rests on objective threats really be reconciled with a theory that focuses on the social and political construction of threats only? Or else, why is JST a progression and not a perversion of the Copenhagen School's securitization theory?[21] There are two parts to my answer. First, leading proponents of securitization theory including Ole Wæver (2011: 472) and Thierry Balzacq (2011) acknowledge that real threats exist. This is important simply because it shows that there is no insurmountable ontological chasm that divides securitization theory(ies) and JST (cf. Floyd, 2019a: 10–12).

Second, the element of social and political construction is not lost from JST. Here as in other versions of securitization theory, security threats are and remain socially and politically constructed by securitizing actors. The difference is that in JST what matters is that securitized threats refer to real/objective threats. Notably, securitization cannot be morally permissible, let alone required, unless there is a real existential threat. Even if some critical (in the broadest sense) scholars accept that real threats do exist, most consider them epistemologically inaccessible ergo: we cannot know for sure whether a threat is real or not. Drawing on work by the late Derek Parfit (2011), I hold that objective is to be understood in the evidence-relative sense, never the fact-relative sense. This means that judgements about the real existence of threats cannot result from the requirement to know *all* 'the relevant, reason-giving facts', but instead on knowing all the relevant, reason-giving available evidence, which must suggest decisive reasons

---

[20] To be clear when I use the term levels of analysis, I do not use it to suggest that just or mandatory securitization positions itself on one or more of the levels; I use it merely to locate different actors. In the words of Buzan et al.: 'Levels [of analysis] are simply ontological referents for where things happen rather than sources of explanation themselves' (Buzan et al., 1998: 5).
[21] My thanks to Cian O'Driscoll for this formulation.

that the beliefs we hold about the threat are true (Parfit, 2011: 163). To be sure, this does not allow for sloppiness or individual limitations on the part of the securitizing actor, or the scholar examining the justice of securitization; instead, evidence must approximate the facts (I elaborate on this below).

Moving on, how exactly securitization plays out is hugely contested in the relevant literature. The upside of these disagreements is that any scholar working with securitization is at liberty to develop her own nuanced approach of what securitization means, which can be vexing, but also advantageous and productive (cf. Wæver, 2003). In this book – and in JST more generally – securitization refers *not* to the construction in language of issues into security threats, but to the adoption of exceptional, often issue-specific security measures following rhetorical threat articulation.[22]

My interpretation of securitization as the exception also partially explains why I have chosen to work with the just war tradition. Thus, securitization and war are both forms of exceptional politics and consequently display some of the same characteristics (i.e., they harm people, including beyond threateners also beneficiaries and innocent bystanders), but also that they can be used and abused by policymakers to further their own ends. The similarities between war and securitization also mean that if one develops a theory on the morality of securitization it is impossible to ignore a theory that has done the same for war for centuries (cf. Floyd, 2019a).

In recent years, there has been a surge of interest in the just war tradition. Changes in the practice of war (including the proliferation of civil wars and the decrease of inter-state wars) but also, according to the leading just war scholar Jeff McMahan, changes in philosophy (a move away from a focus on language towards practical moral issues) have ushered along a new type of just war theory (McMahan,

---

[22] Rhetorical threat articulation is also called the securitizing move. It refers to the identification of an existential threat; in JST, relevant securitizing moves are those by securitizing actors which amount to either a warning to threateners and/or promises for protection to referent objects. Threateners and referent objects in turn are the audiences of securitizing moves. They can influence securitizing actors, but because they do not categorically do, they do not play a decisive role in securitization and consequently JST. In any case, JST is concerned with the ethics of securitization not with right procedure (i.e., with who ought to ideally be involved).

2018: x–xi). The revisionist school led by McMahan questions long-held assumptions by the legalist school, who likens the morality of war to the legality of war, as codified in, for example, the Geneva Conventions of 1949. Despite these internal disagreements, I consider the just war tradition authoritative on the issue of the ethics of war, and by extension emergency politics. Following Cian O'Driscoll and Anthony Lang (2013), this is down to two factors: (1) its legacy (not merely that it has been around for hundreds of years, but also the sheer number of people who have intersubjectively agreed the baseline principles that are relevant when discussing the justice of war) and (2) its usage in practice (notably, the fact that the principles of the just war are well known and that they shape public discourse about the permissibility of war) (O'Driscoll and Lang, 2013: 1–16). Of course, its usage in practice is not always benign. The theory has been used and abused by policymakers to justify their unjust wars. While this is problematic, including for just and morally mandatory securitization, it is also the case that just war theory offers guidance enabling understanding why some wars are unjust (see, e.g., Morkevicius, 2022, on the injustice of Russia's war in Ukraine). While the abuse of moral theories of war and securitization cannot easily be stopped, extensive dissemination of the principles of just and mandatory securitization can enable the public to recognize disinformation for what it is.

Revisionism or legalism, the just war tradition is about curtailing the reasons for which it is permissible to fight (Orend, 2006). Moral philosophers interested in constraining the occurrence and bloody/destructive nature of war have for centuries advanced criteria or principles specifying when wars *may* be fought and how wars *ought to* be fought. They have homed in on a small number of criteria. *Ad bellum* (the just resort to war) requirements usually include just cause, macro-proportionality, right intention, last resort, reasonable chance of success, and legitimate authority, while *in bello* (just conduct in war) criteria focus on proportionality, necessity, and discrimination. Overall, *in bello* criteria suggest that *if* wars are fought then moral codes and rules of conduct obtain. Just war scholars do not advocate that just wars *should* be fought; indeed, as we shall see in Chapter 1, Section 1.2, many theorists of the just war stay away from the issue of obligation altogether. A notable exception is scholars working on armed humanitarian intervention.

Informed by critical security studies which holds a negative view of securitization, I am all too aware of the adverse consequences securitization may have, and thus share just war scholar's view that an ethical theory of emergency measures (be they war or securitization) must ultimately be about curtailing the use and destructiveness of such measures (cf. Orend, 2006). However, like just war scholars, and unlike pacifists, I also think that wars are sometimes justified. We can see this clearly when we consider that political regimes differ in terms of their justness; surely a just regime cannot be required – in all cases – to succumb, without a fight, to the aggression posed to it by an unjust regime? I also think that an ethical strategy that *ceteris paribus* recommends desecuritization – as do Wæver and many others – is not feasible, as this only works when real threats are ignored. Thus, when faced with a real threat a would-be securitizing actor will not be convinced of the wisdom and necessity to desecuritize; the actor would, however, benefit from guidance regarding whether they may securitize and how to do this in an ethically informed way.

I also believe that there is a need for an ethical theory of securitization because there will always be securitizations. Even if the occurrence of war and securitization are curtailable by sound ethical theories, they are recurring features in world politics, not merely because aggression and tribalism are – in my view – a part of human nature, but also because threats can be driven by indirect agential variables (resource shortages, etc.). To my mind, an ethical strategy regarding securitization must rest with the provision of universal moral principles that designate when securitization may be initiated, how actors ought to behave, and when and how securitization must be unmade. My allegiance with universalism is a direct rejection of the critical project in security studies, and one that pushes JST deeply into analytical political and moral philosophy. Informed by the just war tradition, JST develops the following principles designating just securitization:

I.4.1 *Just Initiation of Securitization*

1. There must be an objective existential threat to a referent object, that is to say a danger that – with a sufficiently high probability – threatens the survival or the essential character/properties of either a political or social order, an ecosystem, a non-human species, or individuals.

2. Referent objects are entitled to defend themselves or are eligible for defensive assistance if they are morally justifiable. Referent objects are morally justifiable if they meet basic human needs, defined here as necessary components of human well-being. *Political and social orders* need to satisfy a minimum level of basic human needs[23] of people part of or contained within that order, and they must respect the human needs of outsiders. *Ecosystems* and *non-human species*, in turn, need to make a contribution to the human needs of a sufficiently large group of people. *Human beings* are justifiable referent objects by virtue of being intrinsically valuable; all other referent objects therefore have instrumental value derived from the need of human beings.
3. The right intention for securitization is the just cause. Securitizing actors must be sincere in their intention to protect the referent object they themselves identified and declared.
4. The expected good gained from securitization must be greater than the expected harm from securitization; where the only relevant good is the good specified in the just cause.
5. Securitization must have a reasonable chance of success, whereby the chances of achieving the just cause must be judged greater than those of less harmful alternatives to securitizing.

I.4.2 Just Conduct in Securitization

6. The security measures used must be appropriate and should aim to only address the objective existential threat that occasions securitization.
7. The security measures used must be judged effective in dealing with the threat. They should aim to cause, or risk, the least amount of overall harm possible and do less harm to the referent object than would otherwise be caused if securitization was abandoned.
8. Executors of securitization must respect a limited number of relevant human rights in the execution of securitization.

Just Securitization Theory also develops criteria specifying just desecuritization. These are as follows:

---

[23] In fact, only democratic states can be just referent objects because only such states protect the basic human need of autonomy (cf. Floyd, 2019a: 107).

I.4.3 Just Termination of Securitization

9. Desecuritization of just securitization must occur when the initial
   and related new objective existential threats have been neutral-
   ized, whereas desecuritization of unjust securitization must occur
   immediately.
10. Desecuritization should ideally be publicly declared, and corres-
    ponding security language and security measures should be termi-
    nated with immediate effect.
11. In order to avoid renewed and/or reactionary securitization, dese-
    curitizing actors should undertake context-specific restorative
    measures.

For mandatory securitization, just initiation of securitization is the
most important aspect of JST. Together, principles 1 (the just reason)
and 2 (the just referent) are jointly and sufficiently necessary as the just
cause for securitization. I will expand on just reason below and also in
some detail in Chapter 1, Section 1.3. To be sure, crucial – especially
for the many critical security scholars sceptical of our ability to know
that threats are real – is that I understand objective in the evidence –
not the fact-relative sense (Parfit, 2011), meaning that threats are real
when all the available relevant evidence suggests decisive reasons that
they are.

The just referent is not always explicitly identified in just war theory. Some scholars assert that only just states have a right to self-
defence. Justice here is usually bound to a state's record on human
rights (see, e.g., Orend, 2006: 36). Conversely, I hold that the value of
referents rests with their ability to satisfy basic human needs (except
for human beings themselves when our concern ought to be with their
human needs). One reason for this is that while some referents (e.g.,
ecosystems) can usefully contribute to the satisfaction of basic human
needs they cannot easily be squared with human rights. Thus, while
we may say that there is a human right to the environment, the environment is not a duty-bearer.

Anyone with good knowledge of the just war tradition will
notice that while JST mirrors standard just war theories closely,
some important principles are missing. While it is not surpris-
ing that just conduct in securitization does not specify that international agreements are sacrosanct (there are none explicitly about

securitization), an explanation is needed regarding the absence of legitimate authority and last resort from the just initiation of securitization. Legitimate authority is absent from JST for three reasons. First, much of what legitimate authority does in the just war theory (i.e., guarantee that in a war of two sides, only the legitimate actor has a moral right to defend themselves) is ensured by JST's principle of the just referent object (principle 2), which ensures that only just entities can be secured by means of securitization. Second, in the original Copenhagen School theory securitization is not the prerogative of state actors; hence, just securitization must not be restricted to legitimate authorities (i.e., fully democratic and just states). Third, I reject reformulations of legitimate authority into a principle specifying representative authority (e.g., Finlay, 2015: 182–183), which would emphasize consent by referent objects to securitization, as superfluous because the substantive criteria of just securitization (notably right intention[24]) guard against what I have called elsewhere agent-benefiting securitization (Floyd, 2010). Bearing in mind here that the need to prevent securitizing actor's acting in their own as opposed to the interest of the just referent object is the greatest rationale for representative legitimacy (Floyd, 2019a).

Last resort is, if in a modified and much weakened form, present in JST's principle 5. This criterion specifies that securitization is permissible when it has a reasonable chance of success, whereby reasonable chance is judged comparatively against the consequences of less harmful alternatives to securitizing. Securitization is permissible when it emerges *ex ante* as the best option. As I shall argue in Chapter 1, Section 1.2, a stricter interpretation of last resort – as the last thing to be tried after other viable less harmful options have failed to satisfy just cause (i.e., ameliorated moderate last resort) – is pivotal for the obligation to securitize. Indeed, I hold that just cause + right intention + proportionality + ameliorated moderate last resort together constitute not the permissibility to initiate securitization but equate to a 'must cause' for securitization.

Although my list of principles includes criteria determining just termination of securitization, just securitization and just desecuritization

---

[24] Which can be ascertained by comparing putative securitizing actors' securitizing speech acts with what they propose to do/end up doing.

each has a separate outcome (i.e., securitization leads to a securitized state of affairs, whereas desecuritization leads to a desecuritized state of affairs), and consequently the justice of one process must be judged independently of the outcome of the other process. In short, a just desecuritization does not render a prior unjust securitization just, and vice versa.

Just Securitization Theory is aimed at three distinct audiences, scholars, practitioners of security, and the public. In more detail, JST enables scholars of security to examine the justness of any past or present securitizations, it equips security practitioners with tools helping them decide what they ought to do in relevant situations, and it empowers the public to hold securitizing actors and practitioners accountable for how they practise security. While empowering people is an important part of JST, actual empowerment is limited because while the theory allows the public, etc., to critique past or present security practice, as it stands, it cannot easily be used to demand securitization (Floyd, 2018). This is because the theory as developed in *The Morality of Security* (2019a) is concerned exclusively with the permissibility to securitize, it does not theorize when securitization is morally obligatory. Likewise, JST does not offer guidance to decision-makers and security practitioners on when they must act to secure, let alone securitize against a threat. The present book aims to fill these gaps in the theory and – because JST is the only theory of its kind – in the wider literature.

I.5 Summary: Morally Mandatory Securitization

The theory of morally mandatory securitization shares some common ground with the RtoP norm.[25] In Chapter 5, I argue that mandatory securitization can address some of the problems with RtoP, and above all it can refocus the norm away from armed humanitarian intervention towards other types of action, on a much broader range of issues. Furthermore, I borrow from the RtoP literature the idea of a pillar structure invoking the *duties* to secure of actors placed at different

---

[25] There are also very significant differences. Notably, mandatory securitization does not include war, and mandatory securitization applies to a much broader range of issues, whereas RtoP is restricted to atrocity crimes.

levels of analysis. The pillar structure enables a summary of the argument developed over the course of this book as follows:

Pillar 1: Just states[26] that have satisfied must cause[27] have an overriding duty of self-securitization. In the same situation, unjust states have an overriding duty to secure morally valuable referent objects within their territory, but they are not permitted to defend – by means of securitization – their unjust regime. When states fail to act on objective existential threats or when they pose an unjust threat to a just referent object, relevant non-state actors have a pro tanto obligation to act to secure people within the state, including when they have satisfied must cause, via securitization. These obligations extend to group insiders and outsiders.

States are the primary duty-bearers for mandatory other-politicization and – when they have satisfied must cause – mandatory other-securitization, in cases where they are morally or outcome responsible for the threat that gives rise to the need for politicization/securitization. And they can be primary duty-bearers when they have relevant ties of security friendship with the entity in danger. Powerful or especially skilled states can also be designated primary duty-bearers for other-politicization and other-securitization based on capacity.

Pillar 2: When just sub-systemic collective security actors have satisfied must cause, they are morally obligated to self-securitize. In just collective defence organizations – provided member states seek assistance – this duty is overriding. Unjust collective security actors have a duty to secure morally valuable referent objects within their territory, including – when they have satisfied must cause – with securitization.

On the grounds of friendship and ties of community collectives also bear foremost responsibility for dealing with an unjust threat emanating from a rogue member state to the collective, or – if requested by the member state – to one of its members. Collectives are the primary duty-bearers for mandatory other-politicization and other-securitization when they are morally or outcome responsible for the insecurity. They can also be primary duty-bearers when they have relevant ties of friendship with another state or actor. In cases where individual states and collectives have comparable ties of friendship, the capacity to help trumps, rendering the collective – often – the primary duty-bearer for mandatory other-securitization.

---

[26] Just states are states which satisfy a minimum floor of basic human needs (cf. Chapter 2, Section 2.2).

[27] Must cause = just cause, right intention, macro-proportionality *and* last resort (see Chapter 1 for a detailed explanation and justification).

Sub-systemic- and systemic-level non-state actors are likely to have a duty to politicize and – when they have satisfied must cause – securitize, only when they are morally or outcome responsible for the threat. The exception would be cases where they are the most capable actor.

Pillar 3: When just referent objects have no other protector (e.g., a weak or 'friendless' persecuted just non-state actor), then the UNSC is the designated primary duty-bearer for mandatory politicization and – if they have satisfied must cause – securitization. Moreover, the UNSC is the secondary, or even tertiary duty-bearer for mandatory politicization and securitization where other duty-bearers have failed to act (including because their obligation to securitize is overridden for legitimate reasons, notably by the risk of death, disease, and disability; the risk of instability and insecurity as well as by prohibitive financial costs). The UNSC's duty to secure and/or securitize is overriding, based on the contractual relation, the UN charter creates between the people and the UN/UNSC.

I.6 Method and Methodology

While inspired by critical security studies, especially securitization theory, JST is ultimately steeped in analytical political theory and moral philosophy. This is evident not only from the fact that relativism is rejected in favour of universalism,[28] but also from *how* principles of just securitization are derived. In line with analytical and moral philosophy, I derive these principles by employing the Rawlsian method of wide reflective equilibrium. As a method (opposed to a state of affairs), wide reflective equilibrium involves 'testing theories against judgements about particular cases, but also testing judgements

---

[28] As Caney (2005) explains, moral universalism takes two forms, universalism of scope and universalism of justification. Universalism of scope holds that 'there are some moral values that are valid across the world' (p. 26). The philosopher James Rachels highlights this well. He explains that complex societies can only exist based on communication between members. Since communication is futile unless there is a presumption against lying, a commitment to truthfulness is a universal value. Other universal values necessary for the existence of society are the outlawing of murder (Rachels, 1986). Universalism of justification, in turn, 'claims that there are values that can be justified to everyone in a sense that everyone would accept the justification' (Caney, 2005: 27). Just Securitization Theory and mandatory securitization also affirm this type of universalism. Key here, as in much of moral and analytical philosophy, is the human capacity 'for genuine toleration and mutual respect', or in Rawlsian terms reasonableness (Wenar, 2021); see below.

about particular cases against theories, until equilibrium is achieved' (Blackburn, 2005: 312). As a state of affairs or perhaps better, as a state of mind, reflective equilibrium designates '[a] state in which all one's thoughts about a topic fit together; in which there are no loose ends or recalcitrant elements that do not cohere with an overall position' (ibid: 312).

Scholars developing principles or a theory of just war usually test their own theory against specific cases as well as competing just war theories. Many scholars proceed by grouping likeminded scholars on one or other principle together and test the prevailing view against cases and new judgements against theories. Although many different theories of just securitization are possible, JST currently is the only theory of its kind. This means that I cannot achieve reflective equilibrium by testing judgements about specific cases against competing accounts of just securitization. Moreover, there are no theories of justified securitization concerned with obligation. Given the likeness of securitization and war as forms of extraordinary emergency politics, however, what I can do is utilize theories that make similar points with regard to war. Relevant in particular are scholars that theorize armed humanitarian intervention[29] (i.e., 'military intervention into the jurisdiction of a state by outside forces for humanitarian purposes' (Scheid, 2014: 3)), because unlike national self-defence, humanitarian intervention is – once designated principles are met – not simply optional, but generally considered obligatory (cf. Dobos and Coady, 2014: 78). This means that we can test our judgements about particular issues regarding the obligation to securitize (e.g., regarding when the pro tanto obligation to securitize third parties is overridden) against theories of armed humanitarian intervention that stress the moral costs and risks to interveners.

In addition, my account of the obligation to securitize must achieve reflective equilibrium with JST. This is crucial, because a theory of the duty to securitize flows from a corresponding theory of the permissibility to securitize. A disconnect between these 'two'[30] theories would suggest problems with either logic. This book's theoretical grounding

---

[29] Hereafter simply humanitarian intervention.

[30] In brackets because it is just one theory (JST) developed across two different books.

in JST has consequences for how the theory of mandatory securitization shapes up. Just Securitization Theory adheres to a form of 'weak cosmopolitanism' (Miller, 2007: 28) or else a 'moral cosmopolitanism' (ibid: 43) only; thus – like practically all moral theories – it subscribes to the principle of the equal moral worth of people (cf. Floyd, 2019a). The moral equal worth approach in turn includes the view that there is a general, unassigned duty to alleviate human suffering (Pattison, 2010: 19). Consequently, the theory developed in this book starts from the premise that – in certain circumstances – those able owe those unable and objectively threatened (i.e., insecure), protection and assistance in the form of other-politicization and – when the criteria of just initiation of securitization + (ameliorated moderate) last resort are satisfied – other-securitization. In other words, there is a general unassigned *duty to secure* outsiders that can morph into a *duty to securitize* outsiders.

Who precisely has such duties, how much is owed, and when securitization is obligatory as opposed to 'merely' permissible are the subjects of Chapters 2–5. The point here is that a moral theory on the obligation to securitize that builds on a prior moral theory on the permissibility to securitize that is committed to the equal worth of people cannot logically abandon the idea of duties to outsiders.

Given the theory's focus on obligations to third parties, the theory of mandatory securitization is also part of the literature on global justice. According to Gillian Brock: '[a] problem is often considered to constitute a global justice problem when one (or more) of the following conditions obtain:

1. Actions stemming from an agent, institution, practice, activity (and so on) that can be traced to one (or more) states negatively affects residents in another state.
2. Institutions, practices, policies, activities (and so on) in one (or more) states could bring about a benefit or reduction in harm to those resident in another state.
3. There are normative considerations that require agents in one state to take certain actions with respect to agents or entities in another. Such actions might be mediated through institutions, policies, or norms.
4. We cannot solve a problem that affects residents of one or more states without co-operation from other states' (Brock, 2017).

As will become clear in the Chapters 2–5 that follow, all four of these points are obtained with regards to the theory of mandatory securitization.

Any theory concerned with a global justice problem must be based on sound normative foundations that ground solutions, obligations, and responsibilities (ibid). To do this, I utilize existing theories of global justice that address what we owe to people living outside of our own state's borders. In reflective equilibrium with JST, which not only is needs-based,[31] but also understands human rights as grounded in basic human needs, my approach to global justice shares much in common with scholars that recognize a relatively small number of human rights. The logic of security (including the possibility of the security dilemma) as well as the fact that states are the custodians of the monopoly of violence organically reinforces my positing with 'weak cosmopolitans', otherwise known as a form of communitarianism (Miller, 2016: 161). In line with that position, I set the threshold for unreasonable costs that override pro tanto obligations of mandatory other-securitization lower than many global justice scholars (almost all of whom are strong or even 'radical' cosmopolitans) would. Moreover, I defend the view that special duties and not merely general duties exist.

In addition to reflective equilibrium, I utilize another method employed by philosophers: hypothetical examples. For instance, in Chapter 1 where I consider alternatives to securitizing, I advance an array of hypothetical examples belonging to different threat types (notably I differentiate between agent-intended threats and intent-lacking threats, with the later subdivided into agent-caused but intent-lacking threats and agent-lacking threats),[32] and to make my case, however, I utilize solely hypothetical examples. Several reasons inform this decision. First, as Helen Frowe explains, 'Stripping away the detail can enable us to identify general principles that can be obscured by the intricacies of historical cases' (Frowe, 2014a: 5).

---

[31] Following Doyal and Gough's (1991) JST holds that all human beings are fundamentally social creatures who cannot live meaningful lives as humans if they are unable to participate in social life. To participate in social life, two basic human needs must be satisfied: physical health and autonomy. These two basic needs are thus transculturally valuable. In JST, a referent object's satisfaction of basic human needs is decisive of its justness and hence its eligibility for self- and other-defence via securitization (Floyd, 2019a: chapter 4).

[32] See Chapter 1, Section 1.3, for an explanation.

Second, and again invoking Frowe, the use of hypotheticals does not mean that a theory generated in this way cannot be helpful with 'real-life examples' (ibid: 4). Third, as I go on to explain, this method serves the general ambit of JST. Unlike other normative theories of security, JST is built on the observation that there is a functional distinction between securitizing actors and scholars (Buzan et al., 1998: 33–35). While securitizing actors are the ones doing the securitization, scholars can – if listened to by relevant practitioners – influence securitization processes. In other words, while JST recognizes that securitization is a political choice by securitizing actors (Wæver, 2015), one of the aims of the theory in my 2019 book was to inform such actors when securitization is permissible, and what they need to consider in securitizing. An extension of JST into the terrain of obligation runs the risk of upsetting that balance, because – if such circumstances can be identified – securitization is no longer a choice (i.e., optional), but mandatory. Moreover, once the scholar declares a referent object objectively existentially threatened and in need of being saved or defended by securitization, it would seem that the scholar reduces the gap between the securitizing actor and the analyst. Many in securitization studies would hold that scholars who call for the securitization of or against specific empirical referents or threats are themselves securitizing actors. Whether or not this is true depends on one's understanding of securitization. If securitization equates to rhetorical securitization only as it does for many, then scholars can double up as securitizing actors. If, however, securitization necessarily involves the use of exceptional measures to address a threat, as it does for me here, then scholars are not, simply in virtue of their written text (or spoken word in, e.g., a public lecture), architects of successful securitization. Just as anyone else, however, academics can – by voicing insecurity concerns – *request* securitization, while as epistemic communities they can veto/endorse securitization already underway (Floyd, 2018, 2021).[33]

Given the different conflicting interpretations of securitization in existence, it is helpful to work with hypothetical examples because it allows me to advance generic observations concerning the obligation

---

[33] Elsewhere (Floyd, 2021), I argue that functional actors object to or endorse securitization on behalf of others. By contrast, referent objects, who by being promised protection via the speech act double up as audiences, veto or endorse securitization on behalf of themselves. One category of functional actor is epistemic communities, which often include academics.

to securitize without calling for securitization of/against specific real-life cases – and thus seemingly (though not actually) obliterating the functional differentiation between securitizing actors and scholars. Use of hypothetical examples carries on in Chapters 2 and 3, but in Chapters 4 and 5 I focus with NATO, the EU, and the UNSC, respectively, on real actors, albeit sometimes in hypothetical situations. This is the case because at the sub-systemic and systemic level of analysis the number of securitizing actors that can have a duty to secure via securitization is so limited that it makes little sense to work with hypothetical actors; moreover, not focusing on real actors here would stand in the way of this book's ability to suggest constructive and relevant improvements to current practice.

Some scholars are likely to criticize my choice of two western sub-systemic actors (NATO and the EU) as too narrow and non-inclusive.[34] Even though I repeatedly stress in relevant Chapter 4, that mandatory securitization applies equally to, for example, the African Union (AU), Association of Southeast Asian Nations, or Southern Common Market, I expect that some scholars will take my choice of NATO and the EU as evidence of mandatory securitization's inapplicability to the non-western context. Such an argument will likely be supported by my choice of western analytical/moral philosophy and its – in the cultural relativist's mind – harmful aspiration to universalism (e.g., Lyotard, 1984). Notably, the Copenhagen School's securitization theory has repeatedly, and in my view wrongly, been criticized as applicable only in liberal democratic contexts and latterly (and even more mistakenly) as racist for *inter alia* tying normal politics to western democratic politics (Howell and Richter-Monpetit, 2020). While these claims have been soundly refuted (on limited applicability, see, e.g., Vuori, 2008, or Côté, 2016, and on racism, see Wæver and Buzan, 2020, or Hansen, 2020), cultural relativism's deep-seeded idea that concepts apply only where they originate reigns large. While the argument that origin informs applicability is often meant to ensure that non-western voices on questions of morality are heard, cultural relativists ought to be aware that such claims regarding, for example, human rights 'are politically dangerous and have been regularly used by dictators

---

[34] I would like to thank the two anonymous reviewers for pressing me hard to further developing my arguments on the issues that follow in the remainder of this subsection.

to justify their depredations' (Donnelly, 2003: 64, FN 8). Moreover, it is, as Simon Caney points out, a 'non-sequitur' to hold that '[t]he geographical location of the invention of an idea [determines] its later applicability' (Caney, 2005: 87). If an invention (for instance, human rights or just securitization) seems more applicable in the geographical location where it was invented than another, it is simply because the practice of human rights, etc., is most developed in that geographical context (Donnelly, 2003: 63; Mulgan, 2001). If a scholar choses NATO and the EU over say the AU, it is – as in my case – perhaps simply because this is where their expertise lies or because the institutions are among the most advanced in relevant ways.

Moving on, at key junctures of the argument I invoke the reasonable person and sometimes also common law's reasonable person standard. The reasonable person or citizen is frequently invoked in political and moral philosophy, most notably perhaps in John Rawls' political philosophy where public reason is indicative of democracy (see Rawls, 1997). Throughout the book, I follow Rawls, for whom 'Citizens are reasonable when [...] they are prepared to offer one another fair terms of cooperation according to what they consider the most reasonable conception of political justice; and when they agree to act on those terms, even at the cost of their own interests in particular situations ...' (Rawls, 1997: 770).[35]

---

[35] In Rawls's political philosophy (since the 1980s and especially with *Political Liberalism*), reasonableness 'serves as the fundamental criterion for judging the acceptability and legitimacy of the public conception of justice and all associated "political" claims and decisions – those that place demands upon all citizens of the polity' (Young, 2006: 159). For Rawls, reasonableness refers to citizens ability to 'cooperate with others on terms all can accept' (Rawls 1996, 5, cited in Young, 2006: 160–161). Reasonableness in turn allows decision-making and judgements by overlapping consensus. In other words, Rawls recognizes the fundamentally political nature of, for example, justice (Martin, 2014: 589).
   Reasonable citizens are 'characterized by their willingness to listen to doctrines, arguments and reasons opposed to their own, even if they do not agree with them' (Audard, 2007: 198). Of course, not all humans behave reasonably all the time, but the claim is merely that on the whole human beings' *value* reasonableness. The empirical evidence in support of this is overwhelming. Thus, in many parts of the world, we organize political society accordingly, after all reasonableness (and the idea of an overlapping consensus) is 'the very foundation of a well-ordered liberal democracy' (Young, 2006: 162). Moreover, democracy is transculturally valued. We know this because 'liberal democracies produce less insurrection than any other

Objective existential threats, reasonable persons, and the – for mandatory securitization pivotal – last resort are concepts that will not sit easily with critical security studies scholars and many other constructivists. These scholars will point out that last resort, referent objects, and threats are themselves sites of contestation with no objective content, and on that basis critique the notion that we can have a theory of just, let alone mandatory securitization reliant on these concepts.

I agree that many referent objects (especially identities and orders) are socially and politically constructed. It is also the case that identities manifest or become stronger because of securitization (Ukrainian national identity, for instance, is bolstered by the ongoing war with Russia). However, the fact that something is socially/politically constructed does not mean that we cannot evaluate it.[36] Neither does it mean that all referents are equal,[37] after all, even things that are socially constructed have real consequences for real people (notably: the law). In philosophy, value (goodness and badness) is often assessed in terms of what Joseph Raz calls the 'humanistic principle', which is to say,

---

political system attempted in human history. [...] liberal democracies are "the people's choice", given that every other type of political regime produces enough people with enough motivation to overthrow the system' (J. Floyd, 2017b: 189). Moreover, Rawls does not tell us what justice or truth entails (in *Political Liberalism*, he speaks of a political theory of justice) but what *makes* for justice and 'truth'; in short, what makes for a *fair procedure* that as best as possible approaches the truth (J. Floyd, 2017b). Note here that in Rawls' an overlapping consensus is not achieved by people blindly pushing 'their truth', but by people weighing up their considered judgements against the available evidence (cf. J. Floyd, 2017b). Another way of putting this is that moral truth generated by an overlapping consensus is evidence-relative not fact-relative. In short, not only is universalism of justification possible, but also judgements and political claims rendered intersubjectively can approximate the facts; that is, they are or can be right/true in the evidence-relative sense.

[36] In the 1990s, postmodernist scholars questioned the Copenhagen School's aim to study identities as referent objects seeing that identities are fluid and thus always in flux (McSweeney, 1996). Was the school not guilty of objectifying identity after all? The school's response came in the 1998 book: 'We *do* take identities as socially constituted but not radically moreso than other social structures. Identities as other social constructions can petrify and become relatively constant elements to be reckoned with. At specific points, this "inert constructivism" enables modes of analysis very close to objectivist [...]' (Buzan et al., 1998: 205, emphasis in original).

[37] Note here that the cultural relativists point that 'conceptions of right and wrong differ from culture to culture' is dangerous. It does not allow condemnation of societies that are anti-Semitic, colonialist, or racist (Rachels, 1986: 617).

'from its contribution, actual or possible, to human life and its quality' (1986: 194). Human well-being can be charted in different ways. JST follows Len Doyal and Ian Gough's hugely influential *Theory of Human Needs* (1991) by charting well-being, and hence the value of referent objects, in terms of their ability to satisfy basic needs. For JST, needs are more appropriate than rights because some referents cannot be assessed in terms of their human rights record (ecosystems for example), while all can be assessed in terms of their contribution to basic human needs. Notably where individuals or groups thereof are the referent object, our concern is with their human needs. While just cause (meaning the presence of an objective existential threat to an entity that satisfies basic human needs) is pivotal, it alone does not satisfy just initiation of securitization. Amongst other things, just cause can be too trivial for securitization to be proportionate (cf. McMahan, 2005: 4). For example, in cases where a referent object (an order or an identity) is but one of a range of actors or things that provides objective well-being to the same group of people, the demise of the referent would not significantly compromise well-being.

I now turn to the issue of whether inter alia last resort and the reasonable person can be used for determining moral obligation. In defence of my approach, consider first that what I propose is not particularly contested in analytical or moral philosophy (cf. Caney, 2005: Chapters 1 and 2), suggesting that my epistemological outlook is not wrong, but simply different to that of most critical security studies scholars/constructivists many of whom align with continental political philosophy. I have explained already that, following the late Derek Parfit the objectivity of threats in JST is rendered in the evidence-relative not the fact-relative sense. This means that I acknowledge that we lack infallible access to the facts. However, this does not mean that everything is relative. Instead, it means that we must recalibrate our idea of what objectivity means. For Parfit, there is a perfectly intelligible sense of rightness and goodness that is evidence-relative. And that is the sense that is relevant to practical decision-making.

I said above that I sometimes make use of the reasonable person standard, most notably when settling disagreement on the satisfaction of last resort (see Chapter 1, Section 1.5). The reasonable person standard is a 'standard-setting' service frequently used in common law (Gardner, 2015: 1). The reasonable person is not a real person, but instead a heuristic. The same is used to settle 'whose moral views determine which statements are defamatory [...] which losses are too remote to be recoverable [...] he helps to set standards for both the formation and interpretation of contracts [...] he is the arbiter of dishonesty among those assisting a breach of trust, and in criminal law ([...] he has played a central role in the shaping of various defences)' (2015: 3). Reasonable persons do not set standards by invoking what is socially acceptable; instead, it is their 'job' to count the reasons towards justification (ibid: 9). She does so from an impersonal standpoint, which is to say, 'they do not bend to the varying personal characteristics of those who are judged by them' (ibid: 28). We might say then that the reasonable person is able to render an impartial decision or judgement based on the evidence available.

We can see that in legal practice the reasonable person is not overly theorized. For most lawyers and law scholars, the reasonable person is simply and unproblematically the justified person (Gardner, 2001). However, some law scholars have sought to give the reasonable person standard greater philosophical rigour. After all, 'tort and criminal law raise issues of justice, because both set the limits of acceptable behaviour in contexts in which some balance needs to be struck between one person's liberty and another's security' (Ripstein, 1998: 6). To do this, Arthur Ripstein utilizes Rawlsian ideas of reasonableness to inform the reasonable person standard. He argues, 'the reasonable person needs to be understood as the expression of an idea of fair terms of cooperation' (ibid: 7). To be reasonable is to 'take appropriate regard for the interests of others'. In more detail: 'The concept of the reasonable person makes it possible to take account of competing interests without aggregating them across persons. Rather than balancing one person's liberty against another's security, the reasonable person standard supposes that all have the same interest in both liberty and security' (p. 7). Ripstein's intervention is helpful because it allows us to use the reasonable person standard as a heuristic for settling normative questions, in this book most notably in cases when the satisfaction of last resort is disputed (see Chapter 1, Section 1.5).

I.7 Overview of Chapters

This book consists of five chapters, plus this introduction and an overall conclusion. Chapter 1 is about the conditions when securitization is not merely optional – which is the case when the substantive criteria of just initiation of securitization have been met – but about what must be the case for securitization to be morally obligatory. I suggest that relevant actors are obligated to securitize only when, in addition to just cause, right intention, and macro-proportionality, the – what I call – 'must cause' is satisfied. I argue that this is the case when would-be securitizing actors have tried relevant less harmful alternatives and when these have failed to satisfy just cause.[38] This view is in line with what the philosopher David Heyd calls 'unqualified supererogationism' (2019: 2). A philosophical position that sees value in keeping morality – where possible – free from prescriptive behaviour, whereby every good and right generates a moral obligation. I argue that the value of autonomy that allows relevant actors (limited) freedom to choose on how to respond to a just cause for securitization diminishes as certainty that securitization is the best[39] response increases. Certainty increases subject to evidence that less harmful options than securitization do not work.

By using six hypothetical illustrative examples relating to different threat sources (i.e., agent-lacking, agent-caused, and agent-intended threats) as well as different impacts of these threats (e.g., directly lethal, indirectly lethal, and non-lethal), the Chapter 1 contemplates what less harmful alternatives and securitization would look like in each case. The analysis shows that both securitization and politicization[40] are shape-shifters that are always attuned to the specific context.

From here, I move on to the most challenging parts of Chapter 1; the issue of how long politicization may be tried before must cause is satisfied. I explain that – what I choose to call the 'sufficient time gap' differs depending on the nature of the threat. For instance, whether politicization of climate change is effective takes much longer to establish than it takes to ascertain whether political solutions to an infectious disease are effective. I also consider – and ultimately dismiss – whether lethality of threats influences the length of the sufficient time gap. That is, do lethal threats require a quicker security

---

[38] The corollary of this is that the duty to securitize rests on a prior duty to politicize; that is a duty to act on an insecurity (in short, a duty to secure or rescue).

[39] As will become clear in Chapter 1, best here does not mean absolute best; instead, it is the best response relative to other less harmful responses. In short, it must emerge as a better, but not strictly the absolute best option.

[40] As I will argue usually multiple less harmful measures are tried simultaneously, I also refer to them as politicization.

response than non-lethal threats? Overall, I argue that there is no formula which allows us to reliably determine the length of the sufficient time gap for each case up-front. What matters is that politicization is tried for so long that it is allowed to fail. I suggest that – in practice – in cases where there is no agreement on the satisfaction of must cause between, for example, the public and the government executive (for instance, when the population requests immediate securitization, but the government remains reluctant), the reasonable person standard can help arbitrate the situation.

Chapter 2 is the first of four chapters that considers *who* has a duty to securitize and for what reasons. This chapter is concerned with states. Given that – in line with JST – unjust states are permitted to securitize just referent objects, the logic of mandatory securitization also applies to these actors. However, given that the leaders of unjust states are not permitted to secure their own unjust regime from threat I proceed by considering the obligation states have to insiders invoking just states only. I begin by briefly recounting the well-known arguments of social contract theorists that any state's raison d'être is the provision of security. I argue that the norm of the RtoP (i.e., pillar 1) and the concept of state failure show that this still holds true today, and I suggest that just states have an overriding duty to secure and, when necessary, securitize insiders, because the failure to act could result in the withering away of the state. Notably, if the social contract is broken, then just non-state actors are justified in resorting to self-securitization (Floyd, 2019a, chapter 5).

I go on to discuss individual and sufficiently capable states' obligations to securitize outsiders (just referents in other states) where there is no other protector. By drawing on the global justice literature, I argue that a pro tanto obligation of other-securitization is based on the moral equality of people.[41] Following on from Chapter 1, I suggest that this pro tanto obligation rests on a prior obligation to other-politicize an objective existential threat. After all, relevant actors have a pro tanto duty to securitize only when less harmful (i.e., political) options have failed. To put this another way, the duty of self- and other-securitization is a derivative duty of a wider duty to secure. The prior duty to do something about the threat, in turn,

---

[41] I use 'moral equality of people' and 'moral equality of persons' interchangeably throughout this book.

results – depending on the relationship the would-be securitizing actor and referent object have – variously from contractual obligations (e.g., at state level domestically) or from the moral equality of people.

I go on to discuss three factors that can override the pro tanto obligation to securitize. These are (1) the risk of death, disease, and disability; (2) the risk of instability and insecurity; and (3) financial costs.

Given that mandatory other-securitization can be provided by a range of actors (e.g., individual states, sub-systemic collectives of states (including NATO, the AU), or the international community), it is necessary to discuss what triggers specific actors' remedial responsibility, including – once must cause is satisfied – to securitize. By drawing on David Miller's (2007) connection theory, I argue that remedial responsibility can be triggered by outcome responsibility (including moral responsibility, causal responsibility, and benefit from the insecurity), ties of community and friendship, and finally capacity. By combining Miller's triggers with common-sense morality, I argue for a ranking of triggers that correspond to the above order. For capable individual states (notably hegemonic powers), this means that they are likely to be the primary duty-bearer for other-securitization only in a limited number of cases.

Chapter 3 considers non-state actors (including individuals) and whether these can have a moral duty to securitize. I argue that while securitization by individuals is both possible and can be morally permissible, only organized, not simply aggregate, groups can have a moral duty to securitize. I go on to examine relevant sub-state actors' duties to securitize insiders and outsiders. I argue that sub-state actors are permitted to securitize only when the state they reside in fails in its duty to deliver security. In such cases, relevant actors have a pro tanto obligation to securitize insiders. I further argue that in situations where a quasi-social contract is established this duty evolves into an overriding duty. Regarding outsiders, I argue that outsiders are not – unlike in all the other chapters of this book – people in other states, but rather people not represented by the sub-state actor. I argue that a pro tanto obligation to securitize outsiders here is largely based on capacity.

Regarding non-state actors at the sub-systemic and systemic level, things are a little different. While such actors are morally permitted to securitize, few would be able to do so effectively, as they lack the necessary enforcement mechanisms. In many cases, this voids the duty to securitize. Moreover, I suggest that non-state actors are not morally permitted to employ Private Military and Security Companies that would enable them to have a duty of mandatory securitization because of the adverse consequences for international order, stability, and security. I argue that one exception to this rule is formed by cases where non-state actors are outcome responsible for the insecurity that gives rise to the need for securitization and provided that the relevant affected parties have requested securitization, thus signalling overt consent.

Chapter 4 considers mandatory securitization and state-based sub-systemic actors, specifically collective defence organization and collective security organizations. The two types of organization differ in so far as the former is a formal alliance contractually obligated to perform collective action on external threats to insiders (here member states), while the latter serves to provide peace and security *among* the members of the collective, including by promising to act on internal threats (including a member state posing a threat to other members). For illustrative purposes, I take NATO as indicative of a collective defence organization and the EU before the Lisbon treaty that contains two collective defence clauses, as indicative of a collective security organization. I argue that NATO has, if requested to help by a member country, a contractual (Article 5) – and thus overriding – duty to protect that member state, where necessary (when must cause is satisfied) with securitization. I also suggest and defend the argument that Article 5 is now somewhat outdated and that – going forward – just reason (i.e., the existence of an objective existential threat + macro-proportionality, and not armed attack) should be the threshold for collective political action. The obligation to use securitizing measures, however, rests with the satisfaction of must cause.

By contrast, the EU as a collective security organization has, mostly based on ties of community and friendship, 'merely' a pro tanto obligation to securitize insiders. In short, the obligation to securitize can be overridden. Moreover, the treaties governing the EU and NATO do not foresee a contractual obligation on member states to save either organization if the same is existentially threatened. Indeed, if this was the case Brexit would not have been possible.

Both NATO and the EU and by extension similar organizations have a pro tanto obligation of mandatory other-securitization based on the moral equality of people. I argue that the duty to securitize can be overridden by the same considerations that override it in the context of the state, namely: the risk of dying, disease, and disability; the risk of instability and insecurity as well as by prohibitive financial costs. Given that especially NATO is likely to have more voluntary executors of securitization than individual states, it is less likely that the obligation will be overridden. While this might render NATO the world policeman, I argue that the different triggers of remedial responsibility to rescue alleviate the burden on NATO to act, after all NATO is not morally responsible for all insecurities, neither does it have the most developed ties of security friendship/community with all states, regions, and peoples.

Finally, I examine collectives and burden sharing. I hold that the triggers of remedial responsibility also feature in considerations regarding burden sharing for the costs of securitization in 'collective securitization' (Sperling and Webber, 2017). I argue that moral responsibility for threat creation places a greater share of the burden (notably regarding the financial cost) of securitization on relevant member states.

Chapter 5 considers the impact of the discovery of mandatory securitization on global security institutions. While ties of community and friendship, specifically at the sub-systemic level, ensure that the burden of mandatory securitization on the international community is relatively small, I argue that the international community – in the form of the UNSC – is obligated to act (1) when states or sub-systemic actors fail (note, in other-securitization they may fail for legitimate reasons), or (2) where there is no other designated protector. Given that the notion of needing to act when others have failed to act is not new, after all this tiered structure is central to the RtoP norm, I go on to examine the nature of the duty of the UN/UNSC towards the unprotected. I suggest that the UN charter amounts to a contract between the people of the world and the UN, rendering its duty to securitize – when conditions are met and there is no other protector – overriding. I go on to examine the nature of these duties as they already exist by examining RtoP provisions. I show that even if RtoP was in perfect working order and always acted on, it does not cover the moral duties of the UNSC regarding securitization; notably, it does not cover intent-lacking threats. Much like in Chapter 4 where mandatory securitization is used to update NATO's Article 5, I show how mandatory securitization can refocus and thus help RtoP. Thus, mandatory securitization usefully straddles RtoP's responsibility to prevent and the responsibility to react, while full-scale military intervention/war, which some policymakers, albeit erroneously, see as tantamount to the responsibility to react (Pattison, 2018: 225), is outside of securitization.

The book's overall conclusion summarizes the argument advanced in the book. Despite advancing a theory that utilizes security practice to achieve security as a state of being, I end on a cautionary note. To wit, although we have established the existence of mandatory securitization, the same should not be considered a ready-made solution to the world ills but rather a necessary evil in an insecure world. I argue that decision-makers concerned with improving the world should ultimately concern themselves with eradicating the sources of insecurity and not with fighting fires.

1 | *When Is Securitization Morally Required?*
The Case of Must Cause

1.1 Introduction

This chapter is concerned with the conditions when securitization is morally required. As such, this chapter does not make any claims about *who* has a duty to carry out securitization; consequently, it is silent on *where* specific actors' duties to secure stem from (these issues are covered in subsequent chapters). Instead, it aims to locate the critical juncture when securitization is – from a moral point of view – not merely permitted (and thus optional) but obligatory (mandatory). Already, we can see from this that the critical juncture cannot depend simply on what actors think or believe they must do about a threat. Instead, the moral requirement to securitize is external to the beliefs of securitizing actors; that is, it must relate to the available evidence. I hold that the obligation to securitize arises from what has already been done to address the threat. In other words, the obligation to securitize rests on a prior obligation to politicize, by which I mean not simply the elevation of an issue into political forums where it is discussed but the situation when concrete if ordinary (non-exceptional) measures to address the issue are put in place. In more detail, I argue that securitization is morally obligatory only when other feasible and less harmful options have been tried once and demonstrably failed to satisfy just cause.[1] Conversely, I hold that securitization is morally permissible *before* other less harmful options have been tried, namely when securitization is *anticipated* to have the best chances of achieving just cause compared to the chances of viable, less harmful, alternatives (Floyd, 2019a: chapter 5).

To make this argument, this chapter commences by explaining why in Just Securitization Theory (JST) obligation is bound to what I refer

---

[1] I discuss the sources of the obligation to politicize threats in Sections 2.4 and 2.6.

to as *ameliorated moderate last resort* (the situation when plausible and less harmful alternatives have been tried and have failed to meet the just cause), whereas permissibility is tied to reasonable chance of success, to wit when securitization is anticipated to be the 'best option' for addressing the just cause.

Overall, I show that last resort's function regarding the obligation to securitize is comparable to just cause in the permissibility to securitize (cf. McMahan, 2005: 4 & 5),[2] at least in so far as securitization *cannot* be required unless it is a last resort. In other words – and in a play on words – last resort is the *must cause* for the obligation to securitize.

It is important to note that JST's initial just cause, as well as the other criteria concerning just initiation of securitization, is not replaced by must cause (bar chance of success); securitization cannot be obligatory in the absence of a just cause, or any of the other criteria of just initiation for securitization, because one cannot be morally required to perform an act or to do something that is morally impermissible.[3] Put differently:

> Must cause = just cause, right intention, macro proportionality, *and* last resort.

Once I have laid this groundwork regarding last resort, I examine when last resort is satisfied regarding different threat types. To this end, this chapter works out plausible, less harmful, alternatives for a number of prominent and current threats and considers what factors influence for how long these ought to be tried before securitization is a last resort. The task of this chapter is not to do the impossible and to provide a blueprint that – for every possible threat scenario – reliably tells us when securitization is required. Instead, my aim is to tell users of JST how to go about establishing whether must cause is satisfied and on that basis when a relevant actor has a duty to securitize. The instructive nature of this chapter is an additional reason why all threat scenarios discussed refer to stylized and not real-world examples (cf. Introduction).

---

[2] Unless otherwise stated, last resort hereafter always refers to ameliorated moderate last resort.
[3] Or as Danny Frederick (2015: 158) puts it, morally impermissible acts are 'duty-voiding'.

1.2 The Importance of Last Resort[4]

Regardless of who has a moral duty to securitize and irrespective of the specific nature of the threat, what needs to be the case so that securitization is morally required (of relevant actors)? To answer this question, let us begin with the moral permissibility of securitization. In JST (Floyd, 2019a), securitization is morally permissible inter alia when it is judged ex ante to be the best option for satisfying just cause. To establish whether securitization is the best option, it is necessary to anticipate securitization's chances of achieving the just cause and to compare these chances with those of plausible, less harmful, alternatives (notably politicization and purposeful inaction[5]) at meeting the just cause. Only if securitization emerges as the best/most reasonable option is securitization permissible. In other words, securitization's permissibility depends – in part – on the success condition.

That securitization is permissible when it is the best option is in line with our moral intuitions regarding self-defence. As Seth Lazar (2012: 8) has argued: 'Without taking a position on whether our moral theories should be evidence-relative, fact-relative, or both, it is clear that our primary interest when exploring the ethics of self-defence and war is in the evidence relative perspective, because the judgments it yields are much more in tune with our ordinary thinking about self-defense.' Given that the obligation to securitize rests – like all duties – on finding a balance between the good done (the harm prevented) and the costs/harm incurred, the obligation to securitize could – provided all criteria are met – simply rest with the best option understood as having ex ante the best chances of success. To put this more simply, we might think that whenever all the permissibility conditions are met, it follows that the permissible option is also required – in short, that there is no gap between permissibility and requirement.

In the remainder of this section, I want to explain and defend why – where securitization is concerned – I do not support this inference. In other words, I shall explain why some securitizations that are morally justifiable are merely optional, while other securitizations are

---

[4] I owe special thanks to Jonathan Parry for repeatedly discussing this section with me.
[5] As argued in Floyd (2019a), by inaction I don't mean not reacting but purposefully reacting by not addressing the issue, for example, by choosing to not respond to acts of terrorism.

obligatory, even though any theory of the obligation to securitize must rest on a theory of permissibility. I will also explain why securitizations that are not morally required are – provided relevant criteria are satisfied – morally permissible. Pivotal to my reasoning is the logic of supererogation. A supererogatory act is one that is 'good to do, but not wrong not to do' (Heyd, 2019: 9). By contrast, an obligatory act is right to do and wrong not to do.

Most security studies scholars I consulted on the question whether just cause is automatically a *must cause* agreed with me that there is, or should be, a split between the point when securitization is permissible and when it is obligatory. Although I too am of this view philosophically, the matter is not easy to justify. Hence, if securitization is the best option at point X to achieve just cause, then surely relevant actors at point X are also obligated to securitize (i.e., do the best thing). Or put another way, if there is no obligation at point X, then how can securitization be permissible at point X (cf. Oberman, 2015)?

The case *against* separating out just cause (the point when securitization is permissible) and must cause (the point when securitization is obligatory) in the way I do is strengthened further by the fact that obligation at point X is merely a pro tanto obligation that can be overridden by concerns pertaining to the costs and risks to the securitizing actor. For example, regarding humanitarian intervention, we can say that all just states have pro tanto obligations to save people from grave harm; however, they have this obligation only if the cost (notably in terms of own soldiers sacrificed) is not prohibitive to their state's own flourishing (see, e.g., McMahan, 2010: 57). In other words, separating out just and must cause is not only illogical but it is also unnecessary for developing a theory of the obligation to securitize.

The crux of the objection against separating out permissibility and obligation is this: if securitization is the best thing that can be done to satisfy just cause then surely – from a moral point of view and all other things being equal – it *must* also be done. In what follows I want to first defend my view that – in the absence of a must cause – just securitization is supererogatory.[6] And second, I what to explain what changes the balance so that hitherto optional securitization becomes mandatory.

---

[6] There are at least two kinds of supererogatory acts. Acts are supererogatory if they are morally praiseworthy, which is to say they pose great personal risks to an actor and are therefore 'merely' permissible but not required. In addition to

Supererogationists hold the view that 'supererogatory actions lie entirely and without qualification beyond the requirements of morality and that is the source of their unique value' (Heyd, 2019: 15). The existence of supererogation is contested (see Oberman discussed later in this chapter). The philosopher Nora Grigore (2019) suggests that this contestation comes about because our understanding of morality is wedded to good acts being obligatory to avoid them from not being done. In short, in much of moral philosophy, the realization of the moral deed depends on obligation. However, to claim that all good acts are obligatory also brings problems. For one thing, it makes morality very demanding (Grigore, 2019: 1163). For another, it leaves no room for voluntarily good acts (Heyd, 2019: 23–28). The demandingness point is ameliorated by the fact that moral obligations are pro tanto duties only that can – in many cases – still be overridden by costs to the agents (this will be addressed in Chapters 2–4). The fact that supererogationism leaves room for voluntarily good acts is key. Thus, I concur with supererogationists that there is intrinsic value in human beings having moral choice.[7] That is to say, there is moral value in some things being done voluntarily and actors having, within a certain range of options, a choice on how to respond.[8] Put differently, just

such, in Joel Feinberg's terminology, 'meritorious, super-risky non-duties', acts are supererogatory when they amount to 'duty plus' (1961: 282). An example is when a nurse works a twelve-hour shift as opposed to the contractual eight hours to enable a colleague to attend a funeral. The distinction between the two types of supererogatory acts is important because a just securitization initiated in the absence of a must cause is not automatically morally praiseworthy. Supererogatory securitization can simply be duty plus. Notably relevant actors have a duty to secure those objectively existentially threatened, albeit – at this point – not by means of securitization.

[7] This is in line with JST, which holds that autonomy is one of two basic human needs.

[8] It is worthwhile to cite David Heyd here at lengths: 'What would be missing in such a world is what Tertullian referred to as licentia, that special field of liberty, which allows human beings to exercise their power of moral choice. Even Kant, who suggests the ideal of the Kingdom of Ends in which members of the moral community exercise their free will (Wille) by the necessity of their nature, believes that imperfect moral creatures like us have a free choice (Willkür) between good and evil. In this discretionary power to adopt the moral law (or reject it) lies the particular value of morality, at least for human beings. Going beyond duty might be considered as a display of this power of free choice. The pure or unqualified version of supererogationism highlights the moral potential of good human action not prescribed or commanded, imposed or demanded in any sense' (2019: 28).

cause + other criteria for just initiation of securitization give positive justifications (or deontic reasons) for securitization, but these reasons are not strong enough to override the value of autonomy (cf. Grigore, 2019: 1155). We can see that supererogation is also the reason why a securitization that actors are *not* required to do is still permitted, provided, of course, the criteria for just initiation of securitization are satisfied.[9]

Turning now to the second part of my argument, it is time to examine what changes this balance so that relevant actors no longer have a choice regarding *how* to act on just cause. In what follows I shall argue that a qualitative shift in certainty renders deontic reasons for securitization stronger than the value of autonomy, making securitization mandatory. I shall further argue that the certainty that securitization is the best option increases relative to the amount and quality of the evidence collected in support of that view.

Recall that in JST securitization is morally permissible – inter alia – based on ex ante judgements regarding the success of securitization satisfying just cause in relation to other less harmful options. I contest that while these reasons are (provided other relevant criteria are met) strong enough to render securitization morally permissible, they are not strong enough to trump the value of autonomy. This changes when we have concrete evidence that other options do not work. To achieve sufficient certainty, it is thus important that alternatives are *tried* out, because trying out (not anticipation) is the method to obtain sufficient evidence and consequently to generate sufficiently strong deontic reasons that are able to override the pre-eminence of autonomy.[10] The premise here is that we can truly know (be sufficiently certain) that an action is, out of a set of viable options, the best one only when we have eliminated these other options by trying them first and they have failed to satisfy just cause. In rare cases, it is possible that actors possess sufficient evidence that alternatives are unworkable even without having tried them first. For example, if a state is targeted with ballistic missiles, its government must – capability permitting – respond with anti-ballistic missiles, as it is already too late to try, for example, diplomacy. On this view, in summary, what matters is the

---

[9] I return to this in more detail later, when I discuss Oberman.

[10] Granted in some cases the method might be modelling, for example, regarding success of research vaccines.

actor's evidence about the likely success of their options. Trying out an option is the obvious way of getting that evidence. In exceptional cases, where an actor has evidence without trying out an option, trying out is not required.

This analysis gives way to the following guiding principle:

> In virtue of the value of autonomy, actors are permitted to choose how to respond to threats, provided all the options in that range pass some threshold of working and if there is not a huge disparity between the options in terms of how likely they are to work, and initiation of securitization would be morally permissible. But if the actor has unsuccessfully tried a few non-securitizing options, then the importance of responding to the threats trumps any value of autonomy, and securitization becomes required.

To be sure, while trying alternatives leaves securitization to emerge as the *best* option, it might still only be the best option among several worse alternatives. As Simon Caney (2005: 244) explains, the best option (in terms of the success of satisfying just cause) is not judged against some absolute standard but '"relative" to the other options available'.

In philosophy, the requirement to try alternative, less harmful, options (at least once) first (i.e., before war ensues) is known as the last resort (Frowe, 2011: 64). Last resort does more than to provide actors with greater evidence and thus increased certainty whether securitization is the best option. Importantly, by doing other things first, the need for securitization can decrease, because other options might go some way towards dealing with a threat. This is apposite for a number of reasons. First, the resources for securitization (including money and numbers of security practitioners) that most would-be securitizing actors have at their disposal are finite. Imagine a scenario whereby securitization is judged the best option in ten cases, but the designated securitizing actor has the resources to securitize only in five such cases. How should this actor deliberate between which case must be securitized, especially if all – or more than five cases – would not produce undue costs to the securitizing actor, thus requiring securitization in all or more than five cases, because securitization is anticipated to have the best chances of succeeding in satisfying just cause. We might say that in such cases they ought to do the best that they can and say securitize in five cases. Yet how are actors to deliberate which are the five most important cases given that in all cases securitization is expected to be the best option for satisfying just cause? Additional evidence is likely to assist in whittling down the number of cases that require securitizing, because once other options have been tried, we not only gain greater certainty regarding the best option but also the need for securitization goes down as threats are partially addressed by these other options, in some cases making securitization unnecessary.

Second, a low threshold for the obligation to securitize can increase/ trigger moral dilemmas – that is, 'cases in which doing one thing we're morally required to do rules out doing another thing we're also morally required to do' (Van der Vossen in Tesón and Van der Vossen, 2017: 217) – just states face. Such states are obliged to protect human rights and uphold civil liberties, but a requirement to securitize when it is anticipated to be the best option clashes with these other obligations because securitization often infringes these goods (cf. Floyd, 2019d).

While philosophers in particular might disagree with the differentiation between must cause and just cause, it seems to me that there is a precedent in the just war tradition for what I suggest here.[11] Many just war scholars consider war permissible in line with Lazar's earlier-mentioned view of evidence-relative certainty. However, it is also true that most just war scholars are not concerned with obligation. For the most part, the decision whether to go to war is considered the prerogative of states and not discussed further (cf. Oberman, 2015). The exception is formed by scholars theorizing humanitarian intervention. Most scholars writing on humanitarian intervention do so because they are in favour of the practice (an exception is Jackson, 2000; van der Vossen in Tesón and Van der Vossen, 2017) and because they think that able state actors have a duty to intervene when circumstances are right (see, for instance, Glanville, 2014). In my view, it is telling that many writers concerned with humanitarian intervention include as part of their substantive criteria the requirement of (if not by that name) *ameliorated moderate last resort* (e.g., ICISS, 2001: 36–37; Lango, 2014: 140).[12] It seems to me that while supporters of humanitarian intervention are concerned with the

[11] I do not wish to claim that anyone shares my view but rather that scholars mostly concerned with permissibility tend to share one view while those concerned with obligation have the more stringent view.

[12] This is not categorically the case; as Cater and Malone note, the World Summit Outcome Document from 2005 that launched Responsibility to Protect states that 'enforcement action should occur only after "peaceful means" have been considered and found inadequate' (2016: 125).

plight of people subject to grave human rights abuses, they are also wary of advocating the interference into state's sovereignty. Consequently, for humanitarian intervention to be obligatory, we need sufficient certainty that it is the best thing to do. Sufficient certainty for the obligation to go to war for humanitarian reasons, however, rests with isolating war as actually the best option. This can be achieved only by trying other less harmful options (diplomacy, economic sanctions,[13] etc.) first.

While we can find a split between optional and mandatory wars in the wider just war literature (see, e.g., McMahan, 2010), some philosophers are challenging the view of optional wars or optional rescue killings. Helen Frowe (2018), for example, has advanced the 'Requirement Thesis', which treats 'lesser-evil justifications for harming for the sake of others as rescue cases. [It holds that] unless rescuing imposes a very serious psychological cost on the rescuer, of the sort that will seriously impede her capacity for flourishing, she is required to enact lesser-evil rescues' (2018: 479). While Frowe's formulation seems to challenge the distinction I draw between the permissibility and the obligation to securitize, consider that Frowe makes her case with reference to the well-known trolley dilemma in which a pedestrian is faced with the choice to divert a run-away trolley to save five people, yet whereby diverting the trolley will kill one innocent workman. This is important because it shows that Frowe does not allow for alternative options to killing. That is – in her scenario – last resort is satisfied in virtue of the fact that diverting the trolley is the only and hence actually best thing the pedestrian can do to save the five. None of this is at odds with my proposal. I hold that securitization is required only at the point when other – less harmful – things have been tried to divert the trolley, for example, driving a car onto the track in between the workman and the trolley, from which the driver is able to escape before impact.[14] And that when the car fails to stop the trolley by ramming it out of the way, I think securitization is obligatory.

A different critique is offered by Kieran Oberman. In a 2015 article, Oberman advances the Cost Principle, which holds that 'those in power should not force people to render humanitarian assistance to

---

[13] The issue whether sanctions are less harmful than war is contested with scholars usually invoking the sanctions on Iraq in the aftermath of the Gulf War.

[14] This is for purposes of illustration only; I realize that there might not be time to do this.

those in dire need if the costs exceed that which people have a humanitarian obligation to bear' (2015: 261). Put differently, he argues that it is morally *impermissible* for decision-makers to enact wars that pose unreasonable/supererogatory moral or financial costs on the executors of war (e.g., soldiers) and taxpayers. The flipside of this is that unless an otherwise just war incurs such costs, the war is not merely morally permissible but morally required. In other words, there is no such thing as an optional war. As will become apparent in subsequent chapters, I agree that the expected moral and financial costs to the securitizing actor play a major role in the actual obligation to securitize others (i.e., outsiders). In short, the moral costs and risks are duty-overriding or, as in the case of individual persons (see Chapter 3, Section 3.2), duty-voiding factors. This is the standard view in philosophy. McMahan (2010: 57), for example, argues: 'Among other things, while the question whether an act is permissible does not seem to depend on the cost to the agent of doing it, the question whether an act is morally required or obligatory does seem to depend on the costs.' He makes this point by giving the following example:

Suppose that you and I are strangers walking in opposite directions across a high bridge. You have just dropped a $1,000 bill that is about to be blown off the bridge into the river far below. I can prevent this simply by stepping on it. Since it would cost me nothing to prevent you from suffering a serious loss, it is reasonable to suppose that it is obligatory for me to step on the bill. But suppose that the only way I could prevent the money from being blown away would require me to go over the bridge and fall to my death. No one would say that I would still have the same obligation to save your money but that I am excused for not fulfilling it because of the prohibitive cost to me in this case of saving the money. Rather, what we believe is that in the second case I have no obligation to save your money because of what it would cost me to do so. What it would be obligatory for me to do in the absence of any cost is not obligatory if it would require of me a sufficiently significant sacrifice. So a permissible intervention that would be obligatory if it could be done without cost is not obligatory if the sacrifices it would require are very great. (McMahan, 2010: 57)

Still, Oberman's argument is a tough nut to crack because it requires a defence of government supererogation. Justin Weinberg's (2011) work on the possibility of government supererogation is instructive here. It appears that one way to escape Oberman's argument is to suggest that government supererogation is permissible, provided 'through just procedures (say, some kind of deliberative democracy) we enact a policy which permits our government to perform such acts' (Weinberg, 2011: 275). Alas, for JST, this escape route does not work because the theory does not require legitimate authority or audience consent for just securitization (Floyd, 2019a: chapters 2 and 5). But this need not worry us. Weinberg makes it clear that invoking a procedural account of justice does not allow us to escape Oberman's challenge because 'outcomes of procedure matter, and those outcomes will be measured against a substantive account of justice' (Weinberg, 2011: 275–276). In other words, justice depends also on substantive forms of justice, not merely on just procedure.

While the procedural justice escape route from Oberman's challenge then does not work, a division into different types of justice helps us to realize that government supererogatory acts are not necessarily 'all-things-considered wrong' (Weinberg, 2011: 271). Many people might consider such acts right because they 'maximise the good' (Weinberg, 2011: 278). Some scholars would consider risking our own soldiers' lives to defend third parties virtuous (Kaldor, 2012: 138–139; cf. Chapter 2, Section 2.3). For many, 'Morality cannot be just a matter of considering your own needs and those of your nearest and dearest' (Mulgan, 2001: 135).

If we can accept that supererogatory acts are not necessarily wrong and hence impermissible, why then are they not also obligatory? Weinberg argues that whether or not an act is in fact required depends on the 'theories of justice and goodness' individuals accept (2011: 271). He suggests a test, whereby we must ask of the act in question whether it would 'be unjust to fail to perform the act' (Weinberg, 2011: 271). Given that most people distinguish between permissibility and obligation, I believe that most reasonable people would accept that it would *not* be unjust for a state to fail to encounter harmful costs to itself and its people in order to save persons in other countries (indeed this is why Oberman's account is so persuasive). In short, we can now say that a government's act of supererogation aimed at satisfying a need for security of third parties is justified (here: permissible) because it benefits the insecure;[15] however, because it also produces significant costs to inter alia the executors of securitization, it is not required.

---

[15] In the final section of his important paper Weinberg argues that a version of satisficing consequentialism, which sees agents focus on good enough but not

Another argument against Oberman's argument can be extrapolated from David Runciman's work on the moral agency of states. Runciman argues that the only way to make sense of states as moral agents at all is to consider them corporate as opposed to collective entities. Notably 'a collective entity is nothing more than the sum of its parts, whereas a corporate entity is somehow separate from these [...]' (Runciman, 2003: 41). According to Runciman it is only when considering the state as a corporate entity that we can make sense of the fact that 'states can be acted for by their representatives' (ibid, 41). Indeed, 'states need representatives to act for them' (ibid, 41). Although Runciman does not say this, it seems to me that it would be possible to argue that when representatives perform supererogatory acts that harm the people within the state, they act on behalf of the state as a separate corporate entity from the people, and that it is within their right to do so. In support of this argument also consider Ned Dobos and C.A.J. Coady's (2014) observation (here with regards the role of the electorate in representative democracies) that 'we empower our representatives to make decisions for us, and we do not feel that the government must always consult with us and make whatever decision is most popular' (Dobos and Coady, 2014: 93). Indeed, a third objection to Oberman's position can be found in Dobos and Coady's piece. They argue that since the electorate's preferences are unlikely to be indisputably for or against intervention the public cannot meaningfully exercise its veto 'in which case, we see no reason to think the decision is not covered by the authority vested in a representative government' (Dobos and Coady, 2014: 94).

To summarize the argument of this section, in line with our moral intuitions regarding self-defence I hold that when our concern is with the permissibility to securitize, then evidence-relative relative judgements regarding the success of securitization render sufficient certainty. Given inter alia the cost to securitizing actors and global stability, however, this same level of certainty is *insufficient* for the obligation to securitize. By insisting that other, viable and less harmful options are tried before securitization is obligatory, we increase certainty that

---

best consequences (i.e., utility maximization), is compatible with government supererogation. To be clear, a position of act consequentialism is untenable for supererogation because if 'apparently supererogatory acts maximize the good, then they are not supererogatory; rather, they are required' (Weinberg, 2011: 278).

securitization is the best thing to do to address the threat. Moreover, by trying other less harmful options first, the need for securitization in some cases is likely to decrease as some of these options might deal with the threat already.

1.3 The Nature and Origin of Threats in JST

The most important principle of JST is the just cause. However, 'most important' here does not mean that the satisfaction of just cause alone is sufficient for permitting securitization, instead, its special role arises from the fact that none of the other principles of just securitization can be satisfied unless just cause is (McMahan, 2005). In JST, just cause consists of two interrelated principles. The first is the just reason. The second is the just referent object of securitization. I have focused on the just referent object already in the Introduction; in this section, my concern is with the just reason. Notably, just reason is not about what kind of things may be saved by means of self-or other-securitization, but about when (i.e., under what circumstances) this can be done. I hold that securitization can be morally justifiable only if it concerns a real threat. Recall from the introduction that in JST security threats are socially and politically constructed, but that some security threats refer to real threats whereas others do not. Furthermore, and as also previously mentioned, I understand objective in the evidence-relative not the fact-relative sense. Fact-relativity refers to the situation 'in which people know all of the relevant, reason-giving facts' (Parfit, 2011: 162–163), while evidence-relativity refers to the situation when the available evidence suggests decisive reasons that the beliefs people hold about a given situation are true (Parfit, 2011: 150). This choice is justified because: fact-relative knowledge can, if at all, be obtained only with hindsight (cf. Herington, 2013: 67). Moreover, the evidence gathered must approximate the actual facts, notably the failure to do so renders actors culpable. In life in general, all forward-looking decisions and choices are made in line with fact approximating evidence, indeed unless this is generally considered permissible, we could act only ever after the event. For example, governments plan and develop infrastructure years ahead in line with population projections for any given area, not after radical change in population numbers.

It is important to note that in JST objective existential threats are not tantamount to lethal threats to persons. This is for two reasons.

First, a focus on lethal threats only would deny that some threats (notably some infectious diseases) have severe physically or mentally disabling effects, leaving people unable to be and function as humans should, but are not lethal. Second, regarding security, many relevant threats are not – in the first instance at least – lethal threats to people, but threats to non-human referents (states, political regimes, eco-systems etc.) instead. Such threats may be harmful to humans; indeed, I hold that securitization is proportionate only when the demise of a referent object *as we know it* (e.g., a state) is also sufficiently harmful to people, which in turn is the case when human well-being is severely undermined (i.e., to the point that people are objectively existentially threatened), but such threats are not necessarily lethal. Moreover, in the same way as humans do not have to die for a threat to be classed as existential, non-human referents do not have to be threatened with their actual disappearance to be existentially threatened. An established liberal democracy, for example, is existentially threatened not only when it is at risk at been invaded and annexed by a belligerent neighbouring state, but also when, for example, domestic forces seek to transform it into a dictatorship. In both cases the state *as we know it* will cease to exist, even if its territory, population etc. remain.

For all these reasons then, in JST existential threats refer to threats to the essential properties, character or being of putative referent objects. As such the terminology of 'objective existential threat' refers to:

(1) Direct lethal threats, meaning a threat is lethal to persons.
(2) Indirect lethal threats whereby the demise, or the significant alteration of an entity A (e.g., the state, an eco-system), entails the risk of death of people (e.g., when an aquatic ecosystem that disproportionally supports life of people turns toxic and leads to a famine).
(3) Direct objective existential but non-lethal threat, that is, threats that negatively compromise human well-being to the extent that humans cannot live in the way humans should.
(4) Indirect non-lethal objective existential threats whereby a threat to an entity A causes an objective non-lethal threat to people.

Conceptually the origins of all threats can be grouped into three threat categories. I differentiate between agent-intended threats, which refers to threats that one agent intentionally levels at another actor, order, or entity. An agent-lacking threat, in turn, is a threat that does not originate from human agents, for example, a vector-borne disease. Finally, third are agent-caused threats. This refers to a threat that is a consequence of an agent's behaviour, but unlike in agent-intended threats, it is not intended by the threatening agent. I differentiate between two sub-types of agent-caused threats: (1) those caused by the offending agent's obliviousness, that is, when people do not realize that their (combined) actions are potentially threatening to other entities; (2) such threat can also be caused by harmful neglect that is, when relevant agents fail to protect against the foreseeable[16] harmful events/consequences.

This concludes my discussion of threat types and origins of threats. These differences will become relevant again when we consider the length of time for which alternatives must be tried, for now it is necessary to discuss securitization and other less harmful alternatives on the basis of hypotheticals.

1.4 Securitization and Its Alternatives: Hypothetical Examples for Different Threat Types

In JST securitization is tantamount to the exception. Exceptionalism refers to measures and activities that are not considered acceptable in normal circumstances by reasonable persons, usually because of the risks or harm involved. However, even when we know that securitization refers to the exception the concept (i.e., securitization) is as slippery to grasp as a bar of soap in the bath. Unlike war, which inevitably means some use of kinetic force,[17] securitization is a shape-shifter. Thus, while we are able to say what securitization as the exception involves in the abstract, the nature of extraordinary measures in specific cases of securitization takes different forms. Accordingly, the threat from migration is or can be solved doing different things

---

[16] An outcome is foreseeable when a reasonable person could have foreseen the consequences of her actions (Miller, 2007: 96). 'Thus a man who fires an air rifle in a wood and hits a passer-by cannot escape responsibility by saying that he believed the wood to be empty, or that he did not know that airgun pellets could hurt human beings, even if he says these things in good faith. A reasonable person would know that people can be hidden from view in woods and that pellets can maim them' (ibid., 96).

[17] The emergence of the concept of soft wars changes this drastically (see Gross and Meisels, 2017).

than say the threat from climate change, or that from cyber-attacks. For this reason, it is important that this section must not only discuss plausible, less harmful alternatives to securitization; it must also give some idea what securitization against *different* threats might look like. Given that the argument here follows on from JST, the security measures that make up securitization must at least in principle be justifiable; notably, for example, a lethal response to a non-lethal security threat is unjust (Floyd, 2019a: chapter 6).

Before the start of the analysis, it seems to me that plausible alternatives to securitization fall chiefly into two broad categories: (1) purposeful inaction and (2) politicization.[18] Securitization means both heightened politicization (in a sense that the issue is hyper-politicized) but, confusingly, also de-politicization (in so far as issues are moved out of the democratic process and subject to executive power) (Hansen, 2012: 521; Buzan et al, 1998: 29). Importantly, politicization too is a shape-shifter. Thus, while politicization broadly means dealing with issues through the normal (often democratic political process) the realm of political solutions is vast and varied. Notably illegal unchecked immigration could be addressed by foreign aid and foreign direct investment into immigrant states, while climate change can be addressed by states transforming into carbon-neutral economies. In other words, what concretely politicization means is issue-dependent. This said, at the most basic level it means that issues are addressed using existing legislation that is applicable in normal times (i.e., not emergency legislation), or new – but non-emergency – legislation, that is, laws that are fully compatible with ordinary conduct. Politicization also means that the issue in question is not addressed using the military and traditional security establishment. At the risk of sounding banal, we can recognize politicization when actors do what they usually do in response to a type of issue or problem.

In this section I discuss the nature of securitization on a number of prominent threats across the different threat types (i.e., agent-intended, agent-caused, and agent-lacking). For each case this is followed by

---

[18] It is important here that we are talking of plausible alternatives here. Thus, political responses to threats that have no hope of addressing the threat because they defy scientific laws (for instance, a state-organized gathering in order to collectively praying for rain in *Drought disaster* discussed later) are not considered plausible.

a discussion of the viable, less harmful alternatives. Where agent-intended threats are concerned I focus on cyber-threats and non-state terrorism. For agent-caused but not intended threats I focus on illegal immigration and climate change. For agent-lacking threats I focus on vector-borne infectious disease and natural disasters. It is important to notice that this discussion does not include an assessment of whether the substantive criteria of the just initiation of securitization as specified in JST are satisfied. All threats discussed could satisfy those criteria, however, not all of the examples of security measures used meet the criteria of just conduct in securitization. I use them here purely to aid the reader's understanding of what is at stake in securitization.

1.4.1 Agent-Intended Threats

1.4.1.1 Cyber-Attack

One of the biggest emerging security threats of our time are those from cyber-sphere. Conceptually security scholars differentiate between cyber espionage (e.g., whereby states or firms try and steal industrial or national secrets), cyber-crime (including phishing and scam emails), cyber terrorism and cyber warfare (Dunn Cavelty, 2010). In recent years cyber threats have gained in importance as matters of national security not because they increasingly target individuals or industry, but because they have been used in an effort to undermine institutions and political processes. Evidence suggests that the democratic process in Western Europe and the United States (US) has been tampered with and manipulated, by Russia including by spreading Fake News about candidates, by using fake Twitter accounts and bots, by hacking national state computer systems, and by meddling in elections by boosting pro-Russian candidates (cf. Chertoff and Rasmussen, 2019).

The policy-making community has responded to the increased threats from the cyber-sphere. Already in 2014 at their annual summit Allies of the North Atlantic Treaty Organization (NATO) officially recognized cyber-sphere, alongside air, land and water as a fourth domain applicable for Article 5 mission. Article 5, in turn, is at the heart of the collective defence alliance, it obligates allies to come to the help of other members in case of attack (NATO, 2018, cf. Chapter 4, Section 4.2). Since then, NATO has been working to define when a cyber-attack would trigger this obligation (Scaparrotti, cited in EUCOM, 2018). So far it also remains unclear whether a cyber-attack would trigger an attack in kind only, or a response using conventional weapons as well.

In 2017 President of the European Commission Jean-Claude Juncker during his annual State of the Union address also placed heavy emphasis on cyber security. While previously European cyber security was primarily concerned with keeping European citizens safe from cyber criminals, the Commission new plans foresaw a 'Blueprint for how to respond to large-scale cybersecurity incidents and crises' (Official Journal of the European Union, 2017). In December 2018 the EU signed the Cyber Security Act which commits the EU to building greater cyber resilience.

While threats from the cyber-security sphere come in a variety of forms, I think it makes sense to use the label cyber-attack as a generic term to describe such threats; after all the threats we have in mind are agent-intended. For the purposes of the argument advanced in this chapter consider the following stylized example:

Election
Free and fair democratic elections in region X have for some time been undermined and manipulated by State B. This has been done through cyber-attacks on national Parliaments and also by spreading Fake News and Disinformation in an attempt to undermine the credibility of specific politicians standing for elections before Election Day. State B intends to undermine democratic process so that parties more sympathetic to State B gain a greater share of the vote. Though some domestic parties gain from this, they are not involved in the cyber-attacks. Elections are due to be held in State F located in region X in two months' time.

It should be obvious why a security response on the part of State F is a viable response for dealing with this situation. As regards *Election* securitization could involve executive-led controlled (partial) shutdown of the internet (at least on Election Day and perhaps several days before), for example of all social media websites (West, 2016). Securitization could involve the suspension of online voting. It could involve retaliation using specific kinds of offensive cyber capabilities, not routinized hacking back to stop 'an ongoing DDOS attack by affecting the participating computer systems' (Belk and Noyes, 2012: 23), but by implanting malware on the aggressor state B's computer systems. Securitization could also involve the retaliation with conventional weapons, including air strikes to take out strategic targets. Finally, securitization could involve the use of unilateral sanctions against B, or even multilateral sanctions by region X (as taken by the EU against Russia in response to the Ukraine crisis for example). Overall, we can see that while the issue of a cyber-attack is substantially different from a conventional attack, – in part – a security response to such threats is comparable to securitization against more conventional threats.

So far so good, let us now consider what – if any – plausible alternatives to this course of conduct (i.e., securitization) exist for State F? First, of all it is necessary to stress that there are alternatives. I say this, because in the realm of 'cyber security' the terminology could suggest otherwise. Cyber-*security* as opposed to the securitization against cyber threats taps into the distinction between security as a state of being and security as a social and political practice (Herington, 2015; Introduction). It is possible to achieve cyber security for individuals and states through routine procedures, in fact almost all efforts to achieve cyber-security relate to this (Hansen and Nissenbaum, 2009). The presence, size and importance of the internet demands that states provide cyber-security for their citizens, in the same way as they are obligated to provide security from criminal activity and lawlessness. Neither is necessarily provided by securitization, but it certainly rules out inaction as a viable alternative to a cyber-attack. The existence of cyber-security means that when states are faced with threats as described in *Election* routinized practices kick in to make people; businesses, the economy and the state save from attack. These routinized practices involve damage control and information sharing with allies. Overall, these are largely defensive objectives that is, 'those seeking to secure one's own systems, and preserve freedom of operation' (Belk and Noyes, 2012: 21) Routine procedures can involve a very limited amount of 'hacking back', but it does not contain: 'Offensive objectives are those seeking to coerce rival action, impose harm, or degrade rival capabilities' (ibid, 21). Indeed, full-scale 'hacking back' is a form of securitization. In the US were 'hacking back' is illegal under the 1986 Computer Fraud and Abuse Act, only the Security Services (FBI, NSA etc) are authorized to hack-back (Whyte and Mazanec, 2018: 86–87).

In addition to responding with routinized cyber incident management strategies, political leaders of State F, and perhaps from region X could engage in diplomacy with State B. Thus, while this threat takes place in the cyber-sphere the real or perceived political grievances that give rise to this agent-intended threat lie outside of the cyber sphere.[19] Diplomacy is the medium that allows discussion of grievances and allows trust building. Finally, state F needs to educate citizens on the threat from disinformation and how to avoid it. As part of this F could, for example, provide targeted funding to an impartial public service broadcaster that is free from state interference.

1.4.1.2 Jihadi Terrorism
Jihadi terrorism continues to be regarded as key security threat in many western countries. In order to discuss the securitization against terrorism and plausible alternatives consider the following stylized example.

<u>Jihad Terror</u>
State A is aware that its allies and friends' states B and C have been subjected to repeated jihadi motivated terror attacks. State A has condemned these attacks, declared solidarity with states B and C and offered help with intelligence and military missions abroad in order to free up security personal in B and C, so that these are able to deal with the state of emergency in State B. Reliable intelligence now suggests that terror cells are planning attacks in state A, including in retaliation for the display of solidarity.

How might state A respond to this threat? One obvious way to respond is by means of securitization. In order to understand what securitization entails with regard to terrorism consider that terrorism continuous to be securitized against in many states. In 2010 the United Kingdom's National Security Strategy identified terrorism as a Tier one threat (i.e., threats with the 'highest priority for UK national security looking ahead, taking account of both likelihood and impact' (Cabinet Office, 2010: 27)), while the National Security Strategy and Strategic Defence and Security Review 2015 A Secure and Prosperous United Kingdom states that: 'The threat from Islamist terrorist groups to the UK, including to British nationals and interests overseas, has increased' (HM Government, 2015: 15). What is true of Britain is true of many states in the West and beyond, and in many states, terrorism is securitized against. In the United Kingdom, and in many other European countries, this has taken the form of increased police

---

[19] In the NATO Russia case touched on above they partially lie with the eastward's expansion of NATO into Russia's former sphere of influence.

powers (e.g., stop and search without suspicion, detention without trial, extended pre-charge detention, and control orders), the expansion of state-led surveillance programmes and the request to mandatorily retain data, withdrawal of passports/citizenship of suspects, curfews, the creation of a mandatory monitoring culture in the education sector and much besides. Not all of these are used in all cases, and some are disproportionate. Overall, however, we can see that securitization against terrorism means an increase in the expansion of executive powers at the expense of judicial review and due process. In the United Kingdom, for example, TPIM (Terrorism Prevention and Investigation Measures) award special powers to the Home Secretary to restrict the freedom and movement of terrorist suspects.

The question of interest for our purposes is what alternative less harmful courses of action are feasible for state A? A small number of academics as well as some public intellectuals have suggested not responding to terrorism might the best way forward (Mueller, 2006; Jenkins, 2017). Inaction is considered viable because terrorism works by instilling fear in society. Inaction and depoliticization could deprive terrorism of its power, thus effectively reducing the threat. Such recommendations are easy to advance in the abstract and by those unaffected, but they do not convince in times of emergency. Studies have shown that the securitization against terrorism enjoyed the backing of many national parliaments and among the general population in the days and weeks after an attack (see, for example, Neal, 2013; Evangelista, 2008). It is usually only later, and when no further attacks occur, that the securitization against terrorism becomes contentious. Moreover, as we shall see in Chapter 2, Section 2.2, states have an overriding duty to provide security to their citizens, albeit not necessarily via securitization.

Having dismissed inaction as a viable alternative to the jihadi terrorism threat, it remains to consider politicization. Domestically politicization of terrorism refers to the criminalization as opposed to the securitization against terrorism. The idea is that state A would treat terror offences in the same way as other criminal matters. Terrorism prevention would be ensured by the police using ordinary, routine powers. For example, in the UK this would mean that suspected terrorists could be held for a maximum of 96 hours, not for 14 days; there would be no, or fewer mass surveillance powers; the police would have stop and search powers only with reasonable grounds for suspicion etc.

Politicization could in principle and alongside criminalization also involve trying to strike up dialogue with terrorists,[20] however, in the jihadi case this is made difficult because the IS leadership refused to engage in any kind of dialogue (even with journalists) while lone individuals remain unidentified until they strike.

1.4.2 Agent-Caused Threats

1.4.2.1 Irregular Migration

If, as argued earlier, security threats are not merely those that are intentionally levelled by one actor against another, then unchecked illegal immigration is at least a potential security threat.[21] Consider the following stylized example in which migration is an objective existential threat:

Immigration collapse
Low and middle income states A, B, C, D are suddenly, and through no fault of their own, faced with large numbers of migrants fleeing the political situations and economic hardship in states E and F. States A-D can accommodate and cater for only a small percentage of the total number of immigrants coming in a short space of time, accommodating all would mean the loss of social and political cohesion, conflict between migrants and residents and the collapse of their welfare system, including social services and health care.

In order to understand what securitization would involve we can look – as before with terrorism – at what states that have securitized against migration have done. Australia has securitized against migration since 2001; here securitization includes, or at one point included, the strict refusal to let migrant boats land, mandatory detention for illegal migrants in centres on Australian territory as well as off-shore (including in other countries), the excision of Australia's island territory from migration zones (thus depriving any refugees arriving

---

[20] Tony Blair famously did this during the Troubles.

[21] Some readers have advised against including the example of irregular migration, because of this issue's politically sensitive nature. I have decided to keep the example in part because the securitization of irregular migration is now so widespread. The use of the hypothetical example should make it clear that my text is not a securitizing request on my part. I also think, however, that the view that irregular migration can never amount to a real threat is Euro and western-centric.

their legal routes to asylum) the ban on media reporting from migrant camps and detention centres (Kasic, 2014).

In the United States illegal immigration was securitized against under President Trump. The United States National Security Strategy from 2017 declares that: 'Illegal immigration [...] burdens the economy, hurts American workers, presents public safety risks, and enriches smugglers and other criminals' (Trump: 2017: 9). Security measures realizing rhetorical securitization include the fortification of the US' southern border with Mexico. This includes plans to extend the existing boarder wall across the whole length of the border. Moreover, in 2018 a large group of migrants from El Salvador and Guatemala known as the 'migrant-caravan' was denied access, and border guards supported by 5,900 armed police authorized to use lethal force if necessary (Smith, 2018).[22] Meanwhile in Europe, in the wake of the 2015/2016 refugee crisis a number of countries consider migration a threat to national security, and some have securitized against migration. In Hungary under the leadership of Viktor Orbán this has included the building of razor wire fences along several of its borders (notably with Serbia and Croatia), the detention of all illegal migrants in container detention centres; the immediate expulsion of migrants unwilling to be fingerprinted and photographed, and Hungary has passed a law that criminalizes (including by incarceration) aiding illegal migrants (Walker, 2018). While far from all of these measures conform to the rules of just conduct in securitization, they show that securitization against migration pertains to extraordinary measures whereby migrants are kept out of a state, to the forceful detention of those that make it into the country in controlled camps, as well as forceful deportation.

Let us now consider what plausible, less harmful, alternatives to this course of action exist. It seems to me that at this stage of the analysis we can safely say that inaction is never plausible, because a real existential threat to a valued referent object *requires* responsible entities to act (cf. Chapter 2, Sections 2.4 and 2.6). Therefore, I will not discuss inaction further.

A political solution to *Immigration Collapse* would constitute a multi-pronged strategy primarily aimed at rapidly furthering economic

---

[22] Note here that within the terms of JST this is impermissible; lethal force may only be used to counter lethal threats (Floyd, 2019a: chapter 6).

development in affected states E&F and in neighbouring states home to refugee camps. Betts and Collier (2018)[23] explain that such a strategy cannot simply lie with giving foreign aid to affected countries, but rather must rest with the creation of 'opportunities for meaningful work and entrepreneurship', which in turn would generate a different 'narrative' regarding the prospect for young people convincing them to stay put. Beyond this, Betts and Collier (2017) also suggest developmentisation[24] as opposed to just humanitarianism for refugee camps. They argue – and show on real-life examples from refugee camps in Jordan and Uganda – how, when refugees are awarded with 'all of the things that allow people to thrive and contribute rather than merely survive: education, right to work, electricity, connectivity, transportation, access to capital' (Ibid, 144) they can meaningfully contribute to the host society, while simultaneously helping themselves.

Importantly, politicization does not mean open borders. All countries have a sovereign right to maintain external borders. This means that border checks are still carried out and illegal migrants without valid asylum claims can be rejected. To decide on valid claims, states must designate safe countries of origins. States A-D must also work to negotiate readmission treaties with leaderships of states E&F, allowing the safe return of failed asylum seekers.

1.4.2.2 Climate Change

Since the Intergovernmental Panel on Climate Change (IPCC) Fourth Assessment report in 2007 it is generally accepted that the rise in global temperature is man-made through the increase in carbon dioxide emissions from economic development. Since that time climate change has become widely regarded as a security threat. The European Union's Global Strategy, for instance, lists climate change, alongside terrorism, economic volatility etc. as a threat that 'endanger[s] our people and territory' (EU, 2016: 9). The UK government's National Security Strategy 2015 argues that: 'Climate change is one of the biggest long-term challenges for the future of our planet. It leads to and exacerbates instability overseas, including through resource stresses, migration,

---

[23] Betts and Collier's proposal has been controversial, and I do not mean to suggest that it is harmless, only that it constitutes a less harmful alternative to securitization.

[24] As far as I know the term is McInnes and Rushton's 2013.

impact on trade, and global economic and food insecurity' (HM Government, 2015: 65). Moreover, many experts believe that climate change functions as a threat multiplier, whereby climate change exacerbates existing grievances (e.g., terrorism, poverty, migration) leading to conflict and insecurity. Nevertheless, how climate change affects security is complicated and whether climate change will lead to violent conflict remains contested (Meierding, 2013, Selby et al, 2022).

Inter alia the risk of violent conflict means that climate change is predicted to have consequences for national security. Above all else perhaps climate change, or rather its effects, including extreme weather, environmental disasters, crop failure etc. have huge implications for people (human security).

Climate change is a global problem; but individual states can securitize against the effects of climate change in their countries. For example, given that one of the effects of climate change is expected to be the displacement of persons, states can secure themselves against migration in the way described earlier. Or, to give another example, consider that vector-borne diseases are set to increase and expand geographically northwards with a warming climate. In short, states can secure themselves and their populations against vector-borne diseases in the way discussed later. For the purposes of the discussion here I want to take on the issue whole-sale and work with the following stylized example.

Climate disaster
It is January 2037. In 2036 climate change was reliably identified as the driver of two violent conflicts in Africa. Likewise in 2036 climate change was directly responsible for the outbreak of at least one vector-borne disease epidemic. The combined death toll from these events is 200.000.

Although our hypothetical is situated in the future, I assume that the basic structures and functions of the UN have not evolved from the UN we know today. At this level, securitization would pertain to targeting the root causes of climate change as opposed to simply securing diverse referents against its effects (UN peacekeepers could still be sent to the conflict and diseases zones), as such securitization must – in the main – take the form of a legally binding environmental regime that brings down emissions so that climate change stops or progresses no further. This regime would be mandatory on all UN member-states. It could be enforced by a newly designated body that works in close conjunction with the UN Security Council. Non-compliant states would be hit with heavy sanctions and loss of membership in global and/or regional institutions. It would be important, that powerful states (e.g., the world hegemon) – if of a different opinion regarding the necessity of the securitization against climate change – could not pressure other weaker states into non-compliance, for example, by withdrawing foreign aid.[25] Individual states would need emergency powers to coerce people into less carbon intensive behaviours; this could take the form of additional police powers, including surveillance powers checking for sustainable behaviour and energy use, special police powers enabling them to check on businesses, industry and individuals but also mandatory restrictions on car usage, flying etc.

The alternative to this course of action is a multi-pronged strategy of politicization that is very much akin to what we already witness in current affairs. Since 2007 the UN and other international institutions and governments have rhetorically 'securitized' climate change (i.e., declared it a security threat), but no exceptional emergency measures have followed to address the threat. Instead, the international community has – after much foot dragging – managed to agree a new global climate accord: the Paris treaty signed in 2015. While this treaty sees all signatories agree to keep global temperature rise below 2 degrees Celsius (UNFCCC, 2018), it allows signatories to set their own targets. The nature of these targets and whether targets are met, however, are reviewed in regular intervals internationally enabling peer pressure and 'naming and shaming' to increase too low national targets and to motivate action. As Robert Falkner (2016) has pointed out, these same mechanisms are also set to work at the national level were civil society (e.g., Think Tanks, NGOs, and more recently in select countries school pupils[26]) are already monitoring governments and holding them accountable for their climate action. At the individual state level people are encouraged and sometimes financially enticed to make climate friendly behavioural changes, but nothing is enforced or monitored by police or intelligence.

---

[25] Note that in 2017 US 'President Trump suggested [...] that billions of dollars in U.S. foreign aid could hinge on how countries vote on a U.N. resolution condemning his decision to recognize Jerusalem as Israel's capital and move the U.S. Embassy there' (Morello, 2017).
[26] www.nytimes.com/2019/02/15/world/europe/student-climate-protest-europe.html

Another alternative political solution is a binding regime, in which targets are set centrally. While the UNFCCC has failed to agree such a binding regime, the history of the Montreal Protocol on phasing out ozone-depleting substances shows that such regimes take-off when important players (here the US) are on board, and drive it forward, because in the US major chemical producers had phased out ozone-depleting substances and lobbied the federal government to take international action (O'Neill, 2009: 86). In short, the difference between the securitization against climate change and its politicization lies in large part in the stringency of the regime but also in how it is enforced globally as well as nationally.

1.4.3 Agent-Lacking Threats

1.4.3.1 Vector-Borne Diseases

Agent-lacking threats fall chiefly into two categories: environmental disasters and vector-borne diseases. I want to start with the latter. Vector-borne diseases are parasites, viruses and bacteria that are passed on by blood-feeding insects such as mosquitos, tics, fleas, black flies, lice and tsetse flies (WHO, 2017).[27] The stylized example I use later utilizes Dengue fever and severe dengue. 'Dengue is a mosquito-borne viral infection causing a severe flu-like illness and, sometimes causing a potentially lethal complication called severe dengue' (WHO, 2018). Consider now *Dengue threat*:

Dengue threat
Gabenia is a developing country located in the sub-tropics. The population of Gabenia is faced with an unprecedented outbreak of dengue fever. Beneficial weather conditions have resulted in a larger than usual number of infected insects. Many patients develop severe dengue and there are unprecedented numbers of child mortality.

Following the pattern established in this section, we must at first consider what a securitization against *Dengue threat* might look like. From comparable real-life cases (e.g., the Ebola crisis 2014–2015, Covid-19) we know that security measures aim at keeping the non-infected

---

[27] In some – limited cases – such diseases can become communicable between people, including through sexual intercourse, rendering the threat agent-caused.

parts of the population free from infection while simultaneously fighting the sources of infection using coercion. This could mean compulsory vaccination. Securitization could include curfews during the early morning and evening before dusk when mosquitos are most active. These curfews would be enforced by the police and even the military, as they were in Ebola affected countries (Doherty, 2014). Curfews and mandatory detention could also be placed on infected people to stay in specially created detention areas. Thus, while Dengue is chiefly transmitted by mosquitoes, when infected persons become hosts to mosquitos the virus spreads.[28] The military can also be employed to deal with vector–disease control (WHO, 2012: 1). In Brazil, during the 2016 Zika virus disease the military controlled and executed the large-scale fumigation with the highly potent insecticide pyriproxyfen from specialist fumigation vehicles (Watts, 2016). Another extraordinary measure would be the administration of under-tested vaccines, by which I mean vaccines that have not undergone the standard series and rigour of tests before they are declared safe for use on humans.

The alternative to military/police enforced curfews and disease control would be politicization that aims to achieve the same ends (i.e., reducing infection rates and fighting the sources) using ordinary and non-coercive political measures. A real-world example of this would be Sweden during the first wave of the Corona-virus crisis which resisted national lockdowns and instead asked people to keep their distance in public, to not gather in large groups and so on. A key factor in the spread of Dengue is vector-control, this need not be done by the military, and instead people everywhere need to learn how to reduce the number of mosquitos on a long-term basis. A chief factor in this is tightly sealing water containers of all kinds, and also the regular emptying of all stagnant man-made water bodies. Gabenia could run public education campaigns on how to reduce the vector itself. In addition, Gabenia would need to educate people how to protect themselves, for example, by wearing long sleeve clothing, by voluntarily staying indoors at pertinent times of the day (i.e., at dawn and dusk) (European Centre for Disease Prevention and Control: 2019). Gabenia could also distribute insect repellent free of charge to the general population along with mosquito netting.

---

[28] Also note that at this point the threat is agent-caused not agent-lacking.

1.4.3.2 Environmental Disaster

Environmental disasters take many forms, for example, cyclones, earthquakes, hurricanes, floods, and Tsunamis. Any of these can be caused or accelerated by man-made climate change (McGuire, 2016), however, all of these can and do also occur as natural events. Moreover, even when natural disasters are climate change induced, the policy response concerns it and not the wider underlying cause. In any case, in this section I use the example of a naturally occurring drought to discuss securitization and its alternatives; thus, a drought, 'is a prolonged dry period in natural climate cycle. It is a slow-onset phenomenon caused by rainfall deficit combined with other predisposing factors' (WHO, 2023).

<u>Drought disaster</u>
Millville, a city of 500.000 inhabitants is a sprawling metropole in a developing country. Because of its natural setting Millville is a tourist attraction. Located in a temperate climate, Millville has virtually no rainfall from May to August, but heavy downpours during the wet season from December till February. For the past two years, however, rainfall has remained limited, and Millville is now in a middle of a severe drought.

One difference between politicization and securitization against agent-lacking threats is that the military as opposed to civil emergency response teams become central (we have seen this in the Dengue case, which draws on real-life Ebola and Zika virus crises). In the drought case the military could be brought in to protect remaining water sources as well as to ensure that bans on the usage of water are enforced. The most important ban would be a reduction of the personal use of water to a minimal amount, one that would automatically prohibit the watering of gardens, the use of swimming pools or washing cars. This ban could be enforced using drones etc., but also heavy fines (including criminal records) for those who defy orders. The government could pass new emergency legislation requiring water companies to make available information on individual water consumption. Ultimately water supply could be turned off for most of the week and come on at set times for a short period of time, allowing people to refill containers. The police and military could be awarded special powers to check if farms, for example, comply with the regulations and check for illegal tapping of ground-water aquifers. Finally, Millville could go into lockdown and prohibit leisure tourists to enter the city.

Similar to *Dengue threat* politicization would rest not on coercion but on voluntary action. To cope with the situation a reduction in personal water consumption is key. In order to achieve this a strategy of politicization would rest on educating people on the risks of running out of water altogether. The government could also pass laws to criminalize unnecessary water intensive activities, including washing cars etc. Beyond this the government could focus on fixing leaks in the existing pipe networks, on exploring alternative and new sources of water generation (e.g., ground water exploration), while it could also redistribute water from other areas of the country.

With this I have come to the end of discussing our six illustrative cases. To summarize, we have learnt that inaction can be ruled out as a plausible alternative in all specified cases. The fact that threats are real and sufficiently harmful to human beings in all cases means that inaction is unlikely to ever be a plausible alternative. For the most part, a policy of inaction would simply permit actors to shirk responsibility. We have also seen that politicization – much like securitization – is not a one stop solution (i.e., diplomacy or sanctions), but in most cases politicization refers to multi-pronged approaches that *together* could usefully address the threat. This is important because it goes some way towards answering the inevitable question: How *many* alternatives should be tried before must cause is satisfied? I don't think decision-makers need to conjure new non-securitizing alternatives; after all this would cause unnecessary delay. Instead, in each case the number of alternatives refers to how an actor ordinarily responds to outbreaks of e.g., infectious diseases. Beyond this, would-be securitizing actors may[29] also try out well-known and publicized non-securitizing responses that have been employed by other actors, but which they have not tried before. But there is more, importantly, the cases discussed also show that it is implausible to hold that different political solutions to a threat must be tried and shown to have failed one after the other.[30] In reality, politicization of threats will consist of a myriad of different alternative measures tried simultaneously, not in succession. Given this and considering further that we have excluded

---

[29] Assume here that the actor is reluctant to securitize, after all securitization is – at this point – already morally permissible.

[30] I am grateful to Jeff McMahan for pressing me on this point.

inaction as non-viable I henceforth refer to less harmful alternatives to securitization often simply as politicization.

1.5 How Long May Politicization Be Tried before Securitization Is Mandatory?

Using the six cases discussed earlier I now want to contemplate what needs to be considered when we try and work out how *long* politicization may be tried before securitization becomes – in the actual common-sense meaning of the word– necessary and on that basis mandatory, because we now have sufficient certainty that securitization is *indispensable* for satisfying just cause.

Looking at our six cases again I want to begin this discussion by focusing on the differences among the six cases. I have picked the examples deliberately so that two of the threat scenarios discussed refer to agent-intended threats (*Election* and *Jihad Terror*), two scenarios involve agent-caused but not intended threats (*Immigration collapse, Climate disaster*) and two threat scenarios are agent-lacking (*Dengue threat* and *Drought disaster*).[31] Beyond that, two threats (*Jihad terror* and *Dengue threat*) are directly lethal to persons, two threats (*Drought disaster* and *climate disaster*) are indirectly lethal and the remaining two threats are non-lethal (*Election* and *Immigration collapse*[32]) (see Table 1.1).

These distinctions are potentially important; thus, it seems reasonable to argue that the relative lethality of threats renders securitization more urgent vis-à-vis securitization against non-lethal threats. Suggesting, in turn, that political solutions may be tried for a longer period where non-lethal threats are concerned and for a comparatively shorter period of time where lethal threats are concerned. With a view to our examples earlier, it would mean that the satisfaction of must

---

[31] It should be noticed here that agent-lacking threats often morph into agent-caused threats, or at least that they have agent-caused elements to them. The cases of *Dengue threat* and *Drought disaster* clearly show that while the threat is not caused by people living in the affected areas, people contribute to the threat if they – when infected but symptomless – walk around risking being bitten by mosquitos, or -in our drought case – when they overuse scarce water resources.

[32] Immigration collapse could potentially lead to death after clashes between natives and migrants.

Table 1.1 *Hypothetical threat scenarios and their respective lethality*

	Agent-intended	Agent-caused	Agent-lacking	Direct Lethal	Indirect lethal	Non-lethal
Election	✓					✓
Jihad terror	✓			✓		
Immigration collapse		✓				✓
Climate disaster		✓			✓	
Dengue threat			✓	✓		
Drought disaster			✓		✓	

cause (measured from the onset of politicization) takes necessarily longer in *Election* than *Dengue threat*, and longer in *Immigration collapse* than *Drought disaster*.

A related factor that quite plausibly influences the relative length of time for which alternatives may be tried could be the number of people existentially threatened. It seems plausible to hold that a threat that existentially threatens say 1,000 people needs to be dealt with quicker by means of securitization than one that affects 100 people. Thus, while here both threats are lethal, we might say that the threat bringing with it greater numbers of mortality is comparatively *more lethal* than a direct lethal threat with a small number of death (infectious disease versus terrorism comes to mind here). In this same vein we might also distinguish between direct lethal threats and indirect lethal threat, arguing for quicker securitization against direct lethal threats, on the grounds that the initial referent could be saved by other, less harmful, means before anyone dies.

On the face of it this lethality-qua-time reasoning seems convincing. Because *the harm prevented by securitization is greater* it seems true that lethal threats warrant a quicker response than non-lethal threats. And perhaps it is also true that threats leading to comparatively higher numbers of death must be prioritized. However, as soon as we consider that the lethality-qua-time logic suggests that the borderless threat of *Climate disaster* requires securitization comparably quicker than *Drought Disaster* (recall that our fictitious Millville 'only' has 500.000 inhabitants), doubts should set in. Our moral intuitions tell us that it does seem wrong that the commencement of safe-making by securitization of the 500.000 must necessarily take longer than that of >500.000. But why do such doubts creep in? For one thing, because 500.000 seems a big number, certainly compared to say 500. However, all of this is relative. Thus 500 is a big number compared to 50, while 50 is a big number concerned to just 5 deaths prevented by securitization. Yet we might also say that 500 people saved from being severely harmed because of securitization is 'better' than 15 deaths prevented by securitization. This last point is important; it disproves the idea that the harm prevented by securitization is always greater when lethal threats are concerned. In other words, it shows that lethality does not automatically warrant a quicker response to non-lethal threats in all cases, because the harm that securitization prevents is not always greater for those kinds of threat.

Instead of going on to spell out cases when this is so, recall that when we are discussing length of time for which politicization may be tried, we have already accepted that securitization is permissible. Notably, permissibility includes macro-proportionality that is, we have – at this point – settled that securitization and the harm that it will cause innocent bystanders and threateners is a proportionate response, and also that the threat securitization prevents is sufficiently harmful in its effects to warrant causing such harm. It seems to me that once we have passed this threshold and deemed securitization morally permissible (as we have, for the purposes of argument, in all six hypothetical cases) we are on a level playing field regarding threats and the harm that they cause. In short, once securitization is deemed morally permissible, the actual effects of individual threats (i.e., lethal, or not) do not matter, because we know that securitization is proportionate.[33] One exception here pertains to cases where would-be securitizing actors have insufficient means to successfully securitize against two threats, which affect an equal number of people. *Ceteris paribus* in such cases it seems that the more harmful (usually the lethal threat but depending on numbers not categorically) ought to be given priority.

With lethality out of the way, another issue that needs investigating is whether must cause is satisfied more quickly when threats are agent-lacking that is, when there is no threatener. This argument stems from the

---

[33] I discuss this in Floyd (2019a: chapter 5), where I explain that just securitizations that satisfy all criteria are not more or less just depending on the number of people now not being harmed; instead, we must say that some do more good than others.

observation that where agents are at the source of the threat (either by causing the threat intentionally or unintentionally) there is potentially always room for dialogue. That is, there is space in which would-be securitizing actors can warn agents at the source of the threat of what will happen unless these agents change their threatening behaviour. As such they can and perhaps should try and engage in conflict resolution as part of politicization. In agent-lacking threats, in turn, dialogue is impossible (we cannot reason with vectors), and it is therefore reasonable to suggest that the length of time for which alternatives need to be tried is comparatively shorter.

Looking at the stylized examples earlier, however, we can see that it is not true that dialogue and discussion with threateners is always an option. Notably with regards to lone wolf jihadi terrorists acting on the behalf of or in allegiance with, for example, IS this is impossible. The secret security services usually do not know who the people are (or rather that they will carry out attacks) before they have done so. While talking to Muslim communities (e.g., counter terrorism police and de-radicalisation specialists speaking at schools with majority Muslim pupils) can back-fire. Thus, by being identified as a possible offender, feelings of alienation can set in, which make people more susceptible to becoming radicalized (cf. Abbas, 2019 on PREVENT, see also Breen-Smyth, 2014 on the unintended consequences of counter-terrorism).

Based on this analysis, I would like to suggest that the time for which alternatives to securitizing may be tried before must cause is satisfied can – somewhat unfortunately – not be generated using a formula that takes account of lethality and source of the threat. With this dismissed as impossible, what, if anything, concrete can we say about the length of time for which alternatives may be tried? One concrete thing we can say is that it makes little sense to dismiss less harmful alternatives to securitizing, unless these alternatives have been tried for a period of time that is long enough allowing them to fail. And at the same time short enough though as not to unnecessarily endanger would-be referents by delaying securitization. Let us call this ideal time period: the *sufficient-time gap*. I will return to this more fully in a moment but let us consider firstly what failure means in each of our six cases.

Regarding *Election*, political alternatives to securitizing fail when they prove unable to secure the democratic process; in part this could be established using opinion polls that test for the belief in false facts. Politicization of *Jihad terror* fail when the number of (foiled) attacks (not casualties) does not decrease following the introduction of such measures. Alternatives to securitizing in *Immigration collapse* fail if the number of irregular migrants seeking to enter a given state does not markedly decrease. Political solutions to *Climate disaster* fail unless they manage to reduce carbon emissions, allowing the rise of global temperatures to stabilize. Political solutions to *Dengue threat* fail unless the number of new infections is decreasing in statistically relevant terms. Finally, in *Drought disaster* politicization fails when the water level in aquifers and dams has decreased at a rate incompatible with low water usage by all.

One thing we can observe from these examples is that the time that needs to elapse to establish whether politicization has failed differs widely depending on the nature of the threat. Regarding *Dengue threat*, for example, it should be possible to see relatively quickly (i.e., in a matter of days or weeks) whether politicization manages to generate a much-needed decrease in new infections, the same should be true of *Drought disaster*, in so far as relevant authorities should be able to tell – relatively quickly – whether water levels go down too rapidly. By contrast, at the extreme end, the sufficient-time gap for *Climate disaster* could span months, a year, 18 months or more. This is not only because vast amounts of data need to be collected from different states, but also because unless data is collected for a lengthy period (i.e., over the course of 12 or 18 months) to establish the effectiveness of measures. Moreover, unless a longish time window is allowed it is impossible to discount short-term changes to emissions reductions caused by e.g., economic factors such as temporary downturns, weather factors (i.e., less heating in summer months). In short, short-term data collection would generate an unreliable result.

The analysis of the six cases clearly shows that the *sufficient-time gap* can differ widely in distinct cases. In each case the politicizing actor needs to monitor whether the political solutions are making a sufficient positive change. In some cases – notably infectious diseases – this will be relatively easy as we rely on concrete data (i.e., medical statistics); in others – notably, terrorism – it will be much harder due to known unknowns (i.e., the fact that we can't know for sure who else is out there planning to harm people). What then can be done in cases where, for example, states as politicizing actors-cum-securitizing actors disagree with most of the civil society that sufficient-time gap is closed and must cause satisfied?[34]

I want to suggest that this situation can be resolved with help of the reasonable person standard. Specifically, the would-be securitizing actor ought to defer the decision on whether must cause is satisfied to the reasonable person understood in Ripstein's terms as the normatively justified person (1998: 8 c.f. introduction). Of course, the reasonable person is not a real person but instead a heuristic. In practice it would see the would-be securitizing actor publicly tot up the reasons and the evidence in favour of the satisfaction of must cause in order to determine whether this outweighs reasons for not securitizing. This process would enable the rendering of a plausible, non-biased decision regards sufficient-time gap and hence on whether must cause is satisfied. If reasons are miscounted, and a mistake is made in favour of the satisfaction of must cause, it should be remembered here that at this stage securitization is morally permissible.

The reasonable person standard is associated with common law. The practice of mandatory securitization can benefit from the methods of common-law in another way. In common law countries such as the UK, and unlike in civil law countries such as, for example, Germany, the doctrine of precedent applies. Concretely, '[t]his means that the judgment of each case can bind all subsequent cases depending on the seniority of the court (the court system has a hierarchical structure). As such case law becomes part of the law by either setting legal precedents where there is no legislation or interpreting legislation' (Oxford Lib Guide, 2018). Quite aside from the question whether mandatory securitization should be codified into law; precedents can act as useful guides on how to proceed in similar situations. Moreover, precedents reduce the need for the reasonable person standards. To facilitate this method, any given state, regional body etc. should aim to document the threats, the means and nature of politicization and how long for this was tried. Such databases could then also be used to serve as valuable guides to settle disputed cases regarding the satisfaction of must cause.[35]

---

[34] Note here that the disagreement could be either way.

[35] With a view to R2P Bloomfield (2017) makes the point that 'the *accumulation of precedents*' can help 'entrench a new norm in international customary law' (2017: 27, emphasis in original).

1.6 Conclusion

In this chapter, I have argued that securitization is not automatically obligatory when it is morally permissible, which inter alia is the case when securitization is ex ante judged to be the best way to satisfy just cause. Instead, I have suggested that securitization is a moral duty only when politicization has been tried and when this has failed to satisfy just cause, because only then do we have certainty that is sufficient to override the intrinsic moral value of autonomy. Importantly, the so determined 'must cause' does not replace just cause (notably securitization cannot be mandatory unless it is permissible, and permissibility depends *inter alia* on the satisfaction of just cause, proportionality etc). Rather, what it does do is to specify the critical juncture when circumstances are such that the threat no longer merely permits securitization but *requires* securitization.

The distinction between in Pattison's words merely a 'right' to securitization and a 'duty' to do so (2010: 15ff), raises three outstanding issues in need of discussion in this chapter's conclusion. First, are the criteria for the moral permissibility of self-securitization the same as they are for just other-securitization? Specifically, does the right to other-securitization not also depend on the – at least – tacit consent of the general population in cases where securitizing actors are states? Second, in JST the prospect of success is not gauged in terms of securitization's absolute chances of satisfying just cause, but relative to the chances of the success of other less harmful options. In other words, securitization is permissible even if resistance appears futile. This begs the question whether executors of securitization can be required to partake in securitization that has only a slight chance of succeeding in satisfying just cause? Or is it the case that mandatory securitization requires a more stringent success condition than JST?

And finally, third, are the 'jus in securitization' rules the same for morally permitted and for morally required securitization? Or is it the case that laxer standards should apply to the just conduct in securitization when it is morally required?

The first question arises because of the clear differentiation between self- and other-securitization developed in this book, but merely mentioned in passing in my 2019 book *The Morality of Security*. As already touched upon in the discussion of Oberman's work in Section 1.2, other-securitization can be at odds with public opinion and still justified. Consent is also not required for just self-securitization. As I have explained in my 2019 book, in state-led self-securitization, referent objects (most likely (members of) the public) do not have to consent (tacitly or overtly) to securitization. There are several reasons for this, but the main reason is that the inclusion of beneficiary consent seeks to prevent against agent-benefiting securitization.[36] I hold that the possibility of agent-benefiting securitization is pre-empted by the substantive criteria of just securitization, notably right intention. Given that the general public within the securitizing state is not the primary beneficiary of other-securitization, the phenomenon acutely raises the issue whether or not other-securitization requires the consent of the securitizing state's general population? Or, more realistically whether other-securitization should 'reflect its citizens' opinions in its decision making', whose taxes and man-power are utilized to make it possible (Pattison, 2010: 134). To solve this puzzle let's begin by asking when and why the general public might object to other-securitization. I can see three possible scenarios: (1) we don't think that we should help; (2) we don't care about other (far away) people, and (3) helping will negatively affect us, for example, the cost of other-securitization is too high. The first two fall foul of a general obligation towards others on the grounds of the moral equality of people, which imposes remedial responsibilities (positive duties) on capable actors towards all regardless of place and origin (cf. Chapter 2, Section 2.3). In short, the first two do not stand up at the bar of justice. The third objection is the weighty one. We shall see in Chapter 2, Section 2.5, that the obligation to securitize is overridden when the costs for the would-be securitizing actor are expected to be too high. Also recall McMahan's bridge example from earlier (Section 1.2). Here the passer-by's pro-tanto obligation to rescue the $1000 dollar bill is overridden if this can only be achieved at great costs to himself.[37] The interesting question is whether the passer-by is morally permitted to rescue the $1000 dollar bill even if this means falling to his death? The answer is likely to depend on the

---

[36] An agent-benefiting securitization is a securitization where the primary beneficiary of securitization is the securitizing actor, not the referent object (Floyd, 2010).

[37] $1,000 bills are no longer in circulation. Their rarity means that they may well fetch much more than that sum. To be sure, whatever their value, it does not detract from the argument made.

view one has of the sanctity of life (cf. Section 3.2), as well as on the position the passer-by has in life (e.g., do they have caring duties, for example, for children). However, we believe that individual actors are morally permitted to incur great costs (provided they do so voluntarily) in performing moral acts, but that such acts are supererogatory never obligatory (McMahan, 2010: 58). But are governments morally permitted to perform supererogatory other-securitization without the consent of the public who would be the entities incurring the high costs? The answer is that permissibility depends *also* on the extent of the costs incurred (cf. Frowe, 2014a: 151). That is to say, permissibility does not depend on the view of the majority, but rather on proportionality, which includes the costs to people governments are responsible for (Shue, 2018: 266). In other words, the criteria governing the moral permissibility of self and other-securitization are coterminous.

Turning now to our second question, can one be required to do a harmful act that cannot be expected to succeed in averting the threat? On the face of it this seems not only improbable, but it also raises the issue whether there is a mistake in JST, which does not specify an absolute success condition. Instead, here the prospect of success is judged relative to the success of less harmful options in satisfying just cause. Bluntly put, in JST out of a set of options, securitization simply must be the least hopeless one at achieving just cause. One reason for framing JST in this way is that the theory permits just resistance by the weak against unjust harm by the strong (cf. Floyd, 2022). One way to justify a less stringent success condition is to stress the honour of the victim. Daniel Statman puts this as follows: 'Whenever victims of aggression are overwhelmed by an aggression but, nonetheless, find the courage to rise against him through some form of determined resistance, however hopeless, they are thereby reaffirming their honor' (Statman, 2008: 679).

To my mind this reasoning sits comfortably with the value of autonomy stressed earlier in the context of permissibility and supererogation (Chapter 1, Section 1.2). Where wars and securitizations by collectives (states etc.) are concerned there is however a problem with this logic. Helen Frowe has shown that honour-based accounts don't work for collective defence (war) because collateral damage inflicted on innocent bystanders is morally permissible only if the war has a good prospect of success (Frowe, 2014a: 153–154). While honour-based justifications sit uneasily with, for instance, state-led securitizations,

Frowe shows that futile violence is unjust not because it does not have an absolute chance of succeeding in satisfying just cause, but rather because such action is disproportionate.

> When the chances of achieving the good end are slight, it is hard to see how it can be permissible to inflict serious harm as a side-effect of pursuing that end. It might seem rather hard justice to require restraint out of concern for the citizens of the invading state. But the welfare of those citizens is one of the things that the requirement of proportionality demands we consider before undertaking any war, even a war to resist unjust aggression. (Frowe, 2016: 60)

This means that provided securitization is proportionate, a relative chance of success suffices for securitization's permissibility and its requirement.

Finally, our third question: are the principles governing 'just conduct in securitization' the same for mandatory securitization as they are for merely morally permitted securitization? This question comes about because it seems reasonable to suggest that if securitization is a bona fide last resort then the rules for what kind of emergency measures may be used also are relaxed. While this seems intuitively right, it is to be rejected. It cannot be the case that simply because relevant actors have a duty to securitize that they may do so in any which way they see fit, including in complete disregard of basic human rights of those that are subject or object of securitization. If there is a moral disparity, it pertains to how excusable wrongful acts are only. For instance, while torture is morally wrong, its use in securitization might sometimes be excusable (i.e., under extreme duress). It is almost certainly more readily excusable when securitization was a last resort.

2 | *States and the Obligation to Securitize*

2.1 Introduction

Chapter 1 established with the concept of *must cause* the critical juncture when securitization is not merely morally permissible but obligatory. Chapters 2–5 of this book are concerned with discovering who – that is, which actors – have the obligation to securitize, and whether or not this duty is conditional or overriding.[1] In this context, it is crucial to realize that a duty to securitize rests on a prior duty to act on the threat using ordinary political measures, for short, a duty to secure; after all, if no one has a duty to act (politicize), must cause cannot ever be satisfied. In short, the duty to securitize is a derivative duty.[2]

The present chapter focuses on individual state actors. I argue that regarding national security (encompassing the security of the state and its economy, but also the security of citizens within states), the obligation to securitize can be charted in terms of contractual responsibilities. In other words, I argue that in the context of national security must cause offers definitive guidance for when securitization is mandatory, at least where just states are concerned. The picture is much more complicated when it comes to states and mandatory securitization of outsiders (e.g., citizens of other states). I suggest that to understand why this issue is relevant at all we must commence by consulting the literature on global justice. I show how this literature enables us to understand: (1) why able states have a duty to make the insecure

---

[1] Philosophers differentiate between perfect and imperfect duties, and latterly between positive and negative duties (Varden, 2011: 280–283). While there is some overlap, I stay clear of these terms, for two reasons: (1) an imperfect duty is not simply the inverse of perfect duty (cf. Roff, 2013: 15–6), and (2), as Pattison (2022) has argued in a review of Luke Glanville's *Sharing Responsibility*, duties of mandatory securitization are not imperfect duties at all because the theory assigns them to agents each step of the way.

[2] The deep connection between the duty to securitize and the general duty to secure is reflected in the title of this book.

secure via politicization (i.e., use of ordinarily acceptable/normal measures), as well as (2) how much we owe.

I go on to chart the moral costs and risks that override the *pro tanto* obligation to securitize outsiders. I argue that – in addition to must cause – duty-bearing states have an obligation of other-securitization when: (1) the securitizing/intervening state possesses willing, able, and sufficiently numerous executors of securitization; (2) securitization will not create unreasonable levels of insecurity for the would-be securitizing actor; and (3) the financial costs of securitization do not create security deficits for the securitizing state or its citizens.

I go on to discuss liability and obligation, specifically whether liability for threat creation due to prior poor choices strips putative referent objects of the entitlement to being saved by mandatory securitization. I also discuss what liability for threat creation means for securitizing actors, specifically I am interested in the question whether liability for threat creation means that securitization is morally required *before* must cause is satisfied. That is, in virtue of the fact that they have either created the threat or done nothing/little to avert it, are such securitizing actors morally compelled to do everything possible right away to deal with a threat, or may they pursue a political solution first?

Finally, I discuss the circumstances when individual states are the primary duty-bearers of other-securitization. This is important because if all capable states (and other actors) have a pro tanto moral obligation to remedy the insecurity situation, who – out of the many possible actors – should act? To come by this problem, I suggest a ranking of David Miller's (2007) triggers of remedial responsibility that I derive from common-sense morality. Concretely I suggest that moral responsibility for threat creation trumps, outcome responsibility, which – in turn – trumps 'security friendship', while friendship/community trump pure capacity to act in the ranking of such triggers.

2.2 Just States: Duties to Insiders

States are the most common actors in international relations. While we all know what states are, it is worthwhile to remind ourselves that states 'must possess the following qualifications: a permanent population, a defined territory, and a government capable of maintaining effective control over its territory and of conducting international relations with other states' (Evans and Newnham, 1998: 512). Moreover, a state has 'legal personality and as such in international law possesses certain rights and duties' (ibid: 512).

We can differentiate between just and unjust states. In line with Just Securitization Theory (JST), only just referents, including just states and just collectives of states, are eligible for self-securitization and to being saved via securitization by other states or actors. In accordance with JST, just states are states which satisfy a minimum floor of basic human needs. Unjust states can in principle justly securitize just refer- ent object (notably, JST does not insist on legitimate authority (Floyd, 2019a: 140ff)). This includes just third states, groups of innocent people within third states, but also groups of people within its own territory, notably its citizens. Given that citizens (i.e., a permanent population) are – as we have just learnt – an integral part of the state, it could be argued that securitization of citizens as opposed to the regime/government is a form of self-securitization, and consequently that unjust states are eligible for some forms of self-securitization. Indeed, and as we shall see, all states are not merely permitted to secure their populations from just threats, but – at times – required to do so.[3]

It is probably ultimately hair-splitting whether – when a state secures its population – we call this 'self-securitization', or whether only securitization of the regime (including its economic model, lead- ership, government, ideology) is self-securitization, notably the two are often hard to separate (cf. Buzan et al., 1998: 146). The important point is that legitimate authority (which in much of just war theory takes the form of a state possessing a freely and fairly elected govern- ment) is not a necessary component of the moral obligation to securi- tize. We can see this by analogy. A murderer is not – simply because they have already committed a serious wrong – now somehow perpet- ually exempt from the law and thus permitted to commit further mur- ders. Consider also that according to JST unjust states are permitted to securitize (i.e., make safe via emergency measures) their populations, provided that the population is morally innocent in the relevant sense. Indeed, in such circumstances unjust states have an overriding duty of securitization. Nevertheless, because unjust states do not have the

---

[3] Consider here also that forbidding unjust states to secure their own populations would mean that someone else would have to do this; surely – given the costs and risks – a responsibility no state would wish to have.

moral right to self-securitization narrowly conceived (i.e., as securitization of the regime), and because I need to paint the broadest possible picture, I will work with just states only.

The purpose of the state is considered inseparably linked to the provision of security for its citizens (insiders). This is nowhere more pertinent than in the work of Thomas Hobbes (1588–1679). Hobbes considered the state of nature a perpetual state of war, conflict, and consequently insecurity. A condition that according to Hobbes could only be overcome/ameliorated if people associate and bow to an absolute sovereign, the Leviathan. In Hobbes, thus, the purpose of the state (Leviathan) is to provide otherwise elusive: 'internal security against each other; protection against other groups, or external enemies' (Boucher, 1998: 152; see also Sorell, 2013). In order to enjoy security and peace, people are willing to give up 'certain of their rights' (Boucher, 1998: 152), most notably the right to use force in order to secure themselves and their property.

Other social contract theories have a more positive and benign view of the state of nature. John Locke (1632–1704) viewed it as a pre-political but still moral place, where adherence to god was pivotal and provided a moral baseline. However, the absence of authority meant that when conflict (usually over property) broke out, such conflicts could not easily be settled and continued often indefinitely (Friend, 2004). Ultimately, the need to protect their life, liberty, and property (including of their own bodies) drove people to leave the state of nature and to associate in state-like groupings (ibid). In other words, for Locke too one purpose of the state is to provide security.

The third most significant social contract theorist of early modern political theory is Jean-Jacques Rousseau (1712–1778). Like Locke, he had a positive view of the state of nature, unlike Locke, however, he believed that human ascent out of the state of nature into a social contract has left ordinary people insecure, because the contract serves only the most well off. Rousseau's main aim was to right this condition by providing a normative theory specifying how the social contract would need to change so that people everywhere could become equal (Friend, 2004). Although Rousseau's work is not about security in the way Hobbes' and even Locke's work is, equality, which is to say the ability not to be exploited, abused, or otherwise violated, chimes with our modern-day extended concepts of security as a state of being, notably human security.

In summary, the basic idea of these early modern social contract theorists is that states are, or should be, intrinsically linked to the provision of security as a state of being, because they provide an escape from a permanent state of insecurity, and/or because states can only be deemed good/justified if they provide comprehensive security as a state of being.

I list these early social contract theorists here, because despite how much has been written about them and about the role, function, and make-up of the state since, the inter-linkage between states and security remains fundamental to our conception of the state. In our own time, this is obvious from the principle of the responsibility to protect (RtoP or R2P), which has sought to make state sovereignty conditional on that state's provision of freedom from a small number of atrocity crimes (genocide, war crimes, ethnic cleansing, and crimes against humanity) (see, e.g., Bellamy, 2018; cf. Chapter 5, Section 5.3). It is also obvious from national security strategies where the purpose of the state is irrevocably bound up with the security of its citizens. For example, the first objective of the United Kingdom's National Security Strategy and Strategic Defence Review from 2015 is 'to protect our people – at home, in our Overseas Territories and abroad, and to protect our territory, economic security, infrastructure and way of life' (HM Government, 2015: 11). Finally, it is obvious from the concept of state failure. While this concept is contested with scholars setting different thresholds for state failure, most would agree that states have failed 'when they are consumed by internal violence and cease delivering positive political goods to their inhabitants. Their governments lose credibility, and the continuing nature of the particular nation-state itself becomes questionable and illegitimate in the hearts and minds of its citizens' (Rotberg, 2004: 1).

Because states are responsible for the provision of security for their people, states also possess specific and practically unique capabilities to provide security. Most notably, they hold a monopoly on violence, which is to say, they are – bar some very limited allowances for self-defence – the only entity that can legitimately use coercive and lethal force (discharged most notably by the police, military, and intelligence agencies) within their given territory (Weber, 1946: 1). The right to provide security by force and coercion, however, does not mean that states *must* provide national security in this way. In line with the argument in Chapter 1, securitization is mandatory only when *must cause* is satisfied.

States' raison d'être as security providers means that their duty to self-securitize is overriding, which is to say, no considerations can override their duty to securitize insiders in relevant cases. As we shall see below, in other-securitization (e.g., where one state secures inter alia the population of another state by using extraordinary measures), one prominent consideration able to override the duty to securitize is the risk to the securitizing actor (e.g., in armed humanitarian interventions, most obviously in terms of own soldiers' lives lost). This does not apply in cases of mandatory self-securitization, because in such cases the moral cost – for the would-be securitizing actor – of not providing security is *always* greater than the cost of not providing security.[4] Above all else, the failure to enact mandatory securitization terminates the social contract, which is to say the state itself disappears (hence the notion of state failure). Peter Steinberger has shown convincingly that we can find this in Hobbes. He argues: 'When the state fails to do what it was designed to do – when it threatens, rather than protects, the interests of the citizens [and I would include here by failing to act in appropriate ways] – then the social contract, that is, the original agreement among citizens, is annulled' (Steinberger, 2002: 859). Concretely this means that a just state can use its military and security personnel to securitize. More controversially, it means that if there are insufficient numbers of persons that have voluntarily joined professions (e.g., military, police) in which they might incur the risk of death, dying, and disability (cf. Section 2.5) when defending the just state or its people, then it is within the right of the state to use conscription, including of medical personnel and other specialists.[5] To be sure, conscription is only permissible when the initiation of securitization is morally justifiable, when there is a must cause, and when numbers of executors of securitization are insufficient. This is because conscription is morally problematic. As Pattison has convincingly argued: '[...] a policy of conscription undermines several freedoms. It potentially violates self-ownership, since the individual's body is used in a manner that they do not choose. In addition, it denies freedom of

---

[4] Cf. FN 83.
[5] During the coronavirus, the government of North Rine-Westphalia (Germany) floated the idea of a pandemic law that would have enabled the state to force – against their will – medical personal to work during the pandemic. www .sueddeutsche.de/politik/landtag-duesseldorf-pandemie-gesetz-kritik-von-aerzten-pflegern-und-juristen-dpa.urn-newsml-dpa-com-20090101-200331-99-543802

occupational choice and freedom of movement, which are restricted during the period in which the individual is conscripted' (Pattison, 2014: 122).

These moral problems with conscription smooth the path for the use of Private Military and Security Companies (PMSCs) (ibid: 173). Although the moral problems with employing PMSCs are extensive, Pattison's impressive study ultimately concludes that such groups 'can be permissibly employed in a wide variety of roles when their deployment is likely to have very beneficial consequences for the enjoyment of basic human rights' (ibid: 179; see also example on p. 186). It should be noted here that the right to employ PMSCs and even conscription is not one held only by just states, provided that securitization is just, unjust regimes can – in principle – do likewise. For example, if an unjust regime defends its population (likely a morally innocent group of people and hence just referent) against unjust external aggression, it can – in principle – use PMSCs to do so. The problem is, however, that in this case the unjust regime helps secure itself as a side effect. Here thus a decision would have to be made which – the regime or the external threat – is the lesser evil for the population.

As we shall see below a second prominent factor that can override, the pro tanto obligation to securitize is the risk of instability. Scholars sceptical of humanitarian intervention often juxtapose justice (i.e., when human rights are met including through force) and order (Jackson, 2000; see also Hurrell, 2014; Bellamy, 2018: 247). Or, put differently, cosmopolitan forms of justice with more communitarian forms of justice (Williams, 2015; Bain, 2014). Either way, the assumption of sceptics of humanitarian intervention certainly often is that the same will lead to disorder, instability, and even injustice (Cochran, 2014: 191). While – as explained in Section 2.5 – this is a valid objection to mandatory other-securitization, it has no bearing on mandatory self-securitization of just states. If anything, the opposite is true. Thus, when states fail to act on must cause, it becomes permissible for sub-state actors to defy the state and seek self-securitization (we will return to this issue more fully in Section 2.7) resulting in all likelihood in instability, disorder, and insecurity for many. As Steinberger (2002: 859) explains:

[W]hen the state fails to accomplish the things it was designed to accomplish – when, indeed, it subverts the very ends for which it was created – then the contract that the citizens had entered into with one another has now been abrogated, hence has been rendered null and void, in which case the state is literally no longer. The citizens are no longer citizens but are immediately plunged back into a condition of mere nature, and each individual is obliged only to maximize his or her interests as he or she determines.

Provided that must cause is satisfied, the duty to provide national security (i.e., essentially the security of citizens in virtue of securing the state) via securitization is straightforward; here, no other consideration can override the duty to provide security. Yet, what happens in situations, where states are unable to securitize effectively, for example, because they have insufficient financial means? Recall, from Chapter 1, the example of *Dengue threat*, whereby the population of the fictional sub-tropic, developing state Gabenia was threatened with dengue fever and severe dengue. We said that in this case securitization is required once political measures to tackle the outbreak have demonstrably failed to produce a reduction in new infections. Assume now, for the purposes of argument, that must cause is satisfied and that Gabenia must now securitize, for example, by mobilizing the military to exterminate vector-carrying mosquitos and to enforce curfews at key times of the day. But what if Gabenia does not have a functioning military force that could be deployed for these and other tasks, because there never was money available, or even the need, to sustain this. In other words, what happens if Gabenia recognizes their duty to securitize, but cannot deliver on securitization? It seems to me that if they cannot discharge their duty directly to their citizens, it is their duty to seek help from those who can (e.g., a capable neighbouring state, a regional body or even the international community).[6] I will discuss the issue of who has primary responsibility for other-securitization in Section 2.6, for now the important point to note is this: the inability to fulfil the specific

---

[6] The duty to ask for help with internal securitization also applies in cases when securitization would incur huge costs on the domestic security forces, for example, when securitization of organized crime (internally) would risk the lives of countless police. On this issue, please note that excessively harmful securitizing actions are morally impermissible under the just conduct to securitization principles. However, this does not detract from the duty to securitize, but it merely means that this duty must be fulfilled by other means. My thanks to James Pattison for alerting me to this point.

duty to self-securitize does not exempt states from the related duties to seek and/or to accept[7] help.[8]

Regarding the issue of mandatory securitization and national security, it remains to discuss what happens when would-be referent objects request securitization[9] before must cause is met. Recall the case of *drought disaster* discussed in Chapter 1, Section 1.4.3, where the fictitious 500.000 strong city of Millville is suffering from a severe drought. What if a significant number of the population (for instance, a clear majority of 70 per cent), who would be the referent object of securitization, demand – through peaceful protests, petitions, etc. – securitization *before* must cause is satisfied? In such situations, are not fully democratic states obligated to securitize because it is the will of the majority? Or, in other words, does popular revolt bring forward – in time – must cause. I think not, because while states have a duty to secure their citizens, in the absence of must cause there is no specific duty regarding *how* this is to be done.

To make this clearer, consider the issue of how welfare states provide welfare. We might say that welfare states count as such only if they provide a range of basic needs to their citizens, including one or more of the following sick pay, holiday pay, unemployment benefit, maternity pay, free healthcare, etc. This means that if the governing party of a state wants theirs to be a welfare state, then they must – specifics aside – ensure that a range of basic human needs are satisfied. However, said state is not required to provide, for example, unemployment benefit in accordance with the guidelines of other existing welfare states. In the European Union (EU), for example, how precisely welfare states look after the unemployed, including how much

---

[7] We might think here of President Maduro not accepting help to deal with the famine and economically dire situation in Venezuela in 2019.

[8] As Roberta Cohen (2012) explains that the United Nation (UN) Commission on Human Rights' Guiding Principles on Internal Displacement (1998) 'do not explicitly state that international aid can be provided *without* the consent of the affected country, the obligation imposed on states by humanitarian and human rights law to refrain from refusing reasonable offers of international assistance makes it difficult to dispute the existence of a duty to accept such offers' (Cohen, 2012: 15, emphasis in original).

[9] Securitizing requests are speech acts by actors who speak security, not with the intention to initiate their *own* securitization, but instead with the intention to convince other more powerful actors (most notably in this context governments) to securitize (cf. Floyd, 2018).

money the unemployed are entitled to and for how long, varies widely (cf. Harms and Juncker, 2019). In short, while citizens can demand that welfare states provide welfare, they cannot demand *how* precisely this is to be done. The parallel here to the provision of security is that while citizens can demand that states provide security, indeed as citizens they have a right to security, they do not have a right to security being provided in a specific way. The exception to this is formed by situations when must cause is satisfied.

In summary, we can now say that when must cause is satisfied just states have an overriding duty to provide national security, which includes the security of citizens of the state, via securitization.

2.3 States: Duties to Outsiders

The case of Gabenia shows that not all willing states are always able to act appropriately on a must cause for securitization, mostly because they lack the necessary resources. Part of the following discussion is dedicated to answering what might happen when states cannot act on mandatory self-securitization? In the above, I suggested that Gabenia is duty-bound to ask for help from more able actors. But are more able states and collectives thereof in such cases duty-bound to assist them? If so, where does this duty to assist the insecure come from?

The issue of states and other would-be securitizing actors and mandatory other-securitization[10] is much more complicated than this still. It is one thing to discuss the duty to assist (just) states with securitization who actively want – and may even have requested securitization – that assistance (let us call this *mandatory other-securitization by consent*[11]), but quite another to act (1) against the will of beneficiaries but with the consent of the host state or (2) against states as threateners altogether. Let us call *these mandatory other-securitization without consent*.[12]

---

[10] Following the principle of 'ought implies can', I refer here to states that could carry out securitization the duty as being obligated to do so. Indeed, we may say that circumstances leave an actor incapable to carry out a pro tanto obligation as duty-voiding (cf. Frederick, 2015). I would like to thank Danny Frederick for helpful discussions on this point.
[11] Pattison speaks of the welcoming principle (2018: 60).
[12] Wheeler and Dunne (2012) use similar categories to discuss RtoP; however, I only read their discussion after already coming up with these terms.

Especially, the possibility of *mandatory other-securitization with-out consent* could have very severe consequences for executors of securitization and for the securitizing actor,[13] including embroiling these into violent conflicts, counter-sanctions, and counter-attacks by those objecting to unwanted external interference. As such, we can see that the issue of *mandatory other-securitization without consent* raises the question whether states and other external would-be securitizing actors actually have a duty to intervene and to other-securitize at all? Or is it the case that the moral costs and risks of security intervention void such a general duty?

I want to begin by discussing why able states and other actors have obligations to outsiders.[14] To do this, it is instructive to turn to the literature on global justice, which focuses on how much is owed to poor and disadvantaged people, and why it is owed.

Almost always the justification why states owe to outsiders rests with the 'weak' cosmopolitan principle of 'equal moral worth' of persons (Miller, 2007: 27; see also Risse, 2012: 10; Brock, 2009: 11; Caney, 2005: chapter 4), which, in turn, means that the claims of needy people 'must count with us when we decide how to act or what institutions to establish' (Miller, 2007: 27). Indeed, this principle is at the heart of secular morality. Our very idea of morality and ethics is tied to how our actions impact on the life of humans. It is there-fore unsurprising that, for instance, Miller argues that '[...] *we* find it *morally unacceptable* if the deprived person is simply left to suffer' (2007: 98, emphases added). A crude way of putting all this is to say that any ethical theory that is *not* based on a theory of equal moral worth of persons, and on that basis automatically considers obligations to outsiders, is not a moral/ethical theory at all. Hence, by defini-tion, a moral theory of securitization must start from the assumption that able states and other able actors have at least some obligations

---

[13] I differentiate between securitizing actors and executors of securitization. These can be the same – and in securitizations by sub-state actors are likely to be thus. Generally, however, the securitizing actor is the actor who speaks and initiates securitization (by making new emergency laws, etc.), while executors are those actors who act to enforce the emergency law (police, military, etc.).

[14] Able states would be those that have the necessary capability to securitize should the need arise. This includes unjust states, which is to say, states that do not satisfy a minimum floor of basic human needs (cf. Floyd, 2019a: chapter 4).

to the needy, or better still, to insecure outsiders. This includes just and unjust states, even though it is unlikely that states that undermine basic human needs (including of their own people) and are therefore unjust will act to assist the needy/insecure in other states.

If we accept this definition, it follows that all ethical theories of global justice then necessarily consider a *duty of beneficence.*[15] Despite this unity, there is disagreement on: (1) how much we owe and (2) when such duties kick in (cf. Beauchamp, 2019). Starting with the latter first, most theorists of global justice[16] are wedded to the idea of human rights, because rights place duties on states, institutions, and even individuals. Cécile Fabre explains: '[...] to say that someone has a right is to say that an interest of hers is important enough to impose on third parties duties not to interfere with her pursuit of that or some related interest, as well as duties to promote that interest' (Fabre, 2012: 23).[17] In short, on Fabre's and other similar accounts *pro tanto* obligations to assist outsiders become relevant when their human rights are infringed (cf. Miller, 2007: 164).

While scholars generally agree on the power rights have regarding duties, the origins of human rights and therefore their precise nature (i.e., how extensive they are in terms of the number of human rights identified) are subject to debate. This matters because more extensive lists of human rights entail more extensive corresponding duties than more basic lists of human rights can generate. Some scholars believe that we have human rights because we are human (Griffin, 2008: 36), some think that they make us human (Booth, 2007: 382), and others think that more important than their origin is that they work in practice (Beitz, 2009). Consequently, scholars have advanced lists of different lengths specifying human rights. At the moderate end of a spectrum sits David Miller's non-extensive list because he advocates the grounding of human rights in basic human needs. For Miller, 'something is a human right by showing that having that right fulfils the needs of the right-holder' [while] 'needs are those items or conditions it is necessary

---

[15] The idea that 'even apart from any special circumstance, helping or rescuing strangers is a positive duty, at least in some limited circumstances' (Scheid, 2014: 8).

[16] I include cosmopolitan just war scholars into this group.

[17] Here, the 'why' and the 'when' melt into one, because the fact that people are believed to have human rights already includes why we have obligations to help them.

for a person to have if she is to avoid being harmed' (Miller, 2007: 179). Miller considers the linkage between needs and rights essential. Thus, on the one hand, rights need to be restricted by grounding them in human needs,[18] while, on the other hand, only rights place remedial responsibilities (i.e., duties) on people. Remedial responsibility is as far as I am aware also a term advanced by Miller. Unlike the standard 'outcome responsibility' which tracks agents who are responsible for causing X or Y, remedial responsibility begins 'with a state of affairs in need of remedy [...] and we then ask whether there is anyone whose responsibility it is to put that state of affairs right' (Miller, 2007: 98).

Just Securitization Theory is heavily steeped in needs-based thinking. Notably I argue that putative referent objects are eligible for self-securitization, or for being defended by means of securitization by third parties (for short other-securitization), only when they are morally valuable. Moral value, in turn, depends on their ability to satisfy basic human needs (physical health and autonomy), with thresholds set differently for social and political orders and non-human species and ecosystems (Floyd, 2019a: chapter 4). In other words, Miller's human rights – grounded as they are in basic human needs – offer a valid and coherent way of triggering remedial responsibilities.

While Miller's formulation of combining needs with rights is tempting and, I think, convincing (cf. Floyd, 2011), there are nonetheless reasons to be wary of rights talk. Gillian Brock argues that empirical evidence shows that needs-based justifications of moral duties enjoy greater mass appeal than rights talk, in part because rights are limited by being culturally specific to the West (Brock, 2009: 63–69). Moreover, Brock believes that we do not need to translate needs into rights, because the principle of equal moral worth of people already means that 'we are obliged to ensure that persons are adequately positioned with respect to meeting their basic needs' (2009: 63). Clearly, Brock's account of obligation sits easily (i.e., in reflective equilibrium) with JST which makes use of basic human needs satisfaction to determine whether putative referent objects are morally valuable and as such either permitted to defend themselves via securitization, or eligible to defensive assistance by means of securitization (Floyd,

---

[18] Notably, this enables him to make human rights only about those things that are 'essential' to human beings (Miller, 2007: 18) while being able to ignore other alleged human rights.

2019a: chapter 4). However, because Miller grounds rights in needs, and because JST makes use of human rights to place constraints on security practitioners in their handling of suspects, protesters, and innocent bystanders (Floyd, 2019a: chapter 6), Miller's account is equally compatible.

Important about both is that duties (or to use Miller's term remedial responsibilities) kick in when people are not able to be and function as they should as humans. Or, put differently, when they are unable to live minimally decent lives because they are either directly or indirectly (i.e., when a morally valuable referent object is directly threatened) objectively existentially threatened. This is important, because it corresponds to JST's principles of existential threats, as well as the theory's conception of macro-proportionality. As explained in Chapter 1, Section 1.3, in JST threats must be sufficiently demanding (i.e., existential) to count as just causes for securitization, yet demandingness does not mean that threats have to be either directly or indirectly lethal to human beings. Not only would such a formulation render JST unable to account for existential threats to non-human referents (such threats often do not have lethal consequences for humans), but also it would undermine that some non-lethal threats are – in terms of the harm they cause – comparable with lethality (notably threats that render severe mental or physical disabilities). Thus, if I am threatened by something that would hinder me to be and function as a human and to participate fully in society, I might not be lethally threatened, but I cannot live as a human should. For this reason, JST includes also non-lethal, but nevertheless existential threats[19] to humans.

The issue of the level of harm – in JST– pops up again, namely, with regard to macro-proportionality. In a nutshell, I hold that because securitizations cause harm it can only be used against threats that are sufficiently harmful to humans, which is the case when objective well-being is either directly or indirectly threatened.[20] In summary, we can see that not only is it true that states have some positive duties to outsiders, but also – in reflective equilibrium with JST – states have a pro tanto moral obligation to act on those duties.

---

[19] To reiterate, existential threats are then threats to the essential properties or functions of the referent object, not necessarily threats to its survival.

[20] This concurs with Caney, 2005: 105, who stresses that duties are owned only to individuals not to states.

Recall that above I said that global justice scholars disagree on two issues in particular. One concerns *when* duties kick in (we have seen that this – for different scholars – is the case when rights are infringed or when human needs are unmet), the other relates to *how much* is owed? We have seen that some of this depends on the definition of rights and needs scholars work with, respectively. If, for example, one works with an elaborate list of human rights (e.g., one that includes welfare rights), what is owed to people everywhere would be quite different, to a scholar who worked with a list of only the most basic human rights (e.g., the right to life). Certainly, working with *basic* human needs – as I do – already restricts what one is owed and what one owes. Notably, securitization cannot be justified when people in other countries simply *feel* vulnerable.

But more is at stake here, because how much is owed also rests on a prior mindset/conviction about justice. Let us consider briefly how global justice scholars divide on the issue of how much is owed.

We can imagine the issue of how much is owed as a continuum (cf. Beauchamp, 2019: 3; Scheid, 2014) that has as its respective opposing ends practically 'equal positive duties' to all and 'unequal positive duties'.[21] The former end is populated by radical cosmopolitans, which includes effective altruists who advocate giving as much income away as possible to combat global poverty, but also that people should select jobs that make them high earners, in order to enable them to give more away (Singer, 2013). At the other end of our continuum, we find 'merely' 'moral cosmopolitans', which is to say statists or communitarians who believe in the principle of equal moral worth but who believe that ties of national allegiance mean that we owe more to fellow-nationals than people in other states (Miller, 2007: 30). Holding the centre ground are those global justice scholars who recognize that states and people cannot be required to be impartial to allegiances; however, they are 'permitted to confer greater weight on their own goals, projects and attachments' only once the needy have opportunities for 'a minimally decent life' (Fabre, 2012: 21; see also Brock, 2009: 14–15).

Although this is not a book about the fair distribution of security (as a state of being) and therefore how much security wealthy states

---

[21] Here, the moral equality of people rules out the view that we do not owe anything.

must redistribute, instead one about justified security practice, the trends in the literature are relevant, because scholars located at different points of the spectrum would take different views on whether the pro tanto obligation of other-securitization can be overridden. Certainly, some radical cosmopolitans would discount potential risks to securitizing actors (notably in terms of lives lost) as valid objections to not securitizing. We can see this from the radical cosmopolitan literature on humanitarian intervention. Mary Kaldor, for example, argues that the lives of peacekeepers and of victims are equally important, and that peacekeeping ('cosmopolitan law-enforcement') entails 'risking the lives of peacekeepers in order to save the lives of victims' (Kaldor, 2012: 138). In my view, Kaldor also discounts the risk of global instability caused by intervention aka 'cosmopolitan law-enforcement', not only because intervention must be based on partial consent (ibid: 134–136), but also because there is the implicit assumption that everyone would recognize such interventions as good and unproblematic. Relatively, more moderate cosmopolitans, as here Caney (2005: 253), argue that 'intervention [should] not impose undue costs on the intervening authorities'. For Fabre (2012: 21), undue moral cost is incurred when intervention 'would require of the better off to sacrifice their own opportunities for a minimally decent life' (Fabre, 2007: 369; by contrast see Singer, 1972: 231[22]).

This shows that there is a tangible difference between states' duties to securitize insiders and outsiders. Unlike in the latter, in the former case no consideration regarding moral costs or risks can override the duty to securitize because the costs of not acting are always greater (notably the state ceases to exist, or it fails unless it provides security). In Section 2.5, I will consider in detail the moral costs and risks that override states' duties to act on must cause where third parties are concerned, before this however it is necessary to briefly revisit must cause.

---

[22] Singer argues: '[…]if it is in our power to prevent something bad from happening, without thereby sacrificing anything of comparable moral importance, we ought, morally, to do it. By "without sacrificing anything of comparable moral importance" I mean without causing anything else comparably bad to happen, or doing something that is wrong in itself, or failing to promote some moral good, comparable in significance to the bad thing that we can prevent' (Singer, 1972: 231).

2.4 Must Cause and Mandatory Other-Securitization

I argued in Chapter 1 that securitization is morally required only
once politicization of the threat has been tried and has failed to satisfy just cause. I have also argued that real threats require politicization, because when threats are real, strategic inaction is not a feasible
option. Especially in *mandatory other-securitization by consent*, this
raises the question *whose* political solutions count? Is it those per-
formed by the state/group, etc., in need of help with securitization,
or that of the external actor? In other words, in other-securitization
when precisely is must cause satisfied. I want to suggest that – in other-
securitization – all would-be securitizing actors must establish the satisfaction of must cause anew and independently. This means that, if
A requests help with the securitization against an issue from B,[23] then
B is obligated to securitize only once the political solutions B has to
offer have been tried and failed to satisfy just cause. Provided securitization is just, B is permitted to use exceptional measures before that
point is reached, namely, when securitization is *ex ante* anticipated to
be the best option. But the obligation to do something extraordinary
to counter a threat comes into force only once other less harmful measures B can provide have not worked. Concretely this means that the
duty of other-securitization is a derivative duty, that is, a duty that
rests on a prior duty of 'other-politicization',[24] meaning a duty to save
relevant third parties using ordinary political measures, or in other
words a duty to secure.

The fact that each (including each successive[25]) would-be securitizing actor must establish must cause before they have a duty to
other-securitize is crucial for another reason. A central requirement of
JST is macro-proportionality – the principle that securitization must
not cause more harm than it seeks to prevent. Other-securitization
(especially without consent) is likely to cause more harm than a state
using emergency measures to protect its own people from an external

---

[23] Assume here that A has already started with securitization because they have
exhausted politicization.

[24] That there is a duty to act through politicization in the national context
became apparent in Chapter 1, Section 1.4.

[25] What I mean by successive will become clearer in Chapter 5, where I argue for
a tiered and sequential structure identifying duty-bearers at different levels of
analysis responsible for other-securitization where other actors have failed or
legitimately evaded their duties.

threat. In other words, the threshold for when other-securitization is proportionate is likely to be higher (in terms of the harm prevented by such action) than in cases of self-securitization.[26] This also shows once more that the above-mentioned prior duty of other-politicization does not entail an automatic duty to securitize when politicization fails. Notably, securitization by third parties may be disproportionally harmful to the threat in question, in which case securitization is impermissible.

Finally, one difference between the two types of mandatory other-securitization is that *mandatory other-securitization without consent* can apply only when there is an *unaddressed* objective existential threat to a just referent object, or when the state itself is the threatener, whereas *mandatory other-securitization by consent* applies in cases when states acquiesce to relevant assistance offered or when they request securitization by third parties, and this can happen while the requesting state addresses the threat. To be sure, an unaddressed threat exists when a sovereign state *does not* address a relevant threat to a just referent object, which is the case when the state has *no* relevant and targeted political strategy to address the threat.[27] One reason why outside interference and coercion in such cases are morally permissible is that states that do not protect just referents within their territory have forfeited the right to political self-determination[28] (cf. Wellman in Wellman and Cole, 2011: 15–16; Altman and Wellman, 2009: chapter 4; McMahan, 2010: 57; Tesón, 2014: 71–72). Or, in other words, sovereignty is conditional on good behaviour.

---

[26] We can find this also with regard to RtoP, where the threshold for pillar III measures is that 'a state is found to have "manifestly failed to protect"' (Bloomfield, 2017: 29), not – as it was in the International Commission on Intervention and State Sovereignty's – when states are unwilling or unable to protect. Cater and Malone (2016: 125) speak of 'a high just cause threshold for military intervention'. While here the general thought is correct, the issue is not one of just cause but rather one of proportionality. See also Tesón and Van der Vossen (2017) whose green button experiment shows that proportionality not just cause is the prohibitive threshold to just armed humanitarian intervention.

[27] In principle, such a strategy could be mindful inaction; for reasons discussed in Chapter 1, Section 1.4, however, I assume this not to be the case.

[28] We can understand political self-determination as encompassing two things: (1) an internal dimension whereby states are sovereign regards internal politics and (2) the external dimension that concerns 'relations between the self-defined community and the outside world' (IISS, 1992: 16). Security measures that are launched remotely usually target the latter.

The implications of this are important; thus, my framework can answer Ramesh Thakur's provocative question whether the level of gun violence (32.000 deaths annually)[29] necessitates RtoP-type intervention within domestic US jurisdiction (Thakur, 2017: 291) with a decisive *no*. Thus, while – certainly from a Western European perspective – the United States's efforts at reducing gun violence are poor (i.e., why not simply ban gun ownership altogether?), gun violence *is* addressed. In the wake of the Parkland shooting in February 2018, for example, many states have introduced and tightened gun laws, including by raising of the minimal age for gun ownership, as well as by temporarily (for one year) barring dangerous people from gun ownership (Kramer and Harlan, 2019). In short, in the case of the United States it is simply not the case that the threat is not addressed by relevant authorities, and in the absence of an *unaddressed threat* there is no moral case for a duty to politicize – and if that fails – of mandatory other-securitization. This is so for two interrelated reasons. First, mandatory securitization is triggered either for contractual reasons or because of the moral equality of people. Duties are based on the rights that affected people (or groups thereof) hold against duty-bearers. The obligation of mandatory securitization is however not triggered by a right to a policy that works 100 per cent. For one thing, such a policy may not be available. Instead, affected persons simply have a right to the issue being addressed. Moreover, this brings me to my second point that if a state has not forfeited the right to political self-determination (here because they are addressing a threat) other actors do not have a duty to intervene.[30]

2.5 Factors Overriding Individual States' Duties to Securitize Outsiders

In addition to breaking the normal peacetime rules between states (including, by using tough sanctions, blackmail, subversion, the threat of expulsion from international organizations, etc.), mandatory other-securitizations may see an external actor A act within the sovereign

---

[29] 48.830 in 2021 www.pewresearch.org/short-reads/2023/04/26/what-the-data-says-about-gun-deaths-in-the-u-s/#:~:text=On%20a%20per%20capita%20basis,rising%20sharply%20during%20the%20pandemic.

[30] In the broadest possible sense.

territory of state B in order to protect a just referent object (which can be a social or political order, an ecosystem, a non-human species, or a group of people; cf. Introduction). For example, the external securitizing actor could enforce curfews with the help of its military in *dengue threat* (Section 1.4.3) or they could help enforce restrictions on the use of water resources, as necessary in the hypothetical example of *drought disaster* (Section 1.4.3).

Above I have said that we can distinguish between *mandatory other-securitization by consent* and *mandatory securitization without consent*. The former is perhaps less likely to bring adverse consequences for the external securitizing actor. It is logical to assume, for example, that when aforementioned Gabenia asks for help from another sovereign state to deal with *dengue threat* then – provided they satisfy must cause and that securitization is carried out in line with the principles of just conduct during securitization – such help is likely to be gladly received by the government of Gabenia and its population, in short by the beneficiaries of securitization. This should mean that the risks to putative executors of securitization – for example, in terms of the lives lost due to violent resistance to securitization – are comparatively low as there simply will be little in the way of opposition to securitization. Conversely, a comparable course of action is unlikely to be morally justifiable where would-be securitizing actors do not have the consent of the host state. To be sure, this is not because of the lack of consent, but rather because in the absence of consent by the host state escalation (including into war) is preprogramed. And the high likelihood that other-securitization will lead to violent conflict renders the same morally impermissible on the grounds of the proportionality criterion (cf. Introduction). This means that in most cases, other-securitization without consent by the host state can only take the form of remote action, that is, sanctions, not direct intervention within the state's territory.

This said, there is another form of *mandatory other-securitization without consent*, namely, one whereby the host state (i.e., the government) has consented to rescue, including by other-securitization, but (part of) the beneficiary (the population) has not. Consider as a case in point the Ebola virus crisis in 2014/2015 in West Africa. Here, the affected states requested help from the international community, but many locals rejected the finding that Ebola was a threat, and once they accepted the virus as a threat, they became scared and resentful

of international enforcers of the securitization (Linn, 2015).[31] Some
of these were violently attacked by locals, not to mention the fact
that all these enforcers were exposed to the risk of contracting Ebola
themselves. I do not want to go into the Ebola crisis here in any more
detail, because here the obligation to securitize is further complicated
by the fact that Ebola is not a localized threat. That is to say that
unless contained, Ebola could easily have developed into a pandemic
affecting everyone. The case thus blurs the lines between mandatory
self- and other-securitization. The Ebola case is interesting here merely
to showcase that even in seemingly straightforward uncontroversial
cases of other-securitization executors of securitization can be at risk
of being attacked and even of losing their lives.

Given that most scholars who theorize the permissibility of humanitarian intervention (and those that focus on the justice of non-state
organized violence) insist on consent (usually of the beneficiaries of
the intervention/organized violence) (see, e.g., Kaldor, 2012: 134;
Parry 2017a; Pattison 2010; Finlay, 2015), the idea of *mandatory
other-securitization without consent*, including against the will of
beneficiaries, raises the question why such securitizations are morally
permissible (which we know forms the basis of a theory of mandatory
securitization) at all? Indeed, does not the referent object's refusal to
being saved by securitization serve as a valid reason that voids the
duty of other-securitization?

In JST, I discount the importance of consent of the beneficiary of
securitization for two reasons. First, consent in theories of humanitarian intervention or political violence waged by non-state actors primarily serves to exonerate the intervener in cases gone awry. Second,
consent is meant to guard against interveners being driven by their own
political goals. In JST, however, inter alia the criterion of right intention already guards against that possibility. Having thus discounted
the moral relevance of consent, *mandatory other-securitization without consent* requires our consideration and I will now move on to
discuss the moral costs and risks as well as other practical reasons that
void capable states' pro tanto obligation of other-securitization.[32]

---

[31] Similar problems prevailed during the Ebola crisis in the Congo in 2019.
[32] Some readers will take issue with the paternalism informing this part of
the argument (indeed the issue might very well unite, otherwise conflicting
postmodern and postcolonial critical security scholars and analytical moral

2.5.1 Risk of Death, Disease, and Disability

Without doubt, the weightiest factor against mandatory other-securitization is the risk of the loss of lives on the side of the securitizing actor.[33] It is one thing to say that states are permitted to help other states to fight, for example, jihadi terrorism, but quite another to say that police forces, or military personnel of state A and other executors of securitization, *must* risk their lives in order to combat a terror threat to people of state B. While it is possible to object that there is not always the risk of death involved, it seems to me that the risk of being maimed, the risk of contracting a debilitating disease, and the risk of suffering severe psychological damage[34] weigh equally high, after all both 'jeopardise [relevant individuals] prospects for a flourishing life' (Fabre, 2007: 366). Moreover, short of hindsight we cannot know with absolute certainty that no one would be harmed in this way during securitization. In short, the question remains: do states have a duty of other-securitization, even at the risk of losing or irretrievably damaging the lives of their own soldiers, military personnel, police, doctors and nurses, and other executors of securitization? I think that this issue turns on whether potential executors of securitization voluntarily join professions that include these risks (British infantry soldiers, e.g., know

philosophers). Many philosophers approach paternalism as distinctively wrong (e.g., Parry, 2017b, 2022). While I do not share that view, the charge of paternalism is problematic for a theory (here JST) that considers autonomy one of its basic components, because 'paternalistic actions […] constitute intrusions into individuals' spheres of autonomous agency' (Fox, 2019: 328). Paternalists hold against this that interference can – at times – improve a person's life and in the long durée ensure the continuous enjoyment of autonomy (cf. Dworkin, 2020). It seems to me that failing to save people from an objective existential threat against their expressed preferences is all-things-considered worse than temporarily infringing their autonomy. More importantly still, among groups of people (West Africans suffering from Ebola) will be children and other not fully informed people (cf. Section 2.5.4). This means the rejection by (some) adults of other-securitization against the Ebola virus does not 'merely' affect their autonomy, but it 'violates duties to assignable others' (Flinch Midtgaard, 2021: 8). Indeed, it is generally accepted that provided an interference (here other-securitization) is 'other-regarding' (which is to say, an action that infringes the autonomy of one person, or a group of people A, with a view to protecting a second group of people B, from the adverse effects of A's self-regarding action), is not a paternalist one (cf. ibid).

[33] I differentiate between executor of securitization and securitizing actors; in this case, however, I mean both as well as the populations of the securitizing state.

[34] On this point, see Dobos and Coady, 2014, 84–85.

that they might need to conduct peacekeeping/enforcement operations around the world), or whether they voluntarily sign up to specific missions (e.g., doctors working for Medicines Sans Frontiers, or police who join secondment operations abroad, or the many technical staff who volunteer for organizations like the German Technische Hilfswerk). As Fabre explains: '[...] individuals are not under a duty to incur a high risk of death or injury for the sake of another. But if they volunteer to do jobs which will lead them to incur such risks, then they are under the (contractual) duty to do just that. Thus, I, as a private citizen, am not under a duty to enter a burning building to save the child trapped inside, but you, as a fire-fighter, are' (Fabre, 2007: 371; cf. McMahan, 2010: 69).[35] Provided that state A possesses willing, appropriate executors of securitization who wish to help relevant others and are fully aware of the possible risks involved, then the risk of death, disease, and disability does not override the duty of other-securitization.

But what happens if we turn this on its head. Suppose we have the situation whereby state B requests help from state A but state A does not have voluntary willing executors of securitization. This could be the case if state A only has a conscript army, with soldiers drafted to protect national security (assume here our case of other-securitization is fully outside of that remit).[36] In other words, we have a situation where people not only never volunteered to serve their country, but also never agreed to peacekeeping or peace enforcement missions elsewhere. A shortage of willing executors of securitization could also come about if the situation (the threat) requires besides military personnel also doctors and nurses to step up, but none (or an insufficient number) volunteer. This raises the following question: is state A morally obligated to carry out other-securitization even if this means compelling[37] suitable

---

[35] By contrast, private individuals have duties to help others (including mandatory killing of their attackers) if they do not incur a high risk themselves (Fabre, 2007: 370; see also Singer, 1972: 231). Thus, if one held that only professionals are under a duty to save others: 'one would not be under a moral duty to rescue a child from a pond unless one were a lifeguard' (Fabre, 2007: 371).

[36] In our interconnected world, threats in far-away places often affect our security. Climate change, for example, might lead to long-distance migration or even encourage terrorism. The point here is that if other-securitization actually primarily serves the national interest views on the permissibility of conscription might change (cf. Fabre, 2012: 185).

[37] Assume here for the sake of argument this is possible and permissible; in reality, here the duty is likely to be void.

executors of securitization against their will? The latter brings all sorts of problems I cannot go into here, but the former already settles the case. Consider this that while in *mandatory other-securitization by consent* the risk of dying, disease, and disability may be less than in *mandatory other-securitization without consent* it is not zero. Notably, executors themselves could contract the disease they are fighting, as indeed did many NHS staff during the height of coronavirus crisis in 2020. This means that unwilling would-be executors of securitization cannot be forced to participate, after all participating scuppers their prospects of a good life.

So far so good, but this leaves open the question whether sufficiently wealthy states are morally obligated to employ one or more PMSCs to act on the duty of other-securitization. After all, as James Pattison has argued the use of PMSCs can be morally permissible 'when doing so would be likely to be highly effective at helping to promote the enjoyment of several innocent individuals' basic human rights' (Pattison, 2014: 195). Be that as it may, Pattison's extensive analysis of PMSCs leads him to conclude that there are deep moral problems with the existence of such actors, among other things, their use is likely to increase the occurrence and awfulness of wars, and moreover, the privatization of force will leave some actors more insecure than others. Overall, Pattison recommends that the use of PMSCs should generally be eschewed (ibid: 187). It seems to me that if our goal is the reduction of the awfulness and occurrence of securitization as it is for JST we must concur with this finding. I would therefore suggest that states and other actors may employ such companies (provided securitization is both just and obligatory) only when one of the two following scenarios is apparent: (1) one's duty is overriding (as it is for just states and self-securitization) and when it cannot be met without employment of such groups; and (2) in cases where actors are morally or outcome responsible for the threat, and where they cannot act on the duty of other-securitization unless they employ PMSCs. Let us call this the *exception clause*. The exception clause is based on the understanding that PMSCs have the potential to significantly benefit the provision of security, yet that these organizations can also be dangerous and hence that their utilization needs to be limited. Limiting the use of PMSCs to cases where actors have either an overriding duty or where they are outcome responsible ensures that the issue is acted on by the actor who is the designated primary duty-bearer. In other words, it ensures fairness.

In summary, we can now say that with regard to state actors in mandatory state-led other-securitization, the obligation to securitize is overridden if a state does not possess free-willed and able executors of securitization ready to carry out securitization.[38]

2.5.2 Risk of Instability and Insecurity

We have seen that the risk of dying, disease, and disability overrides a state's obligation to securitize outsiders, when: (1) appropriate executors of securitization are unwilling to incur these risks, or (2) when the number of volunteers is too small. While this seems a new and somewhat alien topic in security studies, it chimes with long-standing objections that scholars, practitioners, and the general public have voiced against armed humanitarian intervention. Notably, armed humanitarian interventions are considered morally problematic if the intervener incurs losses (Wheeler and Dunne, 2012: 93). In more detail: 'Industrial societies, which have material and personnel capacity to contribute to peace operations, are frequently inhibited from doing so by what is labelled the "body-bag backlash" – the concern that if military personnel are killed during humanitarian interventions, the public will question or even condemn the exercise as being insufficiently important to national interests' (Krieger, Mendlovitz and Pace, 2006: 15–16).

The second principled objection against humanitarian intervention is the risk of instability and insecurity (cf. ICISS, 2001: 37). In this section, I want to consider whether the risk of instability and insecurity to itself can override a state's duty to securitize outsiders.

The idea behind just securitization is to reduce harm by causing only necessary and proportionate harm to threateners, beneficiaries, and innocent bystanders. No matter how justified[39] securitization

---

[38] Of course, other-securitization may not entail action in the threat zone but be carried out remotely. Though the chances of being targeted are reduced, it is still possible that executors located remotely would be targeted (including terror attacks, targeted sanctions, kidnapping, cyberattack, drone strikes, or assassinations).

[39] Technically, according to JST, all criteria must be met for securitization to be justified; however, I acknowledge that securitizing actors wilfully securitizing perceived, as opposed to real, threats or wilfully exceeding appropriate measures and micro-proportionality is less excusable and thus morally worse than securitizations where actors mean to do the right thing, but due to mistaken beliefs do not.

is, we have already seen that such conduct *can* lead to counter-securitization and – in agent-intended threats – potentially moral hazard (though see Bellamy and Williams, 2012). Beyond this, securitization can also cause rifts between the external securitizing state and the threatener. For example, Russia imposed a series of counter-sanctions against EU member states,[40] after the EU-imposed sanctions[41] against Russia in defence of 'the territorial integrity, sovereignty, and independence of Ukraine' (Foreign Affairs Council, 2014) following the annexation of Crimea. The risk of instability is thus real, and instability can render (new) and significant security problems for the securitizing actor. The question thus is: does the possibility that mandatory other-securitization can cause insecurity for the securitizing actor and its executors detract from the *pro tanto* duty to securitize?

In JST's criterion, number 5 specifies that securitization is morally permissible only if securitization has a better chance of succeeding in securing the referent object than less harmful alternatives. However, in JST the concern is with the effects of securitization on the referent object (i.e., does it wind up more secure than it would otherwise be), not with the effects of securitization *for* the securitizing actor. In terms of JST, this is fine, because that theory does not demand of actors that they securitize putative referent objects. All it does is to specify *when* actors are permitted to securitize, should they wish to do so (cf. Introduction). By contrast, a theory of mandatory securitization must take much greater account of the effects of securitization on the securitizing actor. In the scholarly literature on global justice, it is generally accepted that unreasonable costs override obligations we have towards others. However, there is no universal definition of what constitutes unreasonable costs. The reason for this is that what

---

[40] For example, it has in place an import ban that 'includes beef and pork of all kinds, poultry and poultry products, smoked foodstuffs and sausages, milk and milk products including raw milk and all foodstuffs containing milk as well as fish, vegetables and fruits' (Fritz et al., 2017: 4).

[41] Including 'measures to restrict Russia's access to EU capital markets, • an embargo on the imports and exports of arms and related material from/ to Russia, • a prohibition of exports of dual use goods and technology for military use in Russia as well as • of products that are destined for deep water oil exploration and production, arctic oil exploration or production and shale oil projects in Russia' (Fritz et al., 2017: 4).

counts as unreasonable costs depends on what we think we owe to others (Cf. Scheid, 2014: 6–10; Beauchamp, 2019). In short, the definition of unreasonable costs depends on individual scholars' theories of justice.[42]

Costs encompass different things. Often it is measured in terms of the lives lost, endangered, or lastingly compromised, but it also refers to consequential financial costs (cf. Dobos, and Coady, 2014: 82). I think that in the context of other-securitization just as with armed humanitarian intervention, costs also refer to the risk of instability and insecurity. To be sure, one consequence of securitization is counter-securitization.[43] In the context of the latter, consider once again the example of *jihad terror* used in Chapter 1 (Section 1.4.1). Here, state A becomes a target for jihadi terrorists as a consequence of siding with its allies and friends (states B and C) in their fight against terrorism.[44] Given that other-securitization can make the *securitizing actor* insecure, is this actor obligated to securitize? The answer, I think, turns on *how* insecure the intervening state and its citizens are likely to become because of securitization. We know that the threshold cannot be the one whereby the putative securitizing state would end up as insecure as those it seeks to protect, let alone more insecure. In such cases, securitization is impermissible on the grounds of macro-proportionality. However, it is also possible that securitization is in principle proportionate (because the harm prevented is greater than that caused by securitization), but that this would come at an unreasonable cost to the securitizing actor. Although this cost will cause less *universal* harmful than the harm that would be prevented by securitization, it still overrides a duty to securitize, because other-securitization cannot come at the expense of the self. Given that the threshold serves to override a powerful and important duty, however, we also know that should-be securitizing actors must incur some costs to themselves. It is hard to

---

[42] Some, like Miller (2007), do not see this as a matter of justice, but as humanitarianism instead.

[43] A securitization launched by A in direct response to a securitization by B.

[44] This example is not far-fetched; Spain, for example, became a target for Islamic jihadists only after José María Aznar declared solidarity with George W. Bush's 'war on terror' (McLaughlin, 2017). Likewise, Bulgaria, Poland, and Hungary were threatened and 'designated as "enemies of Muslims" in a statement issued by Ayman al-Zawahiri' because of their involvement into the Iraq war (Mareš, 2011: 241).

put a finger on what precisely this amounts to. Philosophers usually talk about this issue by invoking Peter Singer's (1972) drowning child example, whereby a person comes upon a drowning child in a pond. It is generally accepted that (1) the person must rescue the child at reasonable costs to himself, for instance, water damage to his expensive clothes and to money in his wallet, but (2) that he has no obligation to rescue the child if so doing puts his own life at risk (cf. Pattison, 2014: 120). This example can be and *has* been made less unequivocal by inserting various extras, for example, that rescuer has all his earthly possessions with him, or that rescuing will break his arm. Variations on the original example *inter alia* show that our understandings of reasonable/unreasonable here can shift according to context. All other things being equal, however, it seems that reasonable costs pertain to costs that – most people – could recover and that do not compromise the flourishing of the rescuer.

Consider now once more our example of *jihadi terror* (Section 1.4.1), wherein the securitizing actor at large is likely to incur harmful counter-securitization (e.g., become *a* target for terrorists). Given that this cost would inhibit the flourishing of some people within the rescuer state, the obligation to securitize is overridden even if there are a sufficiently big number of voluntary executors of securitization ready to carry out their task.[45]

It remains to question whether this argument also works for unjust states? Given that these states are unjust, is it not the case that an intervention that would cause the unjust intervening state significant harm not ultimately a good thing, especially if it would weaken the grip of the regime? In other words, does – in such cases – the risk of instability *fail to* override the obligation to securitize? I think that even in these cases obligation is overridden by the risk of instability and insecurity. This is so because insecurity and instability affect morally innocent (in the relevant sense) people within the state, often much more than the unjust leaders of the regime. If NATO's intervention into Libya teaches us one thing, it is that sometimes an unjust order is better than the removal of that unjust order.

---

[45] Some people might argue that securitization should be forbidden in these circumstances; however, most people think that self-determination is an important element of justice. As ever, securitization might be impermissible because it is disproportionate.

2.5.3 Financial Costs

Often securitization costs money. This is rarely considered in security studies,[46] but the costs of military acts and even short-term policing efforts can very quickly amount to vast sums. For instance, the financial costs of security provision incurred by the German taxpayer when Hamburg hosted the G-20 for two days (7–8 July) in 2017 are estimated to have amounted to at least 130 million euros. Part of this very high cost was made up by the federal province (Bundesland) Hamburg needing to recruit 15.000 police from other federal provinces at the cost of 25.000 euros for a Hundertschaft (groups of 80–120 officers) per day (Dey et al., 2017). Just as there are always financial costs attached to recruiting extra police, there are always financial costs attached to securing borders (e.g., by building physical defences but also staffing costs), to moving equipment and so on. But not only security interventions in another state's territory cost money, remotely orchestrated security measures do too (often in the form of lost revenue). Consider, for example, that Russian counter-sanctions to EU-imposed sanctions following the Russian annexation of the Crimea peninsula led to a 'significant decline in total exports to Russia over the period 2014 to 2016 [...]. In the second half of 2014 EU exports to Russia declined by 17.8 % and thus fell to a value of USD 66.5 bn' (Fritz et al., 2017: 9). The unreasonable financial costs of other-securitization are important. No state has endless funds at its disposal; moreover no state, or for that matter, other actor can be expected to shoulder high and disproportionate costs to protect another.[47] But when are the financial costs of other-securitization prohibitive/unreasonable and thus override the pro tanto obligation to securitize? The obvious answer is this: when the financial costs of other-securitization leave the securitizing actor and/or the people, the state has security responsibility for insecure. To give an example, consider that the already mentioned case of the EU sanctions and Russian counter-sanctions, Italy – as one of the largest food exporters to Russia – is disproportionally adversely affected. Exports of capital goods and food have decreased from

---

[46] By contrast, the cost of war is always discussed.
[47] Thomas G. Weiss (2016: 151) argues this about the United States in the light of the 2014 Quadrennial Defence Review that balanced fiscal challenges against security needs.

$14.5 billion in 2013 to $7.8 billion in 2016, with small businesses worst affected (Coticchia and Davidson, 2019: 77). In short, we can say that the financial costs of other-securitization are too high when other-securitization is likely to leave groups of people, and putative would-be securitizing actors have security responsibility for in significant financial trouble.

To conclude this subsection, we can now say that there are prohibitive costs and risks that override the duty of states to save and secure outsiders. In summary, based on the analysis provided, capable individual states are morally obligated to provide for other-securitization when the following conditions are satisfied:

- The state in question has established must cause.
- The would-be securitizing actor possesses willing, able, and sufficiently numerous executors of securitization.
- Securitization is not likely to create significant insecurity or instability for the intervening state or its citizens.
- The projected financial cost of other-securitization does not risk rendering the securitizing state and/or those it has security responsibility for, insecure.

2.5.4 Liability

So far so good, but what happens if putative referent objects are responsible for the insecurity, they are in. Consider again the case of *drought disaster* examined in Chapter 1. Although in this example the drought is a natural phenomenon and the threat thus agent-lacking, what if we alter the thought experiment so that the drought reaches the level of an existential threat only because the inhabitants of Millville did not adhere to early warnings, but continued to fill their swimming pools, wash their cars, etc. In short, what if they continued to use water for non-essential tasks/pursuits after having been informed that so doing will have adverse consequences? The question is: does outcome responsibility (here liability for threat creation) by the threatened entity (would-be referent object of securitization) override an external states' obligation even if all other conditions for mandatory other-securitization are met?

Many global justice scholars do not venture onto the terrain of responsibilities for poor choices. Fabre, for example, acknowledges the fact that responsibility can affect duties, but excludes it for the purposes of analysis. For her, 'beyond dispute is the thought that *if* individuals are not responsible, *then* they have a claim at the bar of justice' (Fabre, 2012: 21, emphases in original). Most scholars do not venture onto this terrain because it goes against the grain of deeply held cosmopolitan beliefs. Caney, for example, rejects Rawls' claim in *The Law of Peoples* (2001) that political regimes should take responsibility for poor choices and thus have no claim to be bailed out, on the grounds that '[c]osmopolitan principles of justice [...] demand that the wealthy always redistribute their wealth in this way' (2005: 130). Miller is one of the few global justice scholars who argues explicitly against this cosmopolitan principle. He suggests that states whose residents have deliberately lived above their means (e.g., by using up resources at unsustainable speed or by having too many children) and that are now poorer than states who – started from the same baseline – but whose residents have made more prudent choices (e.g., have used resources sparingly and reproduced at more sustainable rates) do not owe redistribution of goods to the poorer state (Miller, 2007: 68–75). Collective responsibility plays a major role in Miller's argument. He suggests that collective responsibility applies when members of a political community (for him a nation) either passively tolerate poor choices, or when passive objectors benefit from poor choices (ibid: 114–121). The only way to escape collective responsibility is to 'take all reasonable steps to prevent the outcome occurring' (ibid: 121).[48] It is important to note here that Miller is concerned with outcome responsibility, which is to say conduct that has 'contributed to producing the outcome', and not moral responsibility, which is to say morally blame or praiseworthy for the outcome (ibid: 86; 89). I am sympathetic to Miller's view, in part because we live in a time when no one wants to take responsibility for the outcomes of either their omissions or their own actions when really, they should. Notably, overweight people increasingly place responsibility for the poor shape they are in with food manufacturers, smokers blame their addiction on the cigarette industry, and there was even a case of a former Oxford law student who decided to hold the university's alleged poor teaching responsible for

---

[48] Note here that minority groups exploited by the regime, or not benefitting from the same, are excluded from charges of national responsibility (ibid: 132).

his own failure to receive a first-class degree. Considering all this, does it follow that liability for threat creation overrides the moral duty of third parties to save liable actors? For at least two reasons it does not. First, in every society there are likely to be innocent people, notably children,[49] while there are also people who will not have used up the water recklessly and those that lived by the rules, but who felt that they were powerless to stop others. There will also be ignorant people.[50] While we can say that it was these people's duty to inform themselves (hence that they are culpably ignorant), what if such people are illiterate or resident in cut-off and backwards rural parts of the country? Second, it is immoral not to assist in relevant situations. Notably, Miller does not argue for non-assistance. Instead, he argues that if B is responsible for not having a resource (read: causing a threat), we cannot hold A under 'a duty of justice to help B' (Miller, 2007: 249). But this does not mean that A does not have a humanitarian duty to alleviate suffering in B (Miller, 2007: 257),[51] especially if 'there is no prospect' of the outcome responsible group discharging responsibility (ibid: 257).

In short, if must cause and all other conditions identified in this chapter are satisfied, able states have a duty to securitize third parties even in cases where third parties are responsible for their own predicament. The issue becomes relevant again, however, when state A (the would-be securitizing actor) is faced with multiple cases in need of other-securitization but has the resources (financially and manpower)

---

[49] James Griffin (2008: 44), for example, argues that children become 'agents in stages', whereby he defines agency as: 'involved in living a worthwhile life' (45).

[50] As a case in point consider that during the coronavirus crisis in 2020 Ultra-Orthodox Jews in Israel were disproportionally affected. The *New York Times* states that: 'Experts attribute the proliferation among the ultra-Orthodox to overcrowding and large families, deep distrust of state authority, ignorance of the health risks among religious leaders, an aversion to electronic and secular media that they believe is mandated by religious law, and a zealous devotion to a way of life centred on communal activity' (Halbfinger, 2020).

[51] If I understand Miller correctly, the difference between a duty of justice and a humanitarian duty is that the former is always enforceable while the latter can be overridden (2007: 258). I cannot comment on the meaning of a duty of justice and whether it must be absolute, but if this chapter is correct, it seems to me true that humanitarian duties or the duty to securitize can be overridden.

to assist with only one. Thus, in such cases priority should be given to the case where referents are not, or less, culpable for threat creation.[52]

More needs to be said about liability. Thus, what about those cases where the 'should-be' securitizing actor is responsible for threat creation, or in Miller's terminology, where the securitizing actor is outcome, or even morally responsible for the threat to third parties? Here, we have no difficulty identifying remedial responsibility to other-securitize, after all we have just said that outcome responsibility is a pivotal element in remedial responsibility. Consider the following example.

Toxic waters

Wealthy state A routinely dumps toxic waste in poor state B. Over time, the toxic waste seeps into the ground and contaminates the water supply. The result is high rates of cancer, but also contamination of fish stocks in rivers and freshwater systems. With fish the main food source, the population of state B now suffers a famine. Social unrest, strife, and conflict become widespread.

The causal link of threat creation in *toxic water* is well understood, and outcome responsible state A has full remedial responsibility. The reason why I roll out this example is because I want to discuss what culpability in threat creation by the securitizing actor does to our four conditions when other-securitization is obligatory. The first condition was that of must cause; I argued that while securitization is permissible when it has a better chance of succeeding in achieving just cause than plausible, less harmful alternatives, securitization is obligatory when these less harmful, plausible alternatives (for short politicization) have been tried and failed to secure just cause. The question is this: is the threshold when securitization becomes obligatory the same in cases such as *toxic water*? Especially, if B demands securitization by state A *before* must cause is satisfied, is A in virtue of being outcome responsible not automatically obligated to securitize? My answer to this question is no. State A in virtue of being outcome responsible has the moral obligation to address the problem, but the people of state B are not entitled to the problem being addressed in a specific way (i.e., through securitization); instead, it is morally permissible for A to try other less harmful options first. Indeed, we must get away from the notion that securitization *is* the best thing simply because it means

---

[52] I thank Jonathan Parry for this suggestion.

trying extraordinary measures; after all, if less harmful/ordinary measures achieve just cause, non-securitization is objectively better.

Another pertinent issue with such cases is this: if must cause is satisfied and state A is under the obligation to securitize, is the duty to securitize automatically overriding?[53] We can turn again to Miller for an answer. It seems to me that here (because of outcome responsibility) the three costs and risks *cannot* override the duty to securitize as readily as it can in other cases of other-securitization. Consider the risks of death, disease, and disability. In *toxic water*, the population of state A (from which executors of securitization would be drawn) is collectively responsible for the insecurity, not because they contributed to the problem by producing toxic waste and shipping it off themselves, but rather because they benefitted[54] from the industry that produced toxic waste (e.g., from jobs, the taxes paid by the relevant industry, or the goods produced). The only way individuals cannot be held collectively responsible is when they can show that they took 'all reasonable steps to prevent the outcome from occurring. What is reasonable in a particular case will depend on how seriously harmful the prospective outcome is, and what costs different courses of action will impose on the dissenter' (Miller, 2007: 121), or if they were generally ignorant. According to Miller, the cost of dissenting is too high when a person endangers herself by dissenting. In the unlikely case that the number of bona fide dissenters is such that it leads to the unavailability of sufficient numbers of executors of securitization, then the obligation to act is overridden. Recall, however, that this case is a paradigmatic example of the *exception clause*. In short, provided the state is just and has the necessary financial means, then the shortfall of manpower may be made up by employing a PMSC.

Collective responsibility also means that residents of state A must be prepared to incur higher financial costs than they do for cases of other-securitization not necessitated by state A's previous actions. To be sure, however, even here there is a limit. Although state A is morally culpable,

---

[53] The difference between this case and other-securitization without liability is that the former is 'not a case of aid [...] it is a case of compensatory justice' (Dobos and Coady, 2014: 80).

[54] For Miller, this is one of the triggers of remedial responsibility. In form of the 'beneficiary pays principle', we can also find this in climate ethics where it is used to hold citizens of states who have benefitted from historic carbon emissions remedially responsible for the harm climate change is causing in less developed countries today (cf. Caney, 2010: 128).

it does not have to incur financial costs that would leave it at risk of becoming existentially threatened. Likewise, state A cannot be expected to face existential insecurity or instability because of aiding state B.

2.6 Individual States as Primary Duty-Bearers for Mandatory Other-Securitization?

One issue this chapter has alluded to but not yet addressed is that capable states are not the only actors that have a pro tanto remedial responsibility of other-securitization on the grounds of the moral equality of people. As will become clear in subsequent chapters, other actors – including sub-systemic collectives of states with a security focus (e.g., NATO) – can also have this remedial responsibility. This begs the question when, if ever, are sufficiently capable *individual* states (and other actors) the primary duty-bearers? By primary duty-bearer, I mean the actor who – among several possible duty-bearers – should be assigned the first duty of other-politicization, evolving – if necessary – into a duty of other-securitization.

To be sure, the duty of other-politicization is a general duty that stems from the moral equal worth of people. This duty is variably described as a duty of justice, a humanitarian duty, or even a duty of assistance (Miller, 2007: 254–256). What matters is that there is a general agreement that there is a duty to help/rescue, or as I would put it secure, if actors are unable to help themselves. Some philosophers argue that there are no such things as special duties, but merely '"distributed general duties" [...] whereby the moral community's general duties get assigned to particular agents' (Goodin, 1988: 678). Regardless of where one stands on this,[55] for the purposes of other-securitization Goodin's view of assigning duties differently to distinct agents is instructive. While Goodin (1988: 678 FN 41) leaves it open *how* duties are assigned to particular agents, Miller argues that remedial responsibility is tied to the following triggers: outcome responsibility (causal responsibility), moral responsibility (causal responsibility + blameworthiness), benefit (beneficiary of situation), capacity (capable

---

[55] I side with Miller's (2007: 42–46) view that special duties to friends and compatriots obtain and that this is not unjust, provided that general duties relate to the extension and respect of key human rights for all (see also Nagel, 2005: 132).

of remedying the situation), and community (i.e., ties of friendship). Miller does not advance a ranking of these in terms of who should be assigned remedial responsibility; one reason for his reluctance is that reality is too messy. It is, for example, often difficult to be certain who has moral responsibility for an outcome, in part because 'moral responsibility is a matter of degree' (Miller, 2001: 467).

A second reason for Miller's reluctance is that he aims to ensure that those in need of help are always helped (ibid: 471). As Wouter Peeters et al. argue, however, this victim-centred view is not only unfair to 'responsibility-bearers' who ought to know why precisely they are being called upon, but also indeterminacy of multiple equally weighted principles means that potential bearers of responsibility can pass the buck (Peeters et al., 2015: 23). Following Peeters et al., one can achieve a sequential ranking when one compares Miller's criteria of remedial responsibility with common-sense morality.[56] In a nutshell, we can summarize common-sense morality as saying that moral responsibility for acts is considered weightier than omissions,[57] while

---

[56] 'Common-sense ethics' refers to the pre-theoretical moral judgments of ordinary people' (Brown, 1998: 1). According to Haworth, it is based on 'two types of ethical beliefs: norms and evaluations' (Haworth, 1955: 251), whereby norms proscribe how one ought to behave in a society, while evaluation concerns investigations about the relative value of prized events.

[57] It should be noted here that in moral philosophy the issue of moral disparity between these action and omission is contested. Consider that omitting does not necessarily equate to inaction (e.g., 'Is someone who is standing rigidly to attention best described as keeping still [an action] or as not moving [an omission/inaction]' (Zimmerman, 2010: 609)?). And yet, the moral distinction in everyday life between doing harm and allowing harm is pronounced. After all, most people think it is worse to kill someone than to let people die. Otherwise, as Zimmerman (ibid) points out how else might we explain that abject poverty (including death from preventable diseases and starvation) is not more effectively dealt with while murder is punished everywhere.

One reason that can explain this difference is that we in Zimmerman's words 'take being casually complicit in the occurrence of some outcome to be morally significant' (ibid: 615; cf. Woollard, 2015: 23). In more detail: 'to kill is to act, whereas to let die is to omit to act, and action and omission are of such a nature that we bear responsibility for our acts in a way in which we do not bear responsibility for our omissions' (Zimmerman, 2010: 607). To me, it seems intuitively correct that responsibility for our actions contributes to our blameworthiness and hence the level of penance. In other words, if one's causal role in an outcome is relevant to culpability, it seems logical that there is a moral difference between action and omission. Moreover, the causal factor also allows for a succinct distinction between doing and allowing harm. Fiona Woollard holds that: 'An agent counts as doing harm if and only if a fact

moral and outcome responsibility are weightier than friendship and ties of community, both of which are considered morally significant. While there are difficulties with establishing moral responsibility, our moral intuitions tell us that those responsible for creating an undesired outcome have a primary duty to alleviate the situation. We can find this, for example, in climate ethics where the polluter pays principle tracks remedial responsibility as outcome, specifically moral responsibility (Caney, 2010: 125–127), and where the beneficiary pays principle tracks remedial responsibility as causal responsibility.

Moreover, in common-sense morality pure capacity to remedy a situation is ranked, behind the obligation to help friends.[58] As Diane Jeske (2014) explains: '[...] Even if a person who is wealthier than me is actually in a better position to aid my friend, [in common-sense morality] it nonetheless seems to be the case that I have some reason to aid my friend that the person at least as well or better causally situated to do so does not have. She may have stronger agent-neutral reason to aid my friend, but she does not have the agent-relative reason arising from friendship that I have'.

Of course, common-sense morality faces its own challenges. Consequentialists, for example, discount the role of friends in favour of the obligation to maximize the greater good. Samuel Scheffler holds against this that special obligations to friends/community obtain when 'persons have reason to value the relationships' (cited in ibid.). To me, it seems intuitively right that persons should be assigned greater responsibility to help their friends than strangers.[59] After all: 'You cannot be

---

about the agent's behavior is part of the sequence leading to the harm'. While an agent 'merely [allows] harm if and only if some fact about the agent's behavior is relevant to, but no fact about the agent's behavior is part of, the sequence leading to harm' (Woollard, 2015: 35).

   Woollard (2016) explains why the distinction between doing and allowing is pertinent to a practicable moral theory. 'Treating doing and allowing harm as equivalent seems to leave us with a morality that is either much more permissive than we normally think it is (permitting us to do harm to others to avoid personal sacrifices) or much more demanding (requiring us to prevent harm to others even at great personal sacrifice)' (Woollard, 2016).

[58] To my mind, this is in equilibrium with communitarianism's recognition of special duties.

[59] See also Berenskoetter who argues that: 'While this relationship [i.e., friendship] can take many forms, the cosmopolitan dream of a bond among all humankind is not suitable to serve as the basis for a serious discussion of friendship. As friends are closer to each other than they are to non-friends, one might say friendship is an intimate relationship' (2014: 3).

somebody's friend unless you understand that this entails giving them certain kinds of priority in your life [...]' (Miller, 2007: 35–36).

The thought that ties of friendship/community are weightier than ties of pure capacity is less likely to be controversial when provisions are made that – when friends cannot or (for whatever reason) will not deliver – ensure that responsibility shifts to capable actors, thus ensuring that 'victims' are cared for. But what does friendship or community mean in the context of mandatory other-securitization? Community is perhaps easier to understand because this term already exists in security studies where a security community describes the situation when war between members of the community has become unthinkable (Adler and Barnett, 1998). Security communities can overlap with the boundaries of formal institutions (e.g., in the EU or NATO) or not, such as 'the West'. Friendship is a fuzzier notion. In international relations, friendships may be motivated by care for the other, but perhaps more so by utilitarian motives. As Felix Berenskoetter (2014: 3–4) explains:

[...] in the case of international friendship it is difficult to argue that we are dealing with a relationship based purely on collectives falling in love with each other. Arguably most friendships form out of an instrumental relationship, where the initial interaction is driven by detached utilitarian motives, which then moves to another level as the actors come to know and appreciate each other's qualities. Yet it would be misleading to read this process as a neat sequence in which 'utility' is entirely replaced by 'care'.

The utilitarian motive means that friendships can serve different ends. This is important. It seems to me that relevant for remedial responsibility in mandatory other-securitization is not whether states are friends *simpliciter* but whether they are 'security friends'. Berenskoetter would probably think that the idea of security friendship is tautological because real friendship is indivisibly bound to security (cf. Wheeler, 2018). Berenskoetter holds that 'friendship is [...] a special relationship of choice which does not simply form on the basis of geographic proximity, close trade links or an otherwise high level of "interaction", but through a mutual commitment to use overlapping biographical narratives for pursuing a shared idea of international order' (2014: 9). Leaving aside the point whether relationships between states based on trade render them friends or merely trade/international business partners or acquaintances, Berenskoetter's wider analysis suggests that we can recognize friendships between states when they voluntarily and trustingly engage in joint practices to shape the world in line with their ideal. States are most obviously security friends when they have formed what Adler and Barnett (1998: 55) have called 'tightly coupled' mature security communities where 'national identity is expressed through the merging of efforts' (ibid: 56).

Overall, Miller's insights combined with Peeters et al.'s suggestion to invoke common-sense morality allow for the following sequential ranking of the various triggers for remedial responsibility for initially other-politicization and – if this fails to have the desired effect – other-securitization: (1) moral responsibility; (2) outcome responsibility (I would include benefit here); (3) friendship; and finally (4) capacity. While moral and outcome responsibility trump the other triggers, it can only be actioned when actors have the relevant capabilities.

What then does all this mean for individual state's moral duty of other-securitization? It means that states are the primary duty-bearers of other-securitization when they are morally or outcome responsible for the insecurity. The ranking further means that states can be the primary duty-bearers when special ties of friendship are present. Given, however, that many states are a part of collective security arrangements and/or friends of collectives (for instance, Ukraine or Georgia with NATO), who are often more capable than individual states, individual states are not likely to be primary duty-bearers on the grounds of friendship very often. Moral responsibility trumps both of the other triggers, even when there are capable friends that could act, provided that the wrongdoer is capable of relevant action. In cases where duties conflict, but where both securitization and counter-securitization are justified (cf. Floyd, 2019a: 176), contractual obligations trump obligations to others.

Lest one should think otherwise this ranking of triggers holds true for mandatory other-securitization by consent as well as without consent. It is crucial to remember that other-securitization is not about large-scale armed military intervention into a friend's territory; instead, it might mean that friends suspend – as part of mandatory other-securitization without consent – diplomatic ties or trade guarantees.

Finally, I have argued (including in Section 2.4) that other-securitization rests on a prior duty of other-politicization. This raises the following question: are morally culpable actors that are obviously incapable of other-securitization (e.g., because they do not have a functioning military) still the designated first outside responder in relevant situations? Against this, we might argue that our focus should be on what is best for those in need of help as opposed to what is best for those that should help.[60] And that by requiring these actors to help first, we risk that a suitable response is delayed during which suffering continues.[61] By contrast, the affirmative case is based on fairness (e.g., solve what you have caused), while it is also informed by the view that we must not overrate the value of securitization. After all, the outcome responsible actor can still do something 'ordinary' to alleviate the situation, and this something might reduce the need for other-securitization (cf. Chapter 1, Section 1.2) by further actors. I lean towards the latter explanation, also because a theory of mandatory securitization insures against unnecessary delay by demanding that when actors have reached 'must cause' but can go no further, they have a duty to request help from other more capable actors.[62]

2.7 Conclusion

This concludes my analysis of the obligations of state actors regarding securitization. To summarize, I have argued that when must cause is satisfied just states are obligated to securitize the state or the citizens within states because the primary function of the state is the provision of security. I suggested that no considerations concerning the risks involved in securitization (e.g., instability) can override just states' obligation of self-securitization because the failure to provide security

---

[60] I assume here that not having to act to save outsiders is considered generally preferable because no costs are incurred.

[61] Note here that exempting wrongdoers with insufficient capacity to securitize does not automatically increase the likelihood of securitization, after all other-politicization can achieve the same goal.

[62] For those interested in fairness and perhaps also deterrence, note that wrongdoers have – if requested to do so – a moral duty to assist desecuritizing actors with just desecuritization. This applies specifically to restorative measures which see desecuritizing actors rebuild relations between parties adversely affected by securitization (Floyd, 2019a: chapter 7). An apology for threat creation is one such thing even severely financially challenged wrongdoers could do. By extension, wrongdoers have a duty to assist with securitization to the best of their ability if requested to do so by secondary duty-bearer of mandatory other-securitization.

The idea that powerless but morally responsible actors can play a supplementary role in securitization and/or desecuritization also suggests that – especially securitization – can be carried out by a group of actors. For example, security friends with insufficient capabilities could team up with capable actors. Indeed, this might even work to create friendship; research

terminates the social contract and thus effectively spells the end of the state. In short, here, when must cause is satisfied, not securitizing is always a greater risk than securitizing.

From here, I have gone on to examine the obligation that able states have regarding securitization of people within less able states. I have shown why they have a duty to help people abroad, and when they have such a duty. I have shown why a number of considerations including – the risk of dying, disease, and disability – can override the pro tanto obligation of other-securitization. In short, unlike self-securitization within just states, the duty of able states to securitize to save third parties is conditional. Finally, I have examined what triggers the remedial responsibility of first mandatory other-politicization and – if must cause is satisfied – mandatory other-securitization. I have argued for a ranking of triggers, whereby culpability for threat creation trumps benefit, which in turn trumps friendship, while friendship trumps pure capacity.

One issue that remains outstanding is whether states and other actors have a duty to actively look for insecurities in other places. This issue comes about, because of the possibility of mandatory other-securitization. It seems, however, that 'the duty of beneficence' does not require this. This is clear from the much-used example of the Good Samarian, wherein 'a would-be rescuer has a duty to aid a victim, even if no special circumstances obtain between them' but without 'a duty to patrol the road seeking to apprehend robbers or looking for other robbery victims' (Scheid, 2014: 9).[63]

Finally, and as before with Chapter 1, the analysis provided in this chapter raises some questions regarding the specifics of JST and whether the theory is allowed to stand, or whether it needs amending in some way. Just Securitization Theory argues that securitization

---

on environmental peace-building, for example, suggests cooperation between foes to tackle a joint problem builds trust and can lead to peace (Conca and Dabelko, 2002).

[63] Some might object that a duty of beneficence can include a duty to patrol, and – in evidence – point to the significance of early warning as part of the UN's work on genocide prevention. With a view to the UN, some analysts go further, Heather Roff's has suggested that a new global juridical body must monitor domestic governments as well as international organizations, including the UN (Roff, 2013: 115). To my mind, however, this is based on a specific cosmopolitan duty of justice that is not only too demanding, but potentially counterproductive. At the state level, for example, it could create a culture of suspicion between security friends, eroding trust and thus friendship.

is morally permissible when there is a current objective existential threat to an objectively valuable referent object. In other words – and provided that all other criteria are satisfied – in those circumstances would-be securitizing actors are morally permitted to use emergency measures against a threatener or a threat. In this chapter, I have argued that other-securitization without consent is not obligatory unless there is an unaddressed objective existential threat. In and of themselves both statements are sound, but they do raise the question whether other-securitization is also only morally permissible when there is an unaddressed real threat? Or is it the case that external powers are permitted to other-securitize when the threat is addressed but when the strategy to deal with the threat is poor? To stick, with the example from above (Section 2.4), would the EU be morally permitted to securitize against gun violence in the United States (e.g., by using sanctions) on the grounds that the United States's strategy of addressing the threat is poor, after all gun violence continues to be a problem?[64] Recall that in the above I argue that in this case there is no obligation to securitize, indeed to act at all, because the issue is – even if poorly–addressed by the sovereign state, and sovereign states can determine how they address issues. And yet, it seems intuitively correct that if, in this case, the EU wants to do something, and if the United States's strategy really is poor, they should be permitted to do just that (note here that proportionality might render securitization unjust anyway). The question ultimately is whether permissible other-securitization can be reconciled with self-determination. The principle of mandatory securitization is really based on the idea that there are some things states are not allowed to do. Most notably if a state endangers an innocent (in the relevant sense) minority – other states, etc., have a duty to come to the rescue. In other words, self-determination is not sacrosanct. This is important because it allows for some much-needed nuance. Thus, while a duty to act does not arise when a threat is addressed by the primary duty-bearer (cf. Section 2.4), if the threat is only partially mitigated by the actions of the primary duty-bearer, nothing prohibits external actors (here the EU) from acting on the issue.

---

[64] It must be acknowledged; this hypothetical is for illustrative purposes only. Lucia Rafanelli offers a comparable real-world example with the EU's export ban of 'lethal injection drugs to the US for the express purpose of getting the country to abolish the death penalty' (2021: 50).

3 | Non-state Actors and the Obligation to Securitize

3.1 Introduction

Since the end of the Cold War, the world has undergone dramatic changes, not only politically (notably: widespread democratization, regionalism, and collapse of the Soviet Union), but also economically (including through unprecedented globalization) and technologically (notably the rise of the Internet). These global transformations have been aided by countless non-state actors, many of which arose, or markedly grew in size and significance (specifically global technology businesses, international and transnational non-governmental organizations, and NGOs at the state level), during this period.

Globalization and cyber space have ushered in, or sped up, a whole host of (new) security threats. The coronavirus pandemic, for example, shows that infectious diseases can become a global pandemic much quicker in the age of international air travel than hitherto possible. Many of these new security threats require deep expert knowledge. Cyberattacks, for example, cannot be addressed easily or effectively using military might; instead, they require cyber expertise of a kind and sophistication available only among computer experts.

Although states and other traditional security actors (e.g., North Atlantic Treaty Organization) can and do employ experts to address these new threats,[1] non-state actors sometimes strive to provide security themselves, including via securitization. Non-state actors can be described as 'organizations and individuals that are *not* affiliated with, directed by, or funded through the government' (ESCR, 2019, emphasis added). Generally speaking, such actors fall into two categories: (1) non-state actors situated below the level of the state and (2) non-state actors active across multiple state borders and thus placed above the

---

[1] North Atlantic Treaty Organization runs a cyber security centre; see here ccdcoe.org/.

124

level of the state, either at the sub-systemic or even at the systemic level. In short, non-state actors do not slot neatly into international relations' levels of analysis.

Non-state actors active only within the state differ in their nature and number according to regime type (e.g., is it democratic or autocratic), stability, and economic wealth of the home state. Notably in failed states, violent resistance movements, warlords, and militia groups are a common sight. In stable, strong, and fully liberal democratic states, there will be very few such groups. Here, non-state actors refer mainly to political groups or movements (e.g., hacktivists, earth liberation fronts), non-governmental organizations, and firms/businesses, a small number of which might also be active in failed states. In free states, the number of non-state actors is also going to be much larger than in unfree/autocratic societies, after all in the latter non-state actors are often banned (no free media) or even forcibly discouraged.

What kinds of non-state actors exist – or are sufficiently able to function as securitizing actors – also depends on the culture of the state in which they act. For instance, church and religious groups and figures matter in religious states but they do not have the same kind of influence in secular states. In traditional societies, unique actors (i.e., actors that do not exist elsewhere) often matter disproportionally. India's officially abolished but still tangible caste system of social stratification, for example, divides all Hindus into a number of casts, each with diminishing amounts of social standing, privilege, hence influence.

At the sub-systemic (e.g., regional and transnational) and systemic (e.g., global) level, we can find transnational non-governmental organizations, international non-governmental organizations (INGOs), global firms, and businesses and business magnates (e.g., Bill Gates, Elon Musk) to name a few. It will be impossible to account for each and every possible non-state actor in this chapter; neither do they all fit neatly into one, or just one of the suggested categories. The point of the categories is rather to simplify a diverse reality to provide proper guidance. Table 3.1 is thus not intended to be comprehensive, but rather it aims to summarize what kinds of actors are possible.

This chapter proceeds as follows. In Section 3.2, I will examine which kinds of non-state actor can meaningfully double up as securitizing actors and as such potentially have an obligation to securitize. In Section 3.3, I briefly consider the kind of roles non-state actors

Table 3.1 *Non-state actors at different levels of analysis*

Level of analysis	Non-state actor
Failed, failing, or weak state	Militia groups, warlords, armed rebels, Private Military Security Companies (PMSCs), traditional actors (e.g., tribes), terrorist groups
Stable, strong, democratic states	Civil society, business, firms, non-governmental organizations, quangos; PMSCs, terrorist groups
Sub-systemic/ systemic	International non-governmental organizations (non-profit organizations); big business, multinationals, philanthropists

can inhabit in the securitization process. I show that even exceptional action does not necessarily render a non-state actor a securitizing actor. In Section 3.4, I consider the duties of sub-state non-state actors to insiders, which is to say to persons/referents within the actor/organization or represented by them, as well as to the actor/organization itself. Section 3.5 considers the duties of sub-state actors to outsiders (i.e., peoples of other states or stateless global referent objects). Section 3.6 examines duties of systemic-level non-state actors to insiders and outsiders, given that many of these actors are global; there is often no meaningful difference between insiders and outsiders. Section 3.7 is the conclusion, where I summarize the findings of this chapter.

3.2 What Kinds of Non-state Actors Can Securitize?

As Table 3.1 shows, the relevant non-state actors we need to consider are either individual persons or organized groups of people but not as states. While the role of organized groups' ability to securitize is now undisputed,[2] the question whether individuals are able to securitize remains poorly understood and rarely discussed (but, see, for instance, Topgyal, 2016). It seems to me, however, that if groups of people are able to securitize by doing exceptionally risky and harmful

---

[2] The Copenhagen School was never meant to be state-centric; it is merely the case that states dominated the security agenda in 1998 when SANFFA was published. Nevertheless, the school cannot seem to shift this stigma (see Burke, 2020: 1010).

things following securitizing moves (i.e., existential threat articulation), then there is no reason to categorically exclude the possibility that individuals can securitize.[3] To be sure, to count as a securitization by an individual, the individual would have to double up as securitizing actor and as executor of securitization; otherwise, our concern would be with a group. I believe that one reason why securitization by individuals is rarely discussed is that in cases where we have a plausible case of individual-led securitization we tend to frame and understand the issue as a crime only.

In evidence, consider the case of Anders Behring Breivik, the perpetrator of the racially motivated 2011 Norway attacks that left sixty-nine people dead. To be clear, I do not want to suggest that what Breivik did is not also an atrocious crime. My point is rather that if we see the event *only* as a crime, we ignore that Breivik conceived of his actions as self- and other-defence (of other Caucasian Norwegians and perhaps Christian Europe at large). Moreover, his actions followed a series of written 'speech acts' that clearly identified the threat (indeed for many securitization scholars, it should be significant that his speech acts were accepted by right-wing audiences around the world). If this is so, should not securitization theory be able to explain Breivik's actions as a case of a securitization by an individual person? I should think yes, but I acknowledge that this is difficult because his actions are first and foremost criminal. Regarding them as securitization instead could be seen as vying for an excuse, which is not my intention.

But is it not also the case that had Oskar Schindler reverted to extreme measures of the kind indicative of securitization to save Jews from certain death in concentration camps (e.g., by killing or detaining Nazi guards without the help of his Jewish workers), that it would be easier to accept the possibility of securitization by an individual.[4]

Given then that securitization by individuals seems possible, to what extent do individuals have a moral duty to carry out securitization? I think it is here, rather than with simply the concept/possibility

---

[3] The idea of the audience in securitization serves as a normative bulwark against this because ordinary individuals are less likely to succeed in convincing an audience.

[4] I mean here securitization where one and the same individual is the securitizing actor and the executor of securitization.

of securitization by individuals, that things become difficult. Here is why. individuals have a moral (negative) duty not to harm other people (including by not omitting to help the drowning child (cf. Chapter 2, Section 2.5.1)), but they do not have a positive duty to risk their own life and flourishing in order to save someone else (note the duty to save the drowning child at the risk of one's own life is only asked of people in relevant professions).[5] Thus, no one can be compelled to join the emergency services or military against their will, at least not to defend people in other places (i.e., outsiders). Yet, what of situations where the state is manifestly unjust (e.g., when it denies minorities their basic human needs) and acts of resistance would no longer be criminal, because law and order have either broken down altogether or are used to defend an illegitimate regime only? In such cases, do individuals who have the necessary means not also have a moral duty to securitize individuals and groups of people against the regime?[6] I do not think they do, because the burden of a duty imposed on an individual is too demanding.[7] I think in such cases it is more apt to say that relevant individuals are permitted to securitize (cf. Floyd, 2019a: chapter 5); however, if they decide to do this, then such acts are supererogatory to what morality requires of individuals, because securitization always spells serious risks (the risk of dying, disease, and disability, but also other risks – in the given case – the risk of incarceration, a charge of treason, etc.) for the securitizing actor and executors of securitization.

But what about a duty of self-securitization as a form of self-defence? It is not clear to me what form this could possibly take, but for the purposes of completeness let us consider this issue by examining whether individuals are morally permitted to commit suicide. For, if they are, then there cannot be a duty to self-securitize. While arguments for and against the permissibility of suicide exist, it seems to me that the majority of philosophers agree that suicide is permissible;

[5] Notably in JST, morally wicked people are those that deliberately inflict harm on innocent (in the morally relevant sense) others. By contrast in order to be a just referent for securitization, individuals do not – unlike states – have positive duties.
[6] This is for purposes of thinking this through; I struggle to think what form this would take.
[7] I am speaking here about securitization only; it is possible that individuals have a duty to contest or request securitization (cf. Delmas, 2018: 151).

indeed, much of the debate now concerns whether or not assisted dying is permissible. Moreover, moral arguments against the permissibility of suicide fail to convince.[8] Thus, sanctity of life arguments are incompatible with the just war tradition that under certain circumstances permits killing. Religious arguments whereby we owe our life to God fail to convince the atheist, while social arguments that consider the duties to others of those committing suicide (e.g., parents to their children) do not amount to a full-on prohibition. Overall, the best justification why suicide is permissible is perhaps that 'the right to suicide is the natural corollary of the right to life' (Cholbi, 2017). In any case, if suicide is not morally impermissible it follows that individuals do not have an obligation to self-securitize (whatever that would look like) in the face of objective existential threats.

This leaves us with groups of people detached from state influence and money as the only plausible should-be non-state securitizing actors. It is important to note that I focus on organized groups only, and aggregate groups of people (i.e., all Parkinson's sufferers or all new mums) cannot have such duties as they are simply aggregated individuals with one unifying feature or hallmark, but no organizational structure or agenda. This follows Toni Erskine. In a widely influential study, Erskine has suggested four criteria that delineate moral agency of collectives: (1) 'an identity that is more than the sum of the identities of its constitutive parts', (2) 'a decision-making structure', (3) 'an identity over time', and (4) 'a conception of itself as a unit' (2003: 24).

Still, even among organized groups not all are relevant in the context of mandatory securitization.[9] For example, Harry Potter fan clubs the world over are irrelevant, and their purpose is the celebration of Harry Potter, perhaps the exchange of further storylines, interpretation of book passages, etc. Equally irrelevant are running clubs, indeed all sports clubs, litter-picking groups, wine clubs, book clubs, and so on. The reason why all of these clubs are irrelevant for our purposes here is that none of them aim to provide relevant forms of security.[10] Or, to put this differently, none of these organizations

---

[8] This paragraph draws extensively on Cholbi, 2017.
[9] The emphasis here is on mandatory securitization; I am not disputing that such actors can – at least in principle – securitize and be permitted to do so.
[10] I say relevant forms, because there can be little doubt that some of these clubs provide ontological security to their participants.

rivals or critiques the state in its ability to provide military, societal, environmental, economic, political, and indeed human security for its citizens.

This changes when we consider, for example, militia groups, which is to say armed organized groups active within states that seek to provide security in areas where states underachieve or are over-whelmed/underfunded (e.g., in the United States, we can find militia groups helping with border security on the US–Mexico border). It is also true of secessionist groups whose ambition it is to break away from states to form independent (often) nation states. It can also be true of green NGOs in the business of ensuring the survival of a particular species or the biosphere as a whole, by fighting those that do not.

The only event when non-state actors not already in the business of security provision can plausibly be expected to protect people via securitization is when they are responsible for threat creation. I will return to this issue in more detail below.

None of these actors enjoy legitimate authority in the way just states do. Legitimate authority is a major feature of most just war theories, as only legitimate states are permitted to wage wars. Given that the nature of war has changed to being fought inside states involving non-state actors, most just war theorists hold that just non-state actors need to enjoy 'representative authority' or 'representative legitimacy' if they act on behalf of people (Finlay, 2015; Pattison; 2010; Parry, 2017a). As mentioned in the introduction, however, in JST I have dis-missed the requirement of representative authority, in part because the criteria of JST already guard against proponents of representative authority's biggest fear, which is that sub-state groups merely further their own political agenda. While consent then does not influence the moral permissibility of securitization, it can influence aspects of the duty to securitize. As I will show later on, if people have freely and fully consented to being protected by one or other actor a quasi-social contract exists; in such situations, the duty to securitize relevant refer-ents is overriding not conditional.

In summary, individual actors and organized groups of people are morally permitted to securitize provided that the criteria for just ini-tiation of securitization are satisfied. Given the harm securitization is likely to cause individual persons, only organized groups can have a corresponding duty to securitize.

3.3 Non-state Actors' Diverse Roles in Securitization Processes

In the Introduction to this book, I argued that where non-state actors are concerned securitization usually refers to those situations when groups or individuals declare something or someone as objectively existentially threatened and then perform otherwise unacceptable (most likely because of the harm risked or caused) deeds in order to protect the referent object. It is important to bear this in mind when considering non-state actors as potential securitizing actors, because often non-state actors are not securitizing actors but one of the following instead: (1) audiences; (2) functional actors; (3) securitization requesters; and (4) securitization pre-emptors. The latter two of these are my own category of actor in securitization processes and require further explanation. The other two are standard concepts for anyone working with the Copenhagen School's securitization framework; however, given that the nature of neither category is conclusively settled in the relevant literature, these two also require further explanation.

3.3.1 Audiences

As I have argued elsewhere, securitization succeeds (in a sense of being complete, not in the sense of actually addressing the threat) *not* when a relevant audience accepts the threat articulation (i.e., the securitizing move), but rather when the securitizing actor changes their behaviour away from routine conduct to the exception in response to a threat and/or when they instruct executors of securitization, they are in a position of power over to act in exceptional ways (Floyd, 2019a, 2016a, 2010). In other words, I consider security action significantly more important than simply securitizing language. Of course, language can cause indirect (non-physical) harm, but this does not compare to the direct harm securitizing action can cause (cf. Floyd, 2018).

The inclusion of speech into my version of securitization theory means that there must also be some kind of audience. Frankly put, it makes little sense to highlight the role of the speaker without – at least –acknowledging the receiver. In ordinary language and everyday life, audiences are those persons to whom speech, music, words are addressed. Drawing on early and unpublished work by Wæver (1989), I hold that in uttering securitizing moves, would-be securitizing actors do one of two things: they utter a warning, and/or they promise protection through relevant and prompt action. Consequently, I suggest that there are two possible audiences for securitizing moves: (1) the threatener who is being warned off and/or (2) the referent object who is promised protection.[11] While audiences can influence the would-be securitizing actor's decision to proceed with securitization, empirical evidence suggests that they do not categorically do so (Floyd, 2016a).[12] Therefore, we ought to exclude the audience as a categorically analytically relevant category from securitization (cf. Floyd, 2019a).

Furthermore, contra to the vast majority of securitization scholars, I hold that securitizing moves are not made to seek legitimation for action from putative audiences. Instead, promises and warning are self-executing statements that tell the world about the position of the would-be securitizing actor on a particular issue/problem.[13]

One reason why the audience has become so important in securitization studies is that it delimits the occurrence of securitization. Many securitization scholars would have a normative interest in this; after all, most believe in the moral superiority of not securitizing (i.e., politicization) or desecuritizing.

In addition, a second reason why the audience became important in the school's own writings is that it serves to foreclose analytical irrelevance. Let me explain. Consider that the original aim of the Copenhagen School's securitization approach was to offer a third way

---

[11] Sections from Wæver's more recent work seem to suggest that for him too referent objects double up as audience. For example, in 2015 he argues: 'Sbisà has argued that Austin's theory of speech acts entails that the illocutionary effect ('done in saying') is co-produced by the audience in a more extensive sense than pure uptake, and the status transformation entailed in, for example, securitization is a redefinition of the rights and responsibilities of actors [...]' (Wæver, 2015: 122). In a paper from 2017, he restates much of this, including the following decisive line: 'The defining event in a securitization is exactly the rights and duties exchanged between the defender and *defended*' (2017: 131, my emphasis).

[12] I have since been wondering whether – especially in intent-lacking threats – warnings may also be issued from say a government to the general public. Indeed, here warnings are likely to go hand in hand with the promise for protection. But even if warnings play out in this way, it does not change the veto power of the audience.

[13] Notably 'security legitimacy' – that is, the ability to 'claim a natural right to survive' (Buzan et al., 1998: 36 and 38) – can be situated with the CS's third facilitating condition: 'features of the alleged threats that either facilitate or impede securitization' (ibid: 33).

between on the one hand detrimentally wide Critical security studies and more myopic traditional security studies on the other (Buzan et al., 1998: 203–212). Yet, the great risk associated with declaring that security is a speech act is that there might be no limit to securitization, rendering the theory analytically weak.[14] But Ole Wæver is clever. From the very beginning of thinking in terms of securitization, he has been acutely aware of the limitlessness-utility problem in security; this much is evident from his refusal to include individuals as referents of security as this would expand 'the security realm endlessly' (Wæver, 1995: 48). More so, over time other 'limiters' have crept into the theory of securitization. One of these is the Copenhagen School's claim that the only important cases of securitization are those that have significant consequences, which is the case when extraordinary emergency measures are adopted (Buzan et al., 1998: 25–26). Another is the – in 1998 novel (see Stritzel, 2007) – requirement that the securitizing speech act must be accepted by a relevant audience. While these moves are clearly able to diminish the number of securitizations in the world, we must recognize that they are not purely a reflection of how the world operates, but rather standards set by analysts to maximize the analytical leverage of a particular theory. There is nothing necessarily wrong with delimiting what a theory can and cannot recognize, provided, however, that we recognize that there is a normative agenda (be they analytical relevance or preference for desecuritization) that drives these limitations.

3.3.2 Functional Actors

Within the Copenhagen School's version of securitization theory, functional actors are 'actors who affect the dynamics of a sector. Without being the referent object or the actor calling for security on behalf of the referent object, this is an actor who *significantly* influences decisions in the field of security' (Buzan et al., 1998: 36, emphasis added). This description is taken from the School's seminal 1998 book *Security: A New Framework for Analysis* (SANFFA). Despite being significant, functional actors feature by that label in only three of the five chapters on sectors. Moreover, most of the time (in the

---

[14] This is a perennial critique of human security (see various in *Security Dialogue* special issue from 2004 journals.sagepub.com/toc/sdi/35/3).

book) when specific examples of functional actors are given, the actors mentioned already fulfil an alternative function in the securitization process. For example, in the environmental sector the School leads with actors 'whose activity is directly linked to the quality of the environment' (i.e., fishing, mining, and other industry) (Buzan et al., 1998: 79). 'These are functional actors whose behaviour affects ecosystems but who generally do not intend to politicize, let alone securitize' (ibid). To my mind, however, the function these industries, etc., fulfil in the environmental sector is that of threatener, even if the threat – in many cases – is not intended. In short, most of the alleged functional actors identified in SANFFA are already accounted for by other actors. This said, at one point the Copenhagen School equates functional actors with actors that object to securitization (ibid: 103). Since the veto has become associated with the audience in securitization studies, this category also seems already accounted for, suggesting that the category functional actor is redundant. This changes, however, if one accepts that audiences are either referent objects or threateners. Thus, not all actors that veto any given securitization are necessarily also referent object or threatener. Among others, the media, academics, but also the general public – at least in free societies – can and do veto or endorse securitization that is already under way and that does not concern them directly as referents (or threatener). The media, for example, plays a prominent role in the securitization against the coronavirus, discussing whether the measures taken are justified, effective, and lawful and much besides. The substantive functional difference between audiences and functional actors is thus as follows: audiences object to or sanction securitization on behalf of themselves as referent objects of securitization, while functional actors endorse or veto securitization on behalf of (i.e., in support of) others, notably those considered threatened and threateners (cf. Floyd, 2021).

3.3.3 Securitization Requesters

To summarize what I have said so far, securitizing actors are those actors whose actions constitute securitization and/or who are in a position of power over those who can exercise securitization (e.g., the executive over the police). Where non-state actors are concerned, securitizing actors are likely to be the same as executors of securitization. The audiences are either referent objects or threateners, while functional actors are actors, *other than* audiences-as-addressees, that veto or endorse securitization during securitization for the sake of others. But securitization is a complex, often lengthy, and convoluted process that involves other categories of actor. Two such actors I and others (albeit not by this name, or indeed explicitly) have identified are securitization requesters. Securitizing requesters seek to convince more powerful/strategically positioned actors of the need to securitize. They do this by uttering repeated threat articulations (including point of no return). Unlike securitizing actors, in doing this they do not promise protection or else aim to warn a threatener ('stop or else'); instead, their purpose is to convince, other more powerful and/or suitable actors (often governments) to securitize against the threat.

Of course, one can recognize securitization requesters as distinct from securitizing actors only when one – like me – differentiates between security speech and security action. For many securitization scholars, securitization succeeds at the point of audience acceptance. For such scholars, securitization succeeds when what I call a 'securitization requester' convinces powerful elites ('audiences') of the need for securitization. There is no right or wrong in this, but there is such a thing as logical deduction. Thus, if – as it does in this book – securitization means a specific kind of behavioural change, speech alone cannot get us there. The important difference between what I call securitizing requesters and securitizing actors is that the former do not plan to carry out securitization themselves. In uttering securitizing moves, they do not, for example, request permission from an audience to be allowed to do this. Instead, they want for the authority to carry out securitization (cf. Vuori, 2008: 76).

3.3.4 Securitization Pre-emptors

The mirror image of securitization requesters is not as, for example, Bourbeau and Vuori (2015) argue, desecuritizing actors, but rather securitization pre-emptors. Securitization pre-emptors seek to pre-empt securitization by discouraging would-be securitizing actors from initiating securitization. The difference between functional actors and either securitization requesters or securitization pre-emptors is that the former inhabit a different time window vis-à-vis securitization than the latter two actors. Functional actors are active when securitization is already under way, that is, when emergency measures are launched and inform the securitizing actors' response. Pre-emptors and request-ers, by contrast, operate *before* securitization occurs.

These four types of actor are analytical categories that are designed to clarify the securitization process. They are not (intended to be) immutable structures. For one thing, it is possible that one and the same actor/organization (e.g., a specific newspaper) acts first as securitization requester and – once securitization is under way – as a functional actor endorsing securitization. Moreover, if securitizing requesters fail to convince more powerful actors of the need to securitize, it is possible that such actors turn – sometimes even justifiably – to self- or other-securitization. Similarly, it is pos-sible that a resistance to securitization can evolve into a case of counter-securitization. In short, functional actors can morph into securitizing actors.

It is important to be clear on the existence of these different actors also because the behaviour non-state actors display in securitization processes does not necessarily mark out these actors as securitizing actors. For instance, violent protests/resistance is used also by func-tional actors, securitization pre-emptors, and securitization request-ers. Moreover, from the Section 3.2 we already know that some kinds of action can be both securitizing behaviour and criminal behaviour. Given that where non-state actors are concerned, action alone cannot always designate actors as securitizing actors; we can see why securi-tizing language and justification of action with reference back to the threat remain important, especially in gauging intention (cf. Floyd, 2016a). Candice Delmas' in her influential *A Duty to Resist* (2018) comes to a similar conclusion. She argues: '[s]ome acts of uncivil disobedience are primarily communicative, but many do not aim to persuade an audience – seeking instead to prevent or redress wrongs – though they may still include communicative elements' (2018: 44–45). And a little later, she sheds further light on acts of principled disobe-dience that are not primarily communicative (i.e., seeking to convince lawmakers to change the law) but where agents take matters into their own hands. Notably, 'agents providing covert assistance to migrants or engaged in vigilante self-defence aim first and foremost to prevent harms' (ibid: 52–53). In my categorization, only the latter are securi-tizing actors.

3.4 Sub-state Actors: Duties to Insiders

Having established that there are no a priori reasons that void non-state organized groups' duties to securitize, we must now consider *when* they have such a duty, as well as the nature of that duty (i.e., is it conditional or overriding). I want to begin by discussing potential duties of sub-state actors to insiders. Insider here is a cumbersome term. Unlike with state actors, we cannot point to a people within certain territorial boundaries that count as insiders. Instead, here insiders are those people and/or referents (e.g., a non-human species) the organized group represents (regardless of whether the referent has consented to being represented). In sub-state non-state actors, this is often – but not always – a minority bound together by ethnicity, culture, or nationality. But other actors too can assume the role of securitizing actor. Patriot hackers, for example, are 'malicious non-state cyber actors whose motivations stem from the desire to help their country during conflict or crisis. Patriot hackers most often aim to disrupt the operations of those perceived to be enemies of the state' (Whyte and Mazanec, 2018: 198). In any case, the actors I have in mind here are groups of people residing *inside* the territory of a given state 'fighting' internal and external threats.

Unlike state actors, non-state actors do not have a duty to provide security as a state of being, even if their raison d'être is the provision of relevant forms of security. This is because unlike with states, members of the ethnicity, culture, etc., have not agreed to being protected by the relevant non-state actor.[15] Put differently, there is no social contract. Indeed, the existence of the social contract at the state level, which awards states a monopoly on violence (cf. Chapter 2, Section 2.2), means that non-state actors below the level of the state are not morally or indeed legally permitted to self-securitize. Members of the minority, just like all other citizens have relinquished the right to provide for their own security to the state. However, in Hobbes, for example, it is also the case that when the state fails to achieve the ends for which it was created, then the social contract is nil and void (Steinberger, 2002: 859). Put differently, when the social contract is broken non-state actors are morally permitted to securitize (Floyd, 2019a: chapter 5). But do such actors also have an obligation to securitize (provided that

---

[15] In states, people do not formerly agree to the social contract; instead, they tacitly agree to obey its laws – provided that it keeps them safe.

initiation to securitization is justified and that must cause is satisfied)? To answer this question, consider the following thought experiment:

Destinia
Destinia is a relatively prosperous state. Porous borders mean that ever more illegal immigrants are crossing into Destinia. Over time, the numbers of immigrants is such that the healthcare and welfare system collapses and violent conflict breaks out between residents and immigrants. Destinia has no longer the money to provide security for its people and innocent immigrant bystanders. Luckily, the militia group Destinia Recon, made up of people who have protested against the government's inaction on migration, can provide security, by ensuring law and order and by securing the border with coercive but proportionate force.

For the purposes of argument, I assume that *Destinia Recon* is morally permitted to securitize (the state has broken down (i.e., the social contract is void)), there is an objective existential threat to a just referent object (securitization seems proportionate, etc.), and they do so in line with the principles of just conduct in securitization. In order to answer the above question – and in the absence of contractual obligations – we must proceed by consulting again the triggers of remedial responsibility as outlined in Chapter 2, Section 2.6. After all, in the absence of contractual obligations, the responsibility to alleviate insecurity must rest on one or more of these.

Given that *Destinia Recon* is not morally responsible for the insecurity, they cannot have an obligation to securitize on the basis of culpability. Moreover, although they ultimately benefitted from the collapse of the state (note, now there is no question as regards their *raison d'être*, whereas hitherto there might have been), we know that members of *Destinia* Recon were not a silent party while *Destinia* (through harmful neglect) caused the threat. In short, the trigger of outcome responsibility by benefit is not applicable here.

What then of community/friendship? Surely members of *Destinia Recon* stand in a relationship of friendship with other Destinians, because by and large, they share the same views and are engaged in joint projects as a people. Indeed, there is also no real division between the militia group and the people, considering that the former will have families and friends among the latter. Moreover, members of the militia are themselves Destinians. Beyond ties of community/friendship, *Destinia Recon* also has the capacity to act. With two of the triggers of remedial responsibility strongly satisfied, it seems to me that they have a duty to act in the relevant way.

To be clear, however, this duty is not overriding. No members of *Destinia Recon* can be forced to risk their own life and well-being in order to save other Destinians. What is more, the risk of instability and insecurity as well as financial overstretch also can override the moral obligation. After all, a failed Destinia without the militia group will be even worse off than one with the group in it.

We can now say that in situations where states have collapsed or manifestly failed, relevant and capable sub-state actors have a pro tanto obligation to securitize insiders. The question is: does this obligation bite only once states have collapsed or manifestly failed? To answer this question, consider once more Peter Steinberger's insightful work on Hobbes. Steinberger notes that Hobbes' understanding of security as a state of being was actually much broader than one might think. He argues '[...] the purpose of the state is not simply to secure the lives of its citizens but to secure as well their liberty and at least a certain minimal level of physical comfort' (Steinberger, 2002: 858). If this is so it follows that the social contract is void not merely when the state has collapsed, but rather when the state fails to address an objective exis- tential threat to a just referent object.[16] This is most obviously the case when the state itself threatens a minority within the state, but it is also the case when state leaders ignore or deny the existence of a threat. One prominent example is the autoimmune deficiency syndrome (AIDS) denialism of the former South African President Thabo Mbeki, who refused to provide expecting mothers 'with zidovudine (or AZT) for prevention of mother-to-child human immunodeficiency virus trans- mission', he denied the link between human immunodeficiency virus and AIDS, and he 'restricted the use of freely donated nevirapine and obstructed the acquisition of Global Fund grants' (Chigwedere et al., 2008: 410). The authors of the influential study from which these quo- tations are taken argue: 'We contend that the South African government acted as a major obstacle in the provision of medication to patients with AIDS' (ibid). They – conservatively – estimate that Mbeki's stance led (between 2000 and 2005) to some 330.000 deaths.

---

[16] Recall that this does not mean when they fail to securitize, but rather when they fail to have a strategy in place to act on the threat. In theory, this could be conscious inaction, however, as we have seen in Chapter 1, Section 1.4, inaction can almost be ruled out as a plausible non-securitization alternative.

This example does not lend itself well to discussing the moral obligations of sub-state securitizing actors, because few if any such actors could take on the state. Nevertheless, we can still say that if there was an actor that could meaningfully do this then they have a pro tanto obligation to act.

While I have argued that relevant and capable sub-state actors have a pro tanto obligation of securitization when states fail, there is a potential exception to this, or rather there comes a point when the duty to securitize cannot easily – or at all – be overridden by other concerns. It seems to me that if a non-state actor like the militia group *Destinia Recon* justly and successfully ensures security in an area, if the people in that area have consented to them doing so, and – most importantly – if said people have agreed among themselves to bear arms only under the banner of the militia, we have in place a quasi-social contract. That is to say, with the transferal of the right to self-defence to *Destinia Recon*, the actor undergoes a status transformation whereby its existence and legitimacy become directly tied to providing security for the in-group. This is important, because, arguably, in such cases, the duty to securitize insiders is overriding. In line with the exception clause (Chapter 2, Section 2.5.1), this means that *Destinia Recon* not only has the moral right to enlist militia fighters compulsorily, but also has the moral right to employ PMSCs (e.g., foreign mercenaries) to assist – in relevant cases – with mandatory securitization

It remains to consider what ought to happen when a morally valuable sub-state actor, and thus just referent object, is objectively existentially threatened? Considering that this actor meets the moral minimum of basic human need satisfaction, should not this actor survive? While the justice of the referent object is crucial to the overall justice of securitization, it is but one of a number of principles designating just securitization. Recall that just initiation of securitization entails also macro-proportionality: the requirement that securitization cannot cause more harm than it seeks to prevent. Among other things, this requirement helps us realize that the disappearance[17] of a valuable referent object might cause insufficient harm to people to warrant the

---

[17] Not necessarily disappearance. To be existentially threatened in one's survival does not mean that the actor or state, etc., will disappear, but rather be changed in its essential properties.

harm securitization inevitably causes. This means that the context in which the non-state actor is situated is relevant. Consider two variations on *Eternal Faith*, a sub-state actor.

Eternal Faith 1

Eternal Faith 1 is a human rights organization in state A. State A is an affluent, liberal democratic state, scoring high in the Human Development Index. In recent years, the private funding that used to sustain Eternal Faith has been donated to the rival organization Faith Forever, and Eternal Faith 1 is now threatened with closing down operations. Faith Forever has the same values as Eternal Faith 1 but a slicker marketing campaign, celebrity endorsement, and a huge X following. Eternal Faith 1 has the means and the manpower to defend itself and those it protects via securitization.

Eternal Faith 2

Eternal Faith 2 is the only human rights organization resident in state B, now governed by a vindictive and autocratic regime. Eternal Faith 2 offers much-needed protection and assistance to minorities persecuted by the regime. As state B becomes increasingly unfree, new emergency legislation is passed proscribing Eternal Faith 2. Eternal Faith 2 has the means and the manpower to defend itself and those it protects via securitization.

In accordance with JST, only *Eternal Faith* 2 in state B is morally permitted to defend itself with recourse to extraordinary measures (e.g., revolutionary action, forcible resistance, radical protest, clandestine operations). Consider that non-state actors are permitted to securitize only when there is an unaddressed objective existential threat. While *Eternal Faith 1 and 2 are* threatened in their existence in both cases, it is also the case that the disappearance of the organization does not cause the same amount of harm. Thus, in state B *Eternal Faith* 2 is the only actor that provides protection and assistance to persecuted minorities, whereas in state A, there is no persecution. Moreover, the state and other organizations (e.g., *Faith Forever*) monitor and protect human rights. To put this another way, in state A the harm that securitization is likely to cause outweighs the harm the disappearance of *Eternal Faith 1* is likely to cause.[18]

---

[18] This example shows that the origin of the threat also matters to macro-proportionality. Thus, if Eternal Faith was treated by the government taking an illiberal turn, it would be permitted to defend itself.

If the argument advanced in this section is correct, we can see that *Eternal Faith 2* not merely permitted to defend itself, but – provided it has the relevant capabilities – it quite feasibly has the moral obligation to do so. Unlike in the case of suicide, the concern here is not with one person who does not have an obligation to save itself, but rather demise of the organization renders serious threats to those it protects. On these grounds, it seems logical to argue that the organization here has a conditional duty of mandatory self-securitization.

3.5 Sub-state Actors: Duties to Outsiders

So far, we have discovered that some organized groups can securitize, that they are sometimes morally permitted to do so, and that in some cases they can even have a moral obligation to do this. The question now is: do sub-state actors have an obligation of other-securitization (i.e., secure outsiders against a threat by means of securitization)? If we think of these others as people or non-human referents in other states only, the question seems almost futile. Thus, in Section 3.2 we have seen that while – in principle – some sub-state actors can securitize, Section 3.3 shows that many will not be able to do this. And if sub-state actors struggle to carry out securitization of insiders, how could they possibly be obligated to act across borders?

This said, just as insiders – in this chapter – do not refer to everyone within a given state, outsiders refer – in the context of non-state actors – not only to people outside the state, but rather to those outside the group, or better outside of those people/entities the non-state actor represents. If this is so, then there are relevant 'outsiders' also within the territory of the state.

This raises the following question: in cases where non-state actors are capable of other-securitization, do they have a corresponding duty? To use an example from above, does *Destinia Recon* have a moral duty to protect a separately organized security-providing sub-state group (within Destinia) that has become existentially threatened by criminal gangs? Unlike in the case in Section 3.2, here the trigger of remedial responsibility is capacity. It seems to me that if *Destinia Recon* has the necessary capabilities, then the equal moral worth of people means that they have a pro tanto obligation to also protect these 'outsiders'. In short, sub-state actors can have a conditional moral obligation to securitize outsiders. Because they are able to do this and because they are already in place, their ability can render them primary duty-bearers for mandatory other-securitization. To be clear, however, this duty can be overridden by one or more of our three risks and costs: the risk of dying, disease, and disability, the risk of instability and insecurity and prohibitive financial costs.

3.6 Sub-systemic or Systemic Non-state Actors: Duties to Insiders/Outsiders

I now want to turn to non-state actors operating at the sub-systemic (e.g., regional) or even the systemic level. When, if ever, do transnational companies and INGOs have a duty to protect insiders? In line with what I have argued so far, insiders here are those people the international non-state actor considers itself responsible for. At this level, this can be a vast number of people. An organization such as the international human rights organization Amnesty International,[19] for example, represents anyone whose human rights are endangered – consequently, potentially everyone. Obviously, no non-state actor can be charged with a duty of defending/rescue – via securitization – all people. In line with what I have said so far, such actors are permitted to securitize when minorities or small groups of people are without a protector (e.g., when groups/minorities made up of morally innocent (in the relevant sense) individuals are designated enemies of an unjust regime). A duty to securitize, however, is more demanding than mere permissibility. Here as in other cases, it rests on the moral equality of persons and is triggered by either: moral or outcome responsibility, ties of friendship or capacity. In the given example, moral/outcome responsibility is not applicable. Friendship is I think also not applicable as there is likely to have been no prior relationship between the INGO and the individuals now threatened. This leaves capacity. INGOs are for the most part, unlikely to be the most capable actor able to protect just referents. States and collectives of states simply have too much power and influence, especially in collectives. However, the same is not impossible. The most likely situation is perhaps where a unique technological advantage renders an INGO the most capable actor, for example, if the Bill and Melinda Gates Foundations had developed

---

[19] Mostly, such actors are not securitizing actors; instead, their modus operandi is to request politicization or securitization of particular situations/threats through targeted campaigns. In other words, they are securitizing requesters.

readily deployable solar radiation technology, and if they would be the only ones to have this at the ready when must cause is satisfied. In such cases, actors may well be morally required to deploy their technology on the grounds of unique capability.

Moving on slightly, we have seen that capability is a factor that stands in the way of non-state actors acting. If this is so, and given that the UN – who is or should be the natural protector of threatened minorities – frequently eschews interfering (often even simply just vocally) into the internal affairs of other states (Pattison, 2018), should sub-systemic and systemic non-state actors have the moral right to employ PMSCs so that they could act in order to protect just referent objects? I think the answer to this question must be no. Bestowing non-state actors with the moral right to use PMSCs directly challenges states' monopoly on violence and could lead to chaos and anarchy (see Pattison, 2014: 191). Notably, it could embolden some such actors to look after their own security permanently. Moreover, the possession of capacity might see non-state actors play a more active role in other-securitization more generally drawing the wrath of other states and potentially weakening their home state due to counter-securitization. So overall the employment of PMSCs in securitization must be limited. Above I have suggested that the use of PMSCs is permissible only when an actor has an overriding obligation to provide security or when the actor is morally or outcome responsible for the insecurity, and – for both cases – when rescue would otherwise not go ahead. I repeat this here because it also means that PMSCs themselves can have a pro tanto obligation of other-securitization only when they are morally or outcome responsible. Given that PMSCs are contractors that work for someone else (usually a state), they are not the ultimate bearers of responsibility but rather their employer is. In short, PMSCs do not usually have an obligation to securitize.

So far, I have argued that sub-systemic and systemic non-state actors do not (usually) have a duty of other-securitization. This is so for two reasons: (1) they are not permitted to employ PMSCs that would provide them with the physical means to carry out securitization effectively, and (2) they are unlikely to be the primary or secondary duty-bearer for other-securitization. By secondary duty-bearer, I mean the actor that has a moral duty to act on other securitization when primary duty-bearers fail. In Chapter 5, I will argue that the UN is the default secondary duty-bearer when states or collectives of states fail. Before I can conclude, there is one exception that breaks with both points made above. We already know that – if it can be attributed – then moral and outcome responsibility weighs heaviest in remedial responsibility than either friendship or capacity. One reason for this is that it goes some way towards putting the 'moral imbalance' between threatener and referent object right (Miller, 2007: 100). But it is also fair that those who have committed a wrong have to alleviate it, and not some other actor who has the means, but who has not contributed to the wrong. Bearing this in mind, consider a variant on an example already utilized in Chapter 2.

Toxic Firm
Multinational company Macrocom routinely dumps toxic waste in poor state B. Over time the toxic waste seeps into the ground and contaminates the water supply. The result is high rates of cancer, but also contamination of fish stocks in rivers and freshwater systems. With fish the main food, the population of state B now suffers a famine. Social unrest and conflict become widespread.

Macrocom is obviously responsible for the insecurity caused. As one of the world's wealthiest organizations, it also has the financial means to deliver rescue via securitization; however, as a business it does not employ the kind of people who could meaningfully intervene (in this case other-securitization would likely involve actions on the territory of state B, notably to calm conflict). The question thus is this: should primary responsibility for other-securitization shift to another actor (e.g., wealthy neighbouring state and friend A, or even the international community), or should Macrocom be permitted to employ a PMSC, which would enable them to address the situation. I think that in part at least the answer to this question hangs on whether state B consents to help with securitization or whether securitizing intervention would be without consent. I think that if it was a case of *mandatory other-securitization by consent* then Macrocom may be permitted to employ PMSC to deal with the security fall-out from their actions. By contrast, I do not think that Macrocom ought to be permitted to employ hired guns to securitize without consent. As mentioned above, non-state actors simply do not have the same standing as states in international order. Of course, international order leaves much to be desired, but allowing non-state actors to employ PMSCs and mercenaries to conduct mandatory other-securitization without consent would challenge our rules-based order to the core. Specifically, it would give rise to the possibility that non-state actors wilfully and intentionally create a threat, in order to orchestrate forceful intervention. So, in the interest of stability and security the idea that non-state actors should be permitted to employ PMSCs to conduct mandatory other-securitization without consent is to be rejected.

3.7 Conclusion

In contemporary international relations, non-state actors can be found at all levels of analysis. Within states, relevant non-state actors refer to NGOs, liberation movements, militia groups, pressure groups, firms and businesses, etc.; at the sub-systemic level, it includes INGOs, international firms, and at the systemic level we have global businesses and INGOs and many others besides. Although the number of non-state actors is large, their role in mandatory securitization is surprisingly small. This is for a number of reasons. Sub-state actors are morally permitted to securitize only when states have manifestly failed to address a threat, or when the state is the threatener.

As we have seen, non-state actors' duty to protect can pertain to outsiders, whereby outsiders refer to persons not part of the in-group the non-state actor represents, but that may be present inside the territory of a given state. The situation whereby sub-state actors could securitize outsiders in other states is unlikely to arise, but if it does the same rules apply as they do for sub-systemic and systemic non-state actors. The inside/outside distinction works even less well for sub-systemic and systemic non-state actors than it does for sub-state actors. Thus, where, for example, human rights organizations are concerned, threatened persons everywhere are insiders. I have argued that while – in principle – such actors can have a duty of 'other-securitization', they are unlikely to be either the primary or the secondary duty-bearer. If, for example, the UN – on its own – fails and requests help with securitization from non-state actors, the latter are executors of securitization not securitizing actors. The exception is when transnational or global non-state actors are responsible for threat creation. I have argued that in cases where the state in which the referent object resides requests help, other-securitization is obligatory provided that must cause is satisfied.

I anticipate that some critical security studies scholars will object to the findings that non-state actors play a comparatively small role in mandatory securitization. Jonna Nyman (2018), Gunhild Hoogensen Gjørv (2012), and Matt McDonald (2012) are just some of the scholars who have a generally positive view of non-state actors in securitization processes. The important thing to note is that while non-state actors above and below the level of the state have few obligations as regards securitization, this does not exclude such actors from securitizing. After all, within JST such actors are permitted to securitize provided securitization is just.

4 | *Sub-systemic Collective State Actors and the Obligation to Securitize*

4.1 Introduction

This chapter is concerned with collective state actors situated above the state level (i.e., sub-system-level actors) and their obligation to securitize. I am chiefly concerned with two types of actors: (1) collective defence organizations and (2) collective security organizations. It would be tempting to follow the pattern established in the Chapters 2 and 3 and make my case using hypothetical places/examples. Given, however, that at the sub-systemic level fewer actors can be found, so doing not only would be strange and artificial, but it would also detract from the potential for reform that the discovery of mandatory securitization requires of real-world actors.

In this chapter, I take the North Atlantic Treaty Organization (NATO) as indicative of a collective defence organization and the European Union (EU) prior to 2007/2009 as indicative of a collective security organization. Although I focus on real institutions and examine the extent of pre-existing commitments that are in line with mandatory securitization, it is important to stress that my argument is normative. That is to say, my theory pertains to what NATO, the EU, and in Chapter 5 the UNSC ideally ought to do, not to what they will do.

While I focus in this chapter on NATO and the EU only, my comments are not meant to be restricted to these actors, and my findings regarding mandatory securitization allow for extrapolation to other actors at the sub-systemic level, provided that they fulfil the criteria for moral agency of collectives (Erskine, 2003: 24; cf. Chapter 2, Section 2.7), and that they are security providers.[1] As before with states,

---

[1] Diana Panke (2016: 29) identifies nineteen regional bodies with security competencies, namely: Arab League, Association of Southeast Asian Nations, African Union, Caribbean Community, Economic Community of Central African States, Commonwealth of Independent States, Common Market for Eastern and Southern Africa, Collective Security Treaty Organization,

securitization of the organization per se is a narrow interpretation of self-securitization, while a wider interpretation refers to securitization of its member states or populations. Provided that the referent object is just, an unjust collective is permitted to securitize. Working on NATO and the EU – as I do here – avoids some of these conceptual problems. Their respective member states are just referent objects because they satisfy basic human needs, as evidenced, for example, by both organizations' commitment to liberal democracy[2] and human rights.

But first things first, what, if anything, is the difference between a collective defence organization and a collective security organization? In many texts explaining the principle of collective security, the two concepts seem coterminous. Consider, for example, Baylis et al. (2020: 533) who argue in the glossary of the bestselling textbook *The Globalization of World Politics* that collective security:

refers to an arrangement where 'each state in the system accepts that the security of one is the concern of all, and agrees to join in a collective response to aggression' (Roberts and Kingsbury, 1993: 30). It is also the foundational principle of the League of Nations: namely, that member states would take a threat or attack on one member as an assault on them all.

Unfortunately, that book does not contain a glossary entry explaining collective defence; however, when – in said book – NATO is first introduced, contributor Len Scott writes: 'The key article of the treaty – that an attack on one member would be treated as an attack on all – accorded with the principle of collective self-defence [...]' (Scott, 2020: 61). These passages suggest that collective defence is really just another word for collective security. And yet, some analysts suggest otherwise. Williams and Jones argue that 'professional defence planners habitually' distinguish between the two, yet 'governments [often] ignore' the difference (Williams and Jones, 2001: p.88). They further suggest that collective security arrangements are about preventing one

Economic Community of West African States, EU, GUAM Organization for Democracy and Economic Development, Intergovernmental Authority on Development, NATO, Organization of American States, Organization for Security and Cooperation in Europe, Pacific Islands Forum, South American Defense Council, Shanghai Cooperation Association, and Union of South American States (the latter is now practically defunct).

[2] With recent developments in Poland, Hungary, and Turkey, there are some outliers now.

of the member states morphing into a security threat to other member states, while collective defence is concerned with defending against threats from the outside. In more detail:

[A] collective security system [...] is directed towards no predetermined (or clearly defined) enemy, nor can it operate on the basis of a predetermined coalition. In fact, it is a curious doctrine because its success as an operational system depends upon *all* participants becoming *potentially* peacekeepers (rather than actual aggressors!). Should one of the participants of a collective security system become an 'aggressor' nation, then the rest of them must be ready to move against it. In reality, the underlying purpose of collective security is to buttress the status quo against a violent or unacceptable challenge. (Williams and Jones, 2001: 88, emphases in original)

Likewise, as Kegley and Wittkopf explain: 'collective security [is] a security regime[3] agreed to by the great powers that sets rules for keeping peace, guided by the principle that an act of aggression by any state will be met with a collective response from the rest' (2001: 30). Collective defence is different to this. Williams and Jones again explain:

The notion of collective defence implies an 'alliance' which comes into existence to confront a perceived and perhaps very tangible adversary. A military alliance therefore, of course, implies a limited and restricted membership covering a defined geographical area. It also involves a military obligation which is only likely to be activated in a carefully defined set of circumstances. (Williams and Jones, 2001: 88)

This is also the view of Amitav Acharya who argues that collective defence is about '[c]ommon perception of external threat(s) among or by the members of the community; such a threat might be another state or states within the region or an extra-regional power, but *not* from a member' (Acharya, 2014: 16, emphasis added). This difference is important for the argument developed here. As we shall see over the course of this chapter precisely how an international collective actor is organized (i.e., on the basis of collective defence or collective security)

---

[3] Note here that Acharya (2014: 16) draws a distinction between security regimes and collective security. The main difference seems to be that security regimes are not about collective action (e.g., on arms acquisitions, etc.) but simply about rules that reduce conflict between parties.

determines on what grounds individual states within the collective have obligations regarding securitization to other members of the collective. Specifically, I shall argue that the principle of collective defence is akin to the social contract at state level discussed in Chapter 2, while in collective security organizations no contractual relationship exists that generates overriding duties.

I proceed as follows. I begin by discussing NATO's obligations regarding securitization towards insiders and follow this with an analysis of the organization's obligations to outsiders. I shall examine to what extent the concerns that override mandatory other-securitization where states are concerned apply here. As part of this discussion, I consider again the issue of liability for threat creation. Specifically, I examine whether responsibility for threat creation by one member state makes that state liable to carry the larger share of the financial cost of mandatory securitization. In general, I consider whether such culpable member states ought to do more towards 'collective securitization' (Sperling and Webber, 2017, 2019).

From here, I move to discuss the EU to examine mandatory securitization for collective security organizations. I focus on the EU prior to 2007/2009 because with the Lisbon treaty the EU is slowly but surely morphing into a collective defence arrangement. This is not only due to more recent developments regarding Permanent Structured Cooperation, which allows joint permanent defence structures, but also because the Treaty of Lisbon introduced a mutual defence clause (Article 42(7)), which 'provides that if an EU country is the victim of armed aggression on its territory, the other EU countries have an obligation to aid and assist it by all means in their power, in accordance with Article 51 of the United Nations Charter' (Eur-Lex, 2023). Moreover, this is supplemented by the solidarity clause (Article 222) 'which provides that EU countries are obligated to act jointly where an EU country is victim of a terrorist attack or a natural or man-made disaster' (ibid, 2023).

In the conclusion, I show that the sequential ranking of triggers for remedial responsibility lightens the burden on NATO (as the most capable actor) to be the world's policeman. I also argue that ties of community and friendship significantly reduce the United Nations' (UN) Security Council's role in mandatory other-securitization, because relevant ties of friendship are strongly developed at the regional/sub-global level.

4.2 Collective Defence Organizations: Duties to Insiders

This chapter considers mandatory securitization and just collective actors bigger than individual states. The first kind of collective I want to examine in this context is NATO, the world's foremost collective defence organization. NATO was founded in 1949 in response to the Berlin blockade and the Soviet Union's seizure of Czechoslovakia. Its purpose was to defend Western Europe against the threat from Russian/Soviet invasion and subsequently also the nuclear threat. NATO was formulized in its founding Washington Treaty consisting of fourteen articles. The most significant of these is Article 5 which renders NATO a collective defence organization. It holds that:

The Parties agree that an armed attack against one or more of them in Europe or North America shall be considered an attack against them all and consequently they agree that, if such an armed attack occurs, each of them, in exercise of the right of individual or collective self-defence recognised by Article 51 of the Charter of the United Nations, will assist the Party or Parties so attacked by taking forthwith, individually and in concert with the other Parties, such action as it deems necessary, including the use of armed force, to restore and maintain the security of the North Atlantic area. (cited in Medcalf, 2005: 189)

Be that as it may, in the now seventy-three-year long history of NATO Article 5 has been invoked only once, immediately after the terror attacks of 9/11. Operation Eagle Assist from mid-October 2001 to mid-May 2002 saw NATO Airborne Warning and Control System radar aircraft help patrol the skies over the United States, flying over 360 sorties. Most NATO missions since its founding have seen NATO militarily act out-of-area (whereby in-area is defined as per Article 6 of the Washington Treaty) on the basis of Article 4, which holds that: 'The Parties will consult together whenever, in the opinion of any of them, the territorial integrity, political independence or security of any of the Parties is threatened' (cited in ibid: 189). Notable examples of such out-of-area military missions include Bosnia, Kosovo, and more recently Libya.

Moreover, NATO's Strategic Concept from 1999 officially recognized out-of-area missions as part of NATO's remit (ibid: 60). The need for NATO to act out-of-area to protect allies' security was further cemented by the events of 9/11. NATO's 2010 Strategic Concept lists alongside collective defence also crisis management and cooperative security as its principal tasks. None of this means, however, that NATO is no longer a collective defence organization. After all, throughout, collective defence has always remained the 'greatest responsibility of the Alliance' (NATO, 2010: 14). Notably, crisis and conflicts beyond NATO's borders are interesting only in so far as they pose 'a direct threat to the security of the Alliance territory and populations' (ibid: 19). Second, NATO has taken a number of collective defence measures without invoking Article 5. The deployment of NATO troops to the alliance's Eastern border (i.e., Enhanced Forward Presence) agreed in 2016 in the light of Russia's actions in Ukraine is one example of this.

Having thus explained why NATO is first and foremost a collective defence organization, let us now consider NATO's obligations to the members of the alliance. It seems to me that NATO's raison d'être – at least regarding the provision of security – is comparable to that of the state. Thus, if NATO fails to defend the allies against armed attack, NATO itself is likely to cease to exist. There is after all no reason to invest and be a part of the alliance if that alliance does not protect the allies from relevant threats. We can thus see that the relationship between NATO and its member states is contractual (cf. Caney, 2005: 204). The allies commit to defend others in return for the assurance that they – should the situation arise – too will be defended. If that relationship cannot be guaranteed, NATO loses its reason for being.

Unlike with states, however, the end of NATO would not result in anarchy (i.e., chaos and lawlessness) in the affected states; after all, international law permits not only alliances but also individual states to defend themselves against armed attack. Moreover, and quite unlike the case of states and citizens, NATO members do not need to relinquish the ability to defend themselves when entering a contractual relationship of mutual defence. To the contrary, Article 3 of the Washington Treaty requires member states to engage into effective self-help and to develop their individual capacity to resist armed attack.[4] To be sure, '[t]he individual commitment of each and every Ally to maintaining and strengthening its resilience reduces the vulnerability of NATO as a whole' (NATO, 2018). This also means that NATO's duties to insiders (member states) are less than those individual states have to insiders

---

[4] Latterly, this has been captured under the label resilience. See here: www.nato .int/cps/en/natohq/topics_132722.htm

154 Sub-systemic Collective State Actors & the Obligation to Securitize

(i.e., citizens). Specifically, NATO is not under the moral obligation to act on *all* cases of objective existential threats encountered by member states; rather, it is NATO's duty to '*assist* the Party or Parties' (NATO, 1949/2019) when such assistance is sought.[5] In other words, the contractual relationship between allies formalized in NATO means that member states have – when asked by the member state – an overriding moral duty to defend insiders against armed attack.

It is noteworthy, however, that the one and only time Article 5 was invoked, a member state (the United States) arguably, was not subject to an armed attack. Buckley recalls the deliberations at NATO headquarters thus:

Ted Whiteside, head of NATO's Weapons of Mass Destruction Centre, was also present and questioned whether the attack that day had been 'armed': Article 5 contemplated an 'armed attack' against any NATO Ally, but was an aircraft a weapon? [...]. We went through all the issues on our own. We agreed that there had indeed been an armed attack. The aircraft had been used as missiles. (Buckley, 2006)

More recently, cyberattack has been included into NATO's collective defence obligations. However, it remains unclear when cyberattacks have met the relevant threshold for a collective forcible response, neither is the nature of the response (conventional or cyber) clear.[6] All

---

[5] I have found it surprisingly difficult to find reliable information on how Article 5 is invoked. Upon reading NATO official Edward Buckley's account of how Article 5 was invoked after the 9/11 terror attacks, however, it is clear to me that the state in which attacks occur must sign off on the assistance. In the specific case, the possibility of invoking Article 5 was sanctioned by Colin Powell and President George W. Bush before it was debated at the North Atlantic Council (Buckley, 2006).

[6] The BBC's security correspondent Gorden Corera (2019) summarizes the issues succinctly as follows: 'In the Cold War, a missile launch or a tank column advancing would have left little doubt of what constituted an attack. But in the cyber-world it is not always so easy. When Estonia saw its infrastructure hit through cyber-space in 2007, it was blamed on Russia. But was it the Russian state or "patriotic hackers" operating within Russia? And at whose direction? Another issue is the threshold for considering something an attack. Russia is accused of turning off a power station in (non-NATO member) Ukraine in December 2015. The crippling of infrastructure is one possibility for reaching a threshold for Article 5. But what of 2017 when Russia is alleged to have launched the Notpetya computer virus against Ukraine, but which then spilled over into other countries (including Nato members) damaging businesses at a cost of billions of dollars?'

this suggests that NATO's Article 5 with its focus on armed attack is no longer fit for purpose. Nowadays, many objective existential threats do not take the form of armed attack, provided we define existential threats as threats to the essential properties of member states and not purely as lethal threats.[7] Former NATO official Jamie Shea predicts that this is the direction of travel: '[...] from now on, Article 5 could well apply more to threats against transport, power infrastructure, space communications, pipelines, IT networks and civilians sitting on park benches than to tanks crossing borders' (Shea, 2019: 4). If this is so, then Article 5 needs to be revised to better account for today's security landscape.

My theory of mandatory securitization can make Article 5 fit for the twenty-first century. Not only does it take account of all kinds of threats, including intent-lacking ones, but also it does not run the risk of invoking collective securitization too lightly potentially endangering alliance cohesion. I propose that in line with the logic of mandatory securitization, NATO members are morally required to respond via securitization *only* once political measures enacted to address a relevant and sufficiently sizable threat have been tried and failed to satisfy just cause. In more detail, Article 5 so revised holds that:

The Parties agree that a sufficiently harmful objective existential threat to one or more of them in Europe or North America shall be considered a threat to them all and consequently they agree that, if such a threat manifests, each of them, (where applicable – in exercise of the right of individual or collective self-defense recognised by Article 51 of the Charter of the United Nations), will assist the Party or Parties so threatened. Should ordinary political measures to alleviate the threat fail, the Parties will by taking forthwith, individually and in concert with the other Parties, securitizing action, including the use of punitive sanctions and assistance with punitive security measures, to restore and maintain the security of the North Atlantic area.

This revision of Article 5 would enable NATO to act more decisively and varyingly on a range of threats, enabling it to maintain its deterrent function, without the risks of upsetting alliance cohesion or triggering

---

[7] The threat of de-democratization in several NATO countries comes to mind. Thus, such a threat could not only alter the alliance as we know it (after all a commitment to liberal democracy is one of its fundamental values), but according to Wallander backsliding into authoritarianism increases the threat of subversion by Russia (Wallander, 2018).

war-like responses in the adversary. For example, if Russia were to pose an objective existential threat to a member state and Article 5 was invoked, NATO does not need to offer an armed response[8] but may respond using ordinary political means to try and solve the situation peacefully. Only if those attempts fail, does NATO have a moral obligation to securitize, but that too does not mean armed response.

It should be noted here that my proposal is very much in line with General Secretary's Stoltenberg's vision for NATO 2030 outlined in June 2020. He emphasized both a broader view of security and a multitude of ways (he speaks of 'a broad range of tools') to combat insecurity, including 'Military and non-military. Economic and diplomatic' tools, and the importance of resilience (Stoltenberg, 2020). Just and mandatory securitization offers just that.

In summary, provided that a NATO member or members have requested assistance from the alliance and that must cause is satisfied, the contractual nature of collective defence organizations means that the obligation to act, where insiders are concerned, cannot be overridden by potential moral costs or risks. Unless the alliance fulfils its reason d'être of collective defence, the alliance is defunct. Put differently, when assistance is sought by the affected member state(s), the duty to secure, and if must cause is satisfied, securitize is overriding.

More needs to be said about NATO and the securitization of insiders. We need to consider what – from a moral point of view – ought to happen when two member states fall out with each other or when a NATO member state goes rogue and, for example, threatens groups of people living within their territory. In other words, what role is there for NATO when individual member states actively threaten people within their state and thus provide a just cause – and subsequently a must cause for securitization? In line with what I have said so far in this book, it is logical to suggest that someone has remedial responsibility to act, initially by using political measures to address the threat and if necessary (i.e., when must cause is satisfied) by securitization. I want to suggest that in cases where NATO member states misbehave, or when NATO members clash, NATO is the primary duty-bearer for securitization. This said, it is important to realize that NATO does

---

[8] It should be stressed here that the text of Article 5 speaks of 'action as it deems necessary, including the use of armed force' (see above); however, in public debate a NATO response has been reduced to an armed response.

not acquire that role because of contractual responsibilities. Although Article 2 of the Washington Treaty holds that 'The Parties will contribute toward the further development of peaceful and friendly international relations by strengthening their free institutions, by bringing about a better understanding of the principles upon which these institutions are founded, and by promoting conditions of stability and wellbeing' (NATO, 1949/2019), there is no contractual commitment to eliminating conflict *within* and *between* member states. Instead, Article 2 continues with saying that: 'They will seek to eliminate conflict in their international economic policies and will encourage economic collaboration between any or all of them' (ibid). In other words, NATO members are contractually obligated to seek peaceful relations through economic policies as well as commitment to democracy. The view that NATO must act when a NATO member state goes rogue and poses an unjust threat to a just referent object within the alliance is based on the understanding that remedial responsibility is triggered by ties of community and friendship. Moreover, international organizations have unique capacity to rein in wayward member states – after all only the collective can make membership and/or certain benefits conditional on good behaviour.

Finally, what about self-securitization narrow. That is, what ought to happen if there is not a threat to one or more member state, but to the alliance itself? NATO's physical presence, for example, its website, headquarters, or soldiers under NATO command, could be threatened, while NATO per se can also be threatened through disinformation campaigns. In 2017, for example, it emerged that likely Russia spread the false information that German soldiers stationed in Lithuania as part of NATO's enhanced forward presence had raped an underage teenage Lithuanian girl in order to undermine NATO cohesion (Deutsche Welle, 2017). As a just referent object, NATO is entitled to defend itself via securitization against such external threats. The question is whether NATO has a contractual obligation qua NATO to defend itself (provided criteria are satisfied) via securitization. The Washington Treaty does not conceive of threats to NATO per se, suggesting that there is no contractual obligation to act. However, an attack against NATO per se is also an attack against all member states simultaneously thus, if article 5 is invoked, requiring action. To be sure, however, this duty only applies to external threats. If one or more member state undermines the very existence of NATO, for instance when President Trump threatens to pull the US out of NATO, thus depriving the alliance of its most important actor. Considering that there is nothing in the Washington Treaty that prohibits member states from leaving (indeed France withdrew from the integrated military structure in 1966) or working in – matters of European defence – exclusively through NATO, there is also no contractual obligation to save NATO from internal decline. Article 13 of the Washington Treaty holds that:

After the Treaty has been in force for twenty years, any Party may cease to be a Party one year after its notice of denunciation has been given to the Government of the United States of America, which will inform the Governments of the other Parties of the deposit of each notice of denunciation. (NATO 1949/2019)

The irony here is of course that a US withdrawal would pose a genuine existential threat to the alliance, greater than an attack against its website or headquarters, both of which can be rebuilt. Considering this, some readers will protest that NATO is so important for European security that it has a moral obligation to save NATO from Trump. This may well be true, after all NATO is a just referent object. However, even if true, it does not mean that NATO must achieve security (as a state of being) via securitization.[9] Recall from Chapter 2, Section 2.2, that while states have an obligation to provide security to their citizens, they do not have an obligation to provide security via securitization, unless must cause is satisfied. The same is true for NATO qua NATO.[10]

4.3 Collective Defence Organizations: Duties to Outsiders

The purpose of a collective defence organization is to secure an internal area from external threats or from attack by external parties. Purely defensive alliances have no particular duties of collective defence to outsiders (i.e., states that are not part of the alliance). However, and as already touched upon in the previous section, NATO

---

[9] Indeed, in the Trump case this is quite unlikely to have worked, after all his bugbear was the unequal burden sharing. In other words, what would have worked would have been assurances to pay up.
[10] I am grateful to Mark Webber for discussing this subsection with me on more than one occasion.

is more than a purely a defensive alliance. Immediately after the end of the Cold War, NATO's role and purpose were openly questioned. Hence, with the Soviet Union gone, what was the purpose of an alliance whose role it had been to protect against the Soviet threat? Much ink has been spilled trying to explain NATO's continuous existence (for a useful summary, see Webber 2009), and it is clear that – at the time – NATO needed a new raison d'être. Asmus et al. suggested that: 'the only penetrating justification for the continuation of NATO is its direct relevance to the commonly perceived security problems facing the United States and its European allies. If it does not pass that test, it should and eventually will go out of business' (Asmus et al., cited in Medcalf, 2005: 57). Nowadays, security problems pertain to much more than traditional military attack, at least partly motivated by the need to stay in business NATO evolved to take on crisis prevention and humanitarian missions. A change later formalized in the 2010 Strategic Concept. Moreover, after 9/11 NATO came to fully recognize that threats are global. The Final Communiqué of the 2002 meeting of NATO foreign ministers in Reykjavik stated that: '[t]o carry out the full range of its missions, NATO must be able to field forces that can move quickly to *wherever they are needed* [...]' (cited in Medcalf, 2005: 63, my emphasis).

In addition to being more than purely a defensive alliance, NATO – like many other collective actors in international affairs – is ultimately nothing but a group of states that have come together to form a bigger whole. NATO, for example, is constituted by its individual members all of which are sovereign democratic states. Given that capable states have at least a *pro tanto* duty to act on relevant threats to outsiders (cf. Chapter 2, Section 2.3), a collective of such states, whatever their domestic make-up, must have an equivalent duty. In other words, here as with sovereign states, the duty to save third parties, including via securitization, does not result from a contractual obligation, but rather flows from the weak cosmopolitan principle of the equal moral worth of people. This also means that the duty of other-securitization is not – at least in principle – restricted to *just* collectives. Recall that JST does not insist on legitimate authority and there is no reason why unjust collectives of states do not also have a *pro tanto* obligation to do the right thing. Whether they will do the right thing is another issue altogether; for certain, merely acting on mandatory other-securitization does not render unjust actors just ones (Floyd, 2019a: 142).

As stated previously (Chapter 2, Section 2.4), any would-be securitizing actor must establish the must cause independently. This means that relevant collectives have – in the first instance – a duty to provide security (or else, a duty to rescue) using ordinary political measures and only when this fails a duty to use exceptional measures (securitization).

Moreover, the justice of securitization is dependent on whether it is proportionate. Again, as mentioned previously (Chapter 2, Section 2.4) the threshold for macro-proportionality in other-securitization is expected to be higher than in self-securitization, because intervention (especially without consent) into another states' sovereign affairs is likely to be more harmful; notably, it risks conflict and instability of the international system, than self-securitization.

The major difference between individual member states of NATO and NATO as a collective is that NATO is much more powerful and thus better able to help. This is potentially important because the allocation of remedial responsibility also depends on capacity (Chapter 2, Section 2.6). Miller argues: 'If A is uniquely in this position, then he is remedially responsible for P: if I am the only person walking along a river bank when a child falls in, then it is my responsibility to rescue the child. In other cases, where several agents are to different degrees capable, we may assign responsibility to the most capable [...]' (Miller, 2007: 103). One problem with this is that NATO is thus potentially punished for having ensured its, figuratively speaking, 'continuous presence by the river bank', while other actors have not made such provisions (cf. Welsh, 2016: 108). I will return to this below and in the conclusion; I mention it here because we must consider whether NATO's unique capacity means that there are no moral costs and risks that can legitimately override the duty to act on must cause. Put another way, does NATO have a moral duty to be the world's policeman?

In order to answer this question, let us now consider what effect our three established and potentially prohibitive moral costs and risks (i.e., the risk of death, disease, and dying; the risk of instability and insecurity; and prohibitive financial costs) have on NATO's obligation of other-securitization.

4.3.1 Risk of Death, Disease, and Disability

As argued in Chapter 2 the risk of death, disease, and disability is a factor against mandatory other-securitizations, especially when other-securitization takes place in another state's territory (or for NATO 'outside of area'). Indeed, this risk can override the moral obligation to securitize, notably when insufficient executors of securitization (e.g., soldiers, police, but also healthcare professionals, etc.) voluntarily and knowingly sign up to careers, or specific missions that involve this risk (cf. Chapter 2). With a view to NATO, this risk is less acute than for individual states. For infantry soldiers in particular, the risk of death and disability is an occupational hazard (cf. Dobos and Coady, 2014: 84–88). Soldiers serving in NATO member states know that their services might be required not only in missions conducted by their home state individually, but also under the leadership of NATO. In other words, 'NATO soldiers' are under the obligation to incur the risk of death, disease, and disability on NATO missions.[11]

The same would be true of people working in civilian jobs for NATO, or other sub-systematic actors (e.g., the EU or the Organization for Security and Cooperation in Europe), provided that (a) relevant persons joined voluntarily, and (b) they are/were aware of the fact that the risk of death, disease, and disability on NATO (etc.) missions is real.

One interesting quirk with NATO is that the organization cannot force member states to join its external (i.e., Article 4 and 6 missions; conversely, with Article 5 missions there is the contractual duty to act, while here the possibility that member states would refuse to act is low). In NATO, decisions are taken by consensus, not by majority voting. However, this does not mean that all agree on a course of conduct and then need to bow to the consensus; instead, NATO agrees on a course of conduct all find acceptable. This is important because it means that NATO members are under no formal obligation – either towards NATO's other member states or the organization – to join external missions (Germany, e.g., abstained from Operation Unified Protector in Libya) if the consensus is that whoever wants to partake in an intervention can do so, while those that do not can abstain. Indeed, NATO has to accept the decision of member states to opt out. This also means that it cannot force member states to provide personnel to individual missions. In other words, soldiers employed by NATO member states have 'role-based duties' (Pattison, 2014: 63) to face the risk of death, disease, and disability only when their home country decides to join

---

[11] My thanks here to my former student Daniel Jensen for sharing his experiences as a NATO soldier with me.

other-securitization. The consequence of this is that if *no* NATO member wants to act on an objective existential threat to outsiders, NATO cannot force them, even in situations where individual member states breach the moral obligation to act on the principle of moral equal worth of people.

We have seen Chapter 2 that the objection that executors of securitization might die, etc., does not bite when executors have joined voluntarily. In this context, I also argued that a second requirement is that the number of executors of securitization needs to be sufficient to deal with the threat. Thus, if a state does not have sufficient numbers of willing and voluntary executors, then that state is not obligated to act where potential other-securitization is concerned, because it cannot force, against their will, qualified persons to partake (note here that this is different where self-securitization is concerned; thus as argued in Chapter 2, Section 2.2, states can opt for conscription in comparable circumstances).[12] The fact is, however, that provided that NATO is not already engaged and overstretched doing other missions, it probably does have sufficient numbers of willing personnel. This means that the risk of death, disease, and disability is less likely to override the obligation of other-securitization than in individual states. In other words, with great power seemingly comes the duty to be the world's policeman.

4.3.2 Risk of Instability and Insecurity

Securitization can lead to counter-securitization, that is, a securitization launched by 'A' in direct response to a securitization by 'B'. Without a doubt, NATO has made enemies by playing at being the world's policeman. NATO's military intervention in Bosnia, for example, soured relations with Russia a traditional ally of Serbia (Pouliot, 2010: 196–202). Beyond making enemies, NATO missions have also led to instability triggering further security threats to the region and NATO. Operation Unified Protector in Libya serves as an example here. The mission has been condemned because it led to widespread instability of Libya and indeed the wider region. Since the invasion, Libya has been unable to unite and rival factions have formed multiple

---

[12] This is contra Pattison, 2014: 124, who argues that in certain circumstances conscription can be justified to fight humanitarian wars.

competing governments. The instability is such that the country has become a home for terrorist groups and a transit country for illegal migration into European NATO countries. Without a doubt, terrorist groups the world over resent NATO's intervention as well as the inhumane treatment Gaddafi suffered at the hands of the rebels, albeit aided by NATO, giving rise to the possibility of revenge attacks.

As with state actors (Chapter 2, Section 2.5), the risk of insecurity to oneself through mandatory other-securitization can override the pro tanto obligation to securitize third parties. After all, NATO's primary objective, its reason for being, is not to be the world's policeman (which it becomes largely due to failures of other bodies including the UNSC; cf. Chapter 5) but rather to provide collective defence for NATO members. It seems to me that NATO cannot be morally obligated to do something that is contra its purpose just because it can.

There is more. Recall from the above that in NATO decisions are taken by consensus. In other words, if a NATO member objects to a given mission of other-securitization they do not have to partake. While this has the benefit of leaving NATO able to act (unlike the UNSC when veto powers are used; cf. Chapter 5) even where there are disagreements and strongly diverging opinions between member states, it can lead to NATO itself becoming weakened by other-securitization. Notably, other-securitization that is supported by only a few NATO members can lead to disunity, hampering further development of the organization. In IR, some have always warned of the dangers of intervention. Notably, in the Libyan case, as well as in the case of the 2003 Iraq war before, huge rifts emerged between the NATO allies concerning the need to intervene militarily (Clarke, 2011). The pluralist English school scholar Robert Jackson once argued: 'In my view, the stability of international society, especially the unity of the great powers, is more important, indeed far more important, than minority rights and humanitarian protections in Yugoslavia or any other country – if we have to choose between these two sets of values' (Jackson, 2000: 291).

It seems to me that if on all available evidence there are decisive reasons to believe that acting to secure a third party would lead to an unreasonable threat to the populations of one or more NATO member state (which incidentally could trigger Article 5) or to an indirect threat because the alliance becomes disjointed, unstable, and unable to progress, then the risk of instability and insecurity overrides NATO's pro tanto obligation of other-securitization.

4.3.3 Financial Costs

While NATO might be a powerful and comparatively rich organization, its resources are finite. Even if all NATO members were to meet the 2 per cent of gross domestic product target pledged at the Wales Summit (Shea, 2019), NATO is unlikely to be able to act on multiple or indeed all objective existential threats effectively and simultaneously. This is important. In the context of the state, we said that states are not obligated to act if the financial costs of other-securitization render security threats to the securitizing actor and/or the people it has primary security responsibility for. A corollary of this is that NATO too must have the right to balance the moral duty of securitization concerning third parties, against its first duty to provide collective defence for NATO members. In other words, because mandatory securitization of third parties cannot come at the cost of the ability of member states to be able to defend themselves (Article 3) or at the expense of being able to act on collective defence (Article 5), the moral obligation to securitize outsiders is overridden by prohibitive financial costs.

To summarize what was said so far, it appears that NATO has a duty to securitize third parties when the following conditions are met:

- It is the primary duty-bearer for other-securitization or – where applicable – the secondary duty-bearer.
- NATO has satisfied must cause.
- NATO has at its disposal a sufficient number of willing and able personnel.
- When securitization is unlikely to have unreasonable security consequences for the alliance or one of its member states.
- When the financial costs of securitization do not undermine the ability of NATO member states to provide collective defence, or to defend themselves.

But not so fast, we know from Chapter 2, Section 2.6, that even though NATO has a duty of other-securitization when the above is true, NATO may not be, indeed is unlikely to be, the primary duty-bearer in all cases. Thus, while NATO may well often be the most capable actor this does not automatically make them the actor who should be assigned primary responsibility for dealing with the insecurity. In cases where other actors are morally or outcome responsible, these actors are the primary duty-bearers of other-securitization. Moreover, ties of friendship and community trump sheer capability. In Chapter 2, Section 2.6, I defined friendship as the situation when states voluntarily and trustingly engage in joint practices to shape the world in line with their joint ideal. Regarding collectives and non-members, this is most obviously the case when states that are non-members contribute to NATO missions, and where they share NATO's values of liberal democracy, human rights, and the rule of law. A solid example of this is Sweden prior to NATO membership;[13] not only is Sweden a member of the Partnership for Peace initiative but as an Enhanced Opportunity Partner it contributes significantly to NATO missions (NATO, 2019). In short, great capability does not mean that NATO has remedial responsibility to be the world's policeman.

4.3.4 *Liability*

As before, with the case of the sovereign state, I want to end my discussion of NATO on the subject of liability. It is not my aim to repeat arguments already made. To be sure, however, just as sovereign states have a responsibility to securitize even where referents are culpable (not merely culpably ignorant) for needing securitization (e.g., because they have gobbled up resources at unsustainable speed) so does NATO. The issue I want to discuss here is specific to collectives (i.e., to cases where securitization is conducted not by an individual state, but by a collective of states). I am interested how, if at all, threat creation affects whether individual NATO member states ought to pay a larger share of the financial costs of securitization than member states who have not – through their wrongful or ignorant behaviour – contributed to the threat? Put differently, ought member states that have through their behaviour and actions created threats to the alliance or to third parties, pay a greater share of the financial cost of securitization and – if capable – do more towards securitization than member states that are not implicated in the creation of insecurity? I think the answer to this question has to be yes; after all, placing pivotal importance on moral responsibility

---

[13] At the point of writing Sweden is in the process of applying to NATO.

for a wrong is in equilibrium with the triggers for remedial responsibility identified in this book.

Nevertheless, there is a danger with this suggestion. Thus, if individual member states end up having to pay more towards collective securitization (or indeed, as I have suggested previously more towards the upkeep of NATO depending on how they behave (Floyd, 2019c)), does this not stand in the way of curbing free speech? If member states fear repercussions for creating threats that may later require securitization, is it not likely that say the German chancellor will no longer criticize the human rights record of a Saudi Arabia or a China? In other words, liability requires nuance. There is a difference between, on the one hand, a state actor speaking its mind and standing up for human rights and freedom of speech. Even if this risks offending another state so much that this second state starts to pose a threat to the alliance, and deliberately picking a fight with an 'enemy state' through poor foreign policy decisions on the other. It certainly cannot be the case that liability for threat creation leaves NATO members diplomatically ineffective. Yet I do think that consistently reckless behaviour by one alliance member should lead to that member state not only having to pay more for subsequent mandatory securitization but a higher percentage of gross domestic product towards defence and thus NATO than consistently well-behaved members.

4.4 Collective Security Organizations: Duties to Insiders

Moving on from collective defence organizations, I now want to focus on collective security organizations and their obligation to securitize. As we have learnt above, while these terms are often used interchangeably, collective security organizations do not have formalized military structures and binding collective defence clauses, which require them to defend one another against *external* threats. Instead, collective security organizations serve to build common values, friendship, and thus trust between member states, in that way ensuring that no member becomes a threat to another member state. In the event that one member comes to pose a threat to other states within the collective, there is a commitment to collective action.

The biggest problem with this analytical category of collective security organization is that it is not very precise. It includes a vast and very different array of institutions including the EU prior to 2007/2009 but also the League of Nations[14] and the UN, both of which are very different from the EU. This is not necessarily a problem. Although the EU is very different from the UN, the ultimate purpose of both organizations is the building and maintenance of peace between its member states (van Rompuy, 2012: 4; Europa 2019, see also Chapter 5, Section 5.2). In 2012, the EU was awarded the Nobel Prize for Peace for having turned former foes into friends and partners through economic integration and joint projects. Since its formation in 1957 with the signing of the Treaty of Rome that created its forerunner the European Economic Community, the organization evolved into the EU (with the signing of the Maastricht Treaty), defined by the single market and the four freedoms (movement of goods, people, services, and money). Following several rounds of enlargement, the EU has grown from its original six member states to now twenty-seven. As mentioned above, with the signing of the Lisbon treaty in 2007/2009, the Union – at least on paper – is steadily evolving into a collective defence organization. A trend that is further affirmed by more recent developments, for instance, Permanent Structured Cooperation and the plan of a European Defence Union. For the time being, however, and certainly for the period before 2007/2009, we can describe the EU as a security community, that is, a group of states between which war has become unthinkable.

The first issue I would like to discuss is what duties to insiders do security communities/collective security organizations have when it comes to mandatory securitization? It seems to me that the relationship between member states and the EU is markedly different to that of states and citizens or indeed to NATO and its member states; thus, if the EU fails to defend a member state against manifest attack from the outside, the EU is unlikely to cease to exist.[15] Unlike in those other cases, the EU does not have a contractual duty to act. The fact that

---

[14] Admittedly, *The League of Nations* does not fit my categorization well. While this organization coined the term collective security and was mostly about creating peace between member states, Article X of its founding covenant included a mutual defence clause. 'The Members of the League undertake to respect and preserve against external aggression the territorial and existing political independence of all members of the League – the Council shall advise upon the means by which this obligation shall be fulfilled' (cited in Ladenburg, 2007: 54). The obligation to address unprovoked aggression ultimately led to the non-participation of an isolationist United States (ibid).

[15] It might do, if people lose faith in solidarity.

EU member states are on the one hand tightly integrated (notably the currency union), but that there is no contractual obligation to defend members is a major shortcoming; the EU is clearly seeking to remedy with the inclusion of the mutual assistance/defence clause and the solidarity clause. This said, however, the absence of a contractual duty does not mean that the EU does not have a moral duty to secure – where appropriate – insiders via securitization. Recalling Miller's argument for triggers of remedial responsibility explained in Chapter 2, Section 2.6, I hold that in the EU the duty to secure insiders is triggered by ties of community, by which Miller means 'ties of family or friendship, collegiality, religion, nationality and so forth' (Miller, 2007: 104). This is based on the understanding that: 'Communitarian relationships […] involve special obligations to fellow-members, when P stands in need of assistance' (Miller, 2007: 104). It seems to me that in the case of the EU and other security communities – at a minimum – ties of friendship delineate community status after all mature communities entertain a joint vision of world order (Berenskoetter, 2014). If this is so, then the EU has a moral obligation – when this is requested by member states – to assist with securitization against external threats to individual member states.[16] Importantly, this obligation is triggered regardless of the fact whether the EU is in any way partially responsible for the threat (e.g., by harmful neglect). Nevertheless, it can only act when it also has the capacity to do so. That is to say – depending on threat type –the possibility exists that the duty is void.

Moreover, given the obligation to assist members of the Union/community with securitization is not contractual (unlike in NATO or in individual states), it is also the case that this duty is not absolute. In other words, the EU's duty to assist member states with securitization can be overridden, notably when there are an insufficient number of willing executors of securitization (no member state can be forced to assist against their will), when assistance with securitization would – on all available evidence – lead to the destabilization of the Union, and when the financial costs of securitization are such that member states incur prohibitive costs.

Finally, we must consider whether the EU has a duty to secure itself from an existential threat. As with NATO, the biggest threat to the EU

---

[16] This is not to say that an actor liable for threat creation does not have a stronger duty than the security friend.

per se seems to be the disintegration of the intergovernmental institution itself, notably through member states leaving (be this driven by subversion, populism, or dissatisfaction). And yet, Article 50 paragraph 1 of the Treaty of Lisbon 1 states that 'Any Member State may decide to withdraw from the Union in accordance with its own constitutional requirements' (Consolidated version of the Treaty on the European Union: 2012). This means that while member states leaving might pose an existential threat to the EU, the EU is not permitted to stop these member states from leaving. Should the EU be existentially threatened in another way, for example, by subversion from increasingly illiberal member states, the EU has a moral duty to securitize itself only in so far as securitization is morally permissible and must cause is satisfied.

4.5 Collective Security Organizations: Duties to Outsiders

We have said above that collectives of states have a *pro tanto obligation* to act, and where necessary other-securitize (Section 3.3) on the grounds of the moral equal worth of people. We have also seen that whether or not they have to act in any given case depends on whether they are the primary duty-bearer for other-securitization. In line with the ranking of the triggers of moral responsibility I suggested in Chapter 2, Section 2.6, we can say that the EU is the primary duty-bearer for other-securitization where they are outcome and/or morally responsible for the insecurity and when they are connected to the referent by ties of security friendship. In case of the EU, one indisputable example of a security friend is Norway. Although Norway is not an EU member, the EU and Norway have a similar vision of justice and order and their commitments are even institutionalized in the Mission of Norway to the EU.

Finally, the EU is also the primary duty-bearer for other-securitization in cases where no other actor is morally or outcome responsible, where the threatened entity is friendless and where the EU is the most capable actor.

Moving on, it is now time to consider our three duty overriding factors in the context of the EU.

4.5.1 *Risk of Death, Disease, and Disability*

We already know that the risk of death, disease, and disability can override the duty to act on must cause when there are no, or insufficient numbers of, individuals available who knowingly and voluntarily sign up to professions or missions that involve this risk. We also know that the duty of other-securitization is overridden when there are insufficient numbers of individuals available who could carry out such tasks. The EU or a similar actor should as a collective of states be – at least in principle – more able to have such numbers of volunteers than individual states, but the point still stands, if numbers are insufficient the duty of other-securitization is overridden.

4.5.2 Risk of Instability and Insecurity

The risk of instability and insecurity is – where collectives are concerned – twofold. One is when the available expected evidence suggests that other-securitization will lead to significantly harmful counter-securitization adversely affecting one or more member state of the EU or its citizens. The other is the possibility that other-securitization will destabilize the Union. We must remember here that social and political constructs like the EU rise and fall depending on whether its member states have faith in the organization (cf. Buzan et al., 1998: 154, 22). The handling of the 2015 European migrant crisis by Germany and Austria shows that destabilization of the Union is a real possibility. The bilateral decision to open the borders in order to let refugees fleeing the civil war in Syria as well as countless economic migrants from other countries into the country by German Chancellor Merkel let to a destabilization of the Union in several ways: first, the rolling-back of Schengen with many countries (often for years) characterized by the reinstatement of border controls. And arguably without Schengen, the EU does not exist in the way it was intended. Second, arguments over enforced quota of taking migrants let to a rise of discontent between different member states. Third, the number of migrants coming in as well as the suggestion of a quota led to a rise in Euro-sceptic right-wing parties in many countries. Coupled with Brexit, the Union clearly was destabilized by these events. Indeed in 2016 in his annual State of the Union address, the president of the European Commission argued:

Our European Union is, at least in part, in an existential crisis. [...] never before have I seen such little common ground between our Member States. So few areas where they agree to work together. Never before have I heard so many leaders speak only of their domestic problems, with Europe mentioned only in passing, if at all. Never before have I seen representatives of the EU institutions setting very different priorities, sometimes in direct opposition to national governments and national Parliaments. It is as if there is almost no intersection between the EU and its national capitals anymore. Never before have I seen national governments so weakened by the forces of populism and paralysed by the risk of defeat in the next elections. Never before have I seen so much fragmentation, and so little commonality in our Union. (Juncker, 2016 in European Commission: 1)

This example shows that destabilization of the Union is a real possibility. Moreover, given that preservation of the Union and the Peace is the foremost duty of the EU, we can see that the duty of other-securitization can be overridden if all available evidence suggests that it would lead to destabilization.

4.5.3 Financial Costs

From the chapter on the state and the relevant section on NATO above, we already know that securitization can bring with it heavy financial costs. We also know that the duty of other-securitization is overridden if the prospective financial costs threaten to leave member states or people within the member states with security deficits. There is no reason why this should not also apply in the case of the EU and other collective security organizations.

To summarize, we can now say that the EU must act to securitize third parties when the following conditions are met:

- It is the primary duty-bearer for other-securitization or – where applicable – the secondary duty-bearer.
- The EU has satisfied must cause.
- It must have at its disposal a sufficient number of willing and able personnel.
- When securitization is unlikely to lead to conflict between members of the EU destabilizing the union so that the same falls into existential crisis.
- When securitization is not likely to create an objective existential threat to one or more EU member states or its citizens.
- When the financial costs of securitization do not undermine the ability of EU member states to provide comprehensive security for the people living within the EU.

4.5.4 Liability

Collective security organizations orchestrate securitization collectively. Whenever this is the case, liability for threat creation plays a role. It seems to me that morality demands that fully morally culpable – for threat creation – member states ought to pay – provided they can – more towards the overall cost of securitization than non-culpable members. In reality, this will often be hard to disentangle, which is why Miller (2007: 106) does not identify a sequential ranking that puts moral responsibility first. In a previous publication (Floyd: 2019b), I discussed the EU's securitization of borders and whether Germany ought to pay more towards this collective securitization provided we take its open-door policy as the trigger for the securitization of EU borders. The analysis showed that the destabilization of Libya following NATO's Operation Unified Protector boosted the numbers of illegal migrants because Libya lost control of its borders. Unlike France and the United Kingdom, however, Germany was opposed to intervention in Libya. This shows that it will always be difficult to attribute culpability reliably, even if one is in principle in favour of it.

4.6 Conclusion

This chapter looked at sub-global collective actors in the context of mandatory securitization. I divided collective actors into collective defence organizations, which are defined by collective defence clauses that impose contractual obligations on their members, and collective security organizations which are more loosely organized. I have taken NATO as indicative of the former and the EU prior to 2007/2009 as indicative of the latter. Although some observations advanced in this chapter are specific to these two actors, the chapter is written in such a way that extrapolations for other comparable institutions should be possible. In other words, the chapter provides general observations for the types of actors on the examples of NATO and the EU, respectively. Specifically, I have argued that in collective security organizations the obligation to securitize insiders rests with remedial responsibility triggered by ties of community/friendship, while in collective defence organizations the duty to securitize insiders rests with a contractual obligation. This means that one significant difference between these two types of organization is that in collective defence organizations the obligation to securitize insiders is overriding, while in collective security organizations duties to insiders can be overridden. I have suggested that collective defence organizations thus make for superior arrangements regarding security provision for insiders.

I have also shown that both types of actors have remedial responsibility regarding other-securitization based on the moral equality of persons. In line with the differently weighted triggers of remedial responsibility, mandatory other-securitization is acute for both collectives in cases where the organization is morally or outcome responsible for insecurity. It is also acute when security friends are in existential danger. In line with common-sense morality, friendship between subglobal actors and states (or indeed between states) means that collectives are the primary duty-bearers (provided they are also capable) for other-securitization. This is an important insight because it reduces the need for NATO – and other capable sub-systemic security actors – to act as the world's policeman. Notably, NATO does not have the kind of friendship I have in mind here with all states. This is important because NATO's evolution to global policeman is doubly problematic. First, NATO does incur an unfair burden for – to invoke Miller's example – being ready at the riverside. Second and more problematically, NATO's interference upsets any kind of balance in world politics between the powerful and the powerless. The debacle in Libya speaks for itself.

By placing remedial responsibility with security friends, my proposal also reduces the number of times that the international community (in the form of the UN Security Council) will need to become involved and, where necessary, act appropriately on must cause. Not everyone will see this as a good thing. Pattison, who argues for 'a global monopoly on the authorization and provision of military services' (2014: 219), does so – in part – because he believes that 'the fewer actors that can authorize force, the less likelihood there is of international conflict' (ibid, 2014: 220). By contrast, I believe that the likelihood of conflict is greatly reduced if friends and allies deal with insecurities abroad. While it is also the case that the fewer the number of cases the UNSC has to deal with, the smaller the chance that these fall victims to the veto. Chapter 5 argues that the UNSC is the primary duty-bearer for other-securitization when no one is morally/outcome responsible for the insecurity and/or where the referent does not have relevant friends or ties of community. This is most likely the case for just non-state groups. Moreover, the UN is a secondary duty-bearer for securitization when primary duty-bearers for other-securitization fail, cannot or will not act. Rather than attributing sub-systemic actors with 'supplementary responsibility' when the UNSC fails (Erskine, 2016: 178–180), I hold that sub-systemic actors are – because of ties of friendship – often the designated *primary* duty-bearer for other-securitization while the UNSC is a supplementary actor.

It should be noted that my suggestion here is partially at odds with the UN Charter. AlthoughChapter VIII, Article 52 paragraph 1 states that: 'Nothing in the present Charter precludes the existence of regional arrangements or agencies for dealing with such matters relating to the maintenance of international peace and security as are appropriate for regional action provided that such arrangements or agencies and their activities are consistent with the Purposes and Principles of the United Nations' (UN, 2019). The Charter also states that regional arrangements or actors are not permitted to take *enforcement action* without authorization by the UNSC (Wheeler and Dunne, 2012: 96).[17] In other words, morally mandatory other-securitization without consent[18] *in situ* (as opposed to remote) is legally problematic.[19] Given that the veto and political interests often make armed humanitarian intervention impossible (see Chapter 5, Section 5.2), some have suggested that such authorization could come *after* the event with the UNSC acting as 'a global jury', whereby the idea is that: 'The moral and legal responsibility that falls on those who intervene without Council authority is to persuade the Council – and wider global opinion – that its action should be excused or tolerated on humanitarian

---

[17] Article 53 ¶1 'The Security Council shall, where appropriate, utilize such regional arrangements or agencies for enforcement action under its authority. But no enforcement action shall be taken under regional arrangements or by regional agencies without the authorization of the Security Council, with the exception of measures against any enemy state, as defined in paragraph 2 of this Article, provided for pursuant to Article 107 or in regional arrangements directed against renewal of aggressive policy on the part of any such state, until such time as the Organization may, on request of the Governments concerned, be charged with the responsibility for preventing further aggression by such a state' (UN, 2019).

[18] See Chapter 2, Section 2.3, for an explanation.

[19] Note, however, that the Constitutive Act of the African Union, Article 4 section h specifies 'the right of the Union to intervene in a Member State pursuant to a decision of the Assembly in respect of grave circumstances, namely: war crimes, genocide and crimes against humanity' (AU, 2000: 7).

grounds' (ibid: 94–95). In other words, 'the text of the Charter is balanced against the moral necessities of the case' (ibid: 94). This same approach could usefully be adopted here. To be sure, however, the relative weighing of the triggers for mandatory other-securitization, including security friendship before capability, should ensure that the number of cases where mandatory other-securitization is done without consent is hugely reduced. This loosely follows Erskine, who holds that '[r]egional organizations might fare better when it comes to winning the trust of the populations to be rescued, and are less likely objects of external criticism for engaging in coercive intervention without UN Security Council authorization' (Erskine, 2016: 179).

5 | Systemic Actors and the Obligation to Securitize

5.1 Introduction

This chapter is concerned with systemic-level actors and their obligation to securitize. From Chapter 3, we know that while several actors reside at the systemic level, they are – bar one exception – unlikely to be the primary duty-bearers for mandatory other-securitization, because they lack relevant capabilities or the necessary ties of friendship (cf. Chapter 3, Section 3.6). We also know from Chapter 3, Section 3.2, that only actors aiming to provide relevant forms of security can have a duty to securitize, meaning actors who rival or critique the state in its ability to provide military, societal, environmental, economic, political, and human security. Moreover, only organizations with *inter alia* decision-making structures can have moral agency (Erskine, 2003: 24; cf. Chapter 2, Section 2.4). All this means that at this level there is only really one actor that *can* have a moral duty of securitization: the United Nations (UN) (Welsh, 2012: 106). Article 1, ¶1, of the UN Charter specifies the main purpose of the organization as follows:

> To maintain international peace and security, and to that end: to take effective collective measures for the prevention and removal of threats to the peace, and for the suppression of acts of aggression or other breaches of the peace, and to bring about by peaceful means, and in conformity with the principles of justice and international law, adjustment or settlement of international disputes or situations which might lead to a breach of the peace. (UN, 2019)

Looking at the Charter, however, it is immediately clear that it is not the UN at large, but rather the United Nations Security Council (UNSC) that is tasked with the provision of security. Chapter V Article 24 ¶1 endows the UNSC with 'primary responsibility for the maintenance of international peace and security' (ibid). And Chapter VII bestows the UNSC with the power to determine on threat status and defence. Article 39 holds that: 'The Security Council shall determine the existence of any threat to the peace, breach of the peace, or act of aggression and shall make recommendations, or decide what measures shall be taken in accordance with Articles 41 and 42, to maintain or restore international peace and security' (ibid). Articles 41 and 42 list possible solutions to security threats the UNSC can authorize; these range from forcible but non-military action (e.g., economic sanctions) to military action.

In addition to the UNSC, the Charter discusses the General Assembly's (GA) role in the provision of security. It specifies that the GA can discuss issues of peace and security and that the GA may make recommendations to the UNSC.[1] In short, the UNSC is clearly the paramount actor on security in the UN structure. In this chapter, I focus exclusively on the UNSC and its moral obligation to securitize. To be sure, however, within the wider UN structure, other actors, notably WHO, also can have a duty to secure; by and large, however, they will not act without UNSC authorization.

In Chapter 4, Section 4.1, we learnt that collective security arrangements are about preventing one of the member states morphing into a security threat to other member states, while collective defence organizations are concerned with defending against threats from the outside. The UN, and with it the UNSC, are concerned with maintaining relations (peace and security) *between* member states. Given that 195 of the world's 197 states are members of the UN, and that the two non-members are non-member observer states, there is no meaningful outside. In short, all threats come from within. This means that all possible obligations regarding securitization are owed to insiders not outsiders. Practically, the absence of a definable inside and outside means that where the UNSC is concerned, I speak of a duty of securitization, not one of self-securitization and other-securitization.

As a collective security arrangement or institution, the UN/UNSC is not held together by a mutual defence clause, whereby a threat against one obligates member states to act. The UN/UNSC's relationship with its member states also does not take the form of a regular social contract (at least not in secure times). Notably, individual members have not relinquished their monopoly on violence to the UN. To the

---

[1] For more detail, see here www.un.org/en/sc/repertoire/otherdocs/ GAres377A(v).pdf

contrary in the UN Charter, sovereignty is almost sacrosanct. Article 2 ¶ 7 holds that

Nothing contained in the present Charter shall authorize the United Nations to intervene in matters which are essentially within the domestic jurisdiction of any state or shall require the Members to submit such matters to settlement under the present Charter; but this principle shall not prejudice the application of enforcement measures under Chapter VII. (UN, 2019)

This suggests that the UNSC's obligation to securitize is conditional. In more detail, it suggests that the UNSC's obligation to securitize can be overridden, by one or more of the three factors that can legitimately override a moral duty of other-securitization, namely: (1) the risk of death, disease, and disability, (2) the risk of instability and insecurity, and (3) financial costs. Indeed, the veto bestowed on UNSC's permanent member states can quite plausibly be viewed as institutionalized overridability of moral duties. Least we think the case is straightforward, I argue in this chapter that the UNSC's duty to secure, and if necessary, securitize, when other actors cannot or will not act, is in fact overriding. The same is based on the view that the UN/UNSC and its members (people of the world) exist in a contractual situation that – morally – does not permit for non-action. Note here, however, that such action does not mean securitization, but may simply mean politicization. I develop this argument by examining the nature of the UNSC's duties on responsibility to protect (RtoP) responsibilities. This is valid because RtoP duties amount to the UNSC's existing extent of duties to secure and to securitize.

From here, I go on to examine what mandatory securitization and must cause mean for UNSC's existing mechanisms and structures. I show that mandatory securitization improves RtoP, so that the same is more obviously balanced away from armed intervention towards other ways of handling crisis, and on a broader range of threats than atrocity crimes (Axworthy, 2016; Kleine, 2015; Eckersley, 2007). I suggest and defend the view that – at the systemic level – the responsibility to prevent/react using ordinary political measures (politicization) must rest with an unaddressed just cause, and the responsibility to prevent/react by extraordinary means (securitization) with *must cause*.

In other to make this argument, this chapter is structured as follows. I will briefly explain the make-up of the UNSC, including the veto right and ultimately why it is structured the way it is. I will then examine the kind of duties the UNSC has regarding mandatory securitization and where these duties come from. This will reveal a disconnect between the current practice and what morality prescribes. I will explain how my theory of mandatory securitization can overcome some of the persistent problems without major change, thus enabling the UNSC to better fulfil its role for the benefit of people, international order as well as itself, as a timely and relevant actor in international relations.

5.2 The United Nations Security Council

The membership of the UNSC is specified in Article 23 of the Charter. It holds that:

The Security Council shall consist of fifteen Members of the United Nations. The Republic of China, France, the Union of Soviet Socialist Republics, the United Kingdom of Great Britain and Northern Ireland, and the United States of America shall be permanent members of the Security Council. The General Assembly shall elect ten other Members of the United Nations to be non-permanent members of the Security Council, due regard being specially paid, in the first instance to the contribution of Members of the United Nations to the maintenance of international peace and security and to the other purposes of the Organization, and also to equitable geographical distribution. (UN, 2019)

To understand the choice of permanent members as well as their privileged position, one has to understand history. The Council on Foreign Relations website offers the following explanation:

The P5's privileged status has its roots in the United Nations' founding in the aftermath of World War II. The United States and the Union of Soviet Socialist Republics (USSR) were the outright victors of the war, and, along with the United Kingdom, they shaped the postwar political order. As their plans for what would become the United Nations took shape, U.S. President Franklin D. Roosevelt insisted on the inclusion of the Republic of China (Taiwan), envisioning international security presided over by 'four global policemen'. British Prime Minister Winston Churchill saw in France a European buffer against potential German or Soviet aggression and so sponsored its bid for restored great-power status. (CFR, 2018)

In addition to permanent membership, the five permanent members' (P5) privileged position is cemented by the veto power. Article 27,

¶3, states that: 'Decisions of the Security Council on all other matters shall be made by an affirmative vote of nine members including the *concurring* votes of the permanent members' (UN, 2019: my emphasis). This means that if one of the P5 vetoes a resolution the resolution cannot go ahead. The veto has been used and abused by the P5 since the beginning of the UN (McClean, 2014). Indeed, during the Cold War the UNSC was unable to fulfil its functions given that national interest not collective action dominated the agenda (ibid) To this day, the UNSC is subject to 'the competing interests, values, and power relations of its Member States' (Bellamy, 2016: 262). In short, and as Bellamy surmises, the UNSC is a political not a judicial body (ibid: 256). Concretely, the ability to veto means that the UNSC often fails to act on the responsibilities laid out in the UN Charter notably to maintain international peace and security.[2] If this is so, why then was the veto implicitly included into the Charter? Justin Morris and Nicholas Wheeler argue that the veto ensured three things: (1) 'great power participation in the UN'[3] (Morris and Wheeler 2016: 229; see also Bellamy, 2016: 262). (2) Drawing on work by Inis Claude, they argue it prevented another war between great powers because it did not allow for 'a majority to take action so strongly opposed by a dissident great power that a world war [would] likely ... ensue' (Claude cited in Morris and Wheeler, 2016: 229). And (3) the veto ensures 'a level of congruence between proposed action and the power required to bring about its successful execution' because it has the backing of great powers (Morris and Wheeler, 2016: 229). In other words, the veto ensures that there is a UNSC at all.

Beyond the politics of the P5, the UNSC has other shortcomings. Some argue that its deliberations lack transparency, because '[i]t's most important negotiations take place in secret' (Buchanan, 2018: 291; see also Thakur, 2017: 340; Welsh, 2012: 109 and Aust, 2010: 192–193). Moreover, the Council has problems with legitimacy because its membership does not adequately represent the world population. The Global South is chronically underrepresented, while the West takes up

---

[2] But as Jennifer Welsh has pointed out '[n]othing in the UN Charter provides a means for holding the Council to account' (Welsh, 2012: 110; see also Hehir, 2019).

[3] Note that the League of Nations was weakened by the absence of the United States (cf. FN 153).

three of the five permanent seats. Since 1995, there have been many suggestions (by practitioners and academics alike) on how to best reform the UNSC to make it more representative, including proposals that expand permanent and/or non-permanent memberships variously with or without veto rights for the new permanent members (Weiss, 2016: 59). Since none of these have come to fruition, it is reasonable to assume that reform remains a pipe dream. Moreover, some of the reform proposals might make the UNSC less effective. For instance, while increased membership might make for greater legitimacy, it is not clear 'how any of the recommended changes would improve the chances of reaching consensus regarding the use of force or other Chapter VII coercion' (ibid: 59). After all, increased membership also increases the number of competing political agendas and potentially the number of vetoes.

5.3 What Duties to Securitize Exist, and Where Do They Come From?

In this book so far, I have argued that securitization is sometimes not merely morally permissible but morally obligatory. Among other things, I have argued that if specific conditions are met, states and sub-systemic actors can have a moral duty to secure third parties using exceptional (which is to say in normal times unacceptable) measures, not merely when securitization is requested by the threatened party[4] but also without the consent of either the referent object or – if different – states on whose territory other-securitization might play out (recall here that other-securitization is most often remote). I have also argued that states have an overriding duty to provide security for people living within its geographical territory, while collective defence organizations have an overriding duty to secure just member states if these seek assistance. If this system worked perfectly and all states would look after their people, there would be no need to contemplate mandatory securitization at the systemic level. The fact is, however, that many states either cannot or will not look after people within their territorial boundaries and some states/regimes even pose an objective existential threat to (parts of)

---

[4] Strictly speaking, the affected party is entitled to rescue via politicization; mandatory securitization depends on must cause.

their population. It seems to me that if there is such a thing as the moral equal worth of people (Chapter 2, Section 2.3) then someone somewhere must have a moral duty to pick up the pieces and protect people who cannot do so themselves. The philosopher Robert Goodin points us in the right direction. He argues, '[when] someone has been left without a protector. [...] Then, far from being at the mercy of everyone, the person becomes the "residual responsibility" of all' (Goodin, 1988: 684). Implicit here is that the collective has the necessary capabilities to ensure protection.

Chapter 4 showed that while sub-systemic actors are potentially more easily able to provide other-securitization than individual states (because they are more capable and because they are more likely to have relevant ties of friendship) there are several valid reasons that can override such organizations' moral duty to assist third parties by means of securitization, including if such action runs the risk of destabilizing the organization itself. By elimination, this leaves the systemic level, which is to say the international community in form of the UN/UNSC, as the only capable candidate to provide mandatory securitization where others either fail, or where such obligation is overridden for our three – by now familiar – legitimate reasons: (1) the risk of death, disease, and disability; (2) the risk of instability and insecurity; and (3) prohibitive financial costs.

Readers familiar with the UN/UNSC will not find the suggestion that the international community must assume responsibility when states (and other actors) fail odd, after all this is the underlying premise of the 'RtoP' norm. Notably, the RtoP norm holds that where individual states fail to protect populations from mass atrocity crimes (genocide, war crimes, ethnic cleansing, and crimes against humanity), remedial responsibility, thus the moral duty to protect, falls to the international community (Cohen, 2012: 15, Welsh, 2019, Glanville, 2021; cf. Introduction FN3). The UNSC has special responsibility to enforce the RtoP norm (Bellamy, 2016: 253). Paragraph 139 of the 2005 World Summit outcome document states that

The international community, through the United Nations, also has the responsibility to use appropriate diplomatic, humanitarian and other peaceful means, in accordance with Chapters VI and VIII of the Charter, to help to protect populations from genocide, war crimes, ethnic cleansing and crimes against humanity. In this context, we are prepared to take collective action, in a timely and decisive manner, through the Security Council, in accordance with the Charter, including Chapter VII, on a case-by-case basis and in cooperation with relevant regional organizations as appropriate, should peaceful means be inadequate and national authorities manifestly fail to protect their populations from genocide, war crimes, ethnic cleansing and crimes against humanity. (UNGA, 2005: 30)

The veto, or even simply the possibility of the veto, has been a major obstacle in realizing RtoP commitments (Thakur, 2017: 299; Hehir, 2019: 117–148).[5] Some practitioners and scholars have – in this context – advanced various iterations of the 'responsibility not to veto' (see Morris and Wheeler, 2016: 230–236), or 'constructive abstention' (Axworthy, 2016: 974; ICISS, 2001: 51). With the notable exception of France, however, so far, such plans have not been realized with the remaining P4 reluctant to categorically refrain from the use of the veto in relevant situations. But let us start at the beginning, which is to say by examining the RtoP norm's emergence, its significance, and how it has fared since it first appeared in some detail. Responsibility to protect is crucial to the argument advanced in this chapter because RtoP is the actual extent of a commitment to mandatory securitization in the UN system at the present time.[6]

---

[5] A United Nations Association Briefing from 2015 lists the following cases: '(1) 12 January 2007: resolution calling for the cessation of serious human rights abuses in Myanmar vetoed by Russia and China; (2) 11 July 2008: resolution imposing sanctions on Robert Mugabe, President of Zimbabwe – who carried out widespread state-sponsored murder, intimidation, violence, enforced disappearances, and sexual violence – vetoed by Russia and China; (3) 4 October 2011: resolution condemning "grave and systematic human rights violations" perpetrated under the Syrian President Bashar al-Assad vetoed by Russia and China; (4) 4 February 2012: resolution condemning violence in Syria vetoed by Russia and China; (5) 19 July 2012: resolution imposing economic sanctions on Assad regime for failing to abide by the Annan peace plan vetoed by Russia and China. While the Council was able to come to an agreement on a resolution on the destruction of Syria's chemical weapons on 27 September 2013, the threat of further vetoes has marred the likelihood of a resolution on humanitarian access and protection to Syria; (6) 22 May 2014: resolution condemning violations of human rights in Syria and referring the Syrian Arab Republic to the International Criminal Court vetoed by Russia and China; (7) resolution retrospectively condemning the "crime of genocide" in Srebrenica and calling for reconciliation in Bosnia and Herzegovina vetoed by Russia' (UNA, 2015).
[6] I later argue that RtoP contains securitizing action.

5.4 Responsibility to Protect: A Brief Overview

Responsibility to protect emerged in the 1990s against the background of the Balkan wars and the genocide in Rwanda. In these and other cases, the UNSC's response was inadequate, and its moral authority was in the eyes of western liberal democracies in danger of being completely undermined by NATO's unauthorized (by the UNSC) military intervention into Kosovo. This much is clear from Kofi Annan's speech to the GA accompanying the presentation of his annual report.

As Secretary-General, I have made it my highest duty to restore the United Nations to its rightful role in the pursuit of peace and security, and to bring it closer to the peoples it serves. [...] If the collective conscience of humanity – a conscience which abhors cruelty, renounces injustice and seeks peace for all peoples – cannot find in the United Nations its greatest tribune, there is a grave danger that it will look elsewhere for peace and for justice. If it does not hear in our voices, and see in our actions, reflections of its own aspirations, its needs, and its fears, it may soon lose faith in our ability to make a difference. (Annan, 1999)

Importantly, Annan's speech highlighted changes to the notion of sovereignty. 'The State is now widely understood to be the servant of its people and not vice versa' (Annan, 1999). Indeed, the central question he posed was this: '...if humanitarian intervention is, indeed, an unacceptable assault on sovereignty, how should we respond to a Rwanda, to a Srebrenica – to gross and systematic violations of human rights that affect every precept of our common humanity?' (Annan, 2000: 48) Wheeler and Dunne hit the nail on the head when they summarize 'Annan's Intervention Dilemma' (Cater and Malone 2016) as follows: '[...] the United Nations was created to prevent wars, not to become an instrument for their propagation' (Wheeler and Dunne, 2012: 93).

In response to Annan's challenge, the Canadian government swiftly sponsored the International Commission on Intervention and State Sovereignty (ICISS) to examine the '"right of humanitarian intervention": the question of when, if ever, it is appropriate for states to take coercive – and in particular military – action, against another state for the purpose of protecting people at risk in that other state' (ICISS, 2001: vii). The Commission's consolidating final report in 2001 co-chaired by Gareth Evans and Mohamed Sahnoun was called *The Responsibility to Protect*. The report explains that the ICISS deliberately shifted the language away from a right to responsibility, as well as from the contested idea of 'humanitarian intervention' (see also Thakur, 2017: 272–290) to RtoP so that the international community could look again 'with fresh eyes' at this important issue (ICISS, 2001: 9). The landmark report set out the structured approach to humanitarian crisis/catastrophe we still find in RtoP today, whereby states have primary responsibility, while the international community has a responsibility to protect people when states fail, etc.

The ICISS idea of RtoP was restated in subsequent reports published by the UN's High-Level Panel on Threats, Challenges and Change 2004 (created to facilitate realization of RtoP and included inter alia Gareth Evans (Ki-Moon, 2012: 2)) as well as by Annan's 2005 report 'in Larger Freedom: Towards development, security and human rights for all'.

A version of RtoP was adopted by the UN Summit meeting in 2005. However, RtoP now pertained only to genocide, war crimes, ethnic cleansing, and crimes against humanity and did not include other forms of humanitarian crisis (notably starvation and environmental and natural disaster) mentioned by the ICISS (ICISS, 2001: 33; see also Cater and Malone, 2016: 125). The document did, however, contain the tiered approach to the RtoP. Thus, all signatory states accepted responsibility to protect their people and pledged to act in accordance with it. Moreover, paragraph 139 emphasized the responsibility of the UN to act if individual states failed in protecting people from atrocity crimes.

From 2009 onwards, the RtoP's tiered approach is often described as containing three pillars. In the relevant literature, two distinct versions of these pillars circulate. Some – and in my view mistakenly – identify as the three pillars the responsibility to prevent, the responsibility to react, and the responsibility to rebuild, respectively (see, e.g., Chalk, Dallaire and Matthews, 2012: 37; Mahdavi, 2015: 10; 2012: 259). Here, the three pillars are drawn from the ICISS report which identifies these three responsibilities. Most other scholars, however, mean by the three-pillar framework that 'articulated by Secretary-General Ban Ki-moon in his 2009 report to the General Assembly' (Welsh, 2016: 987; see also Bellamy, 2015: 45). In this document, pillar 1 refers to 'The protection responsibilities of the State, Pillar two [to] International assistance and capacity-building [and] Pillar three [to] Timely and decisive response' (Ki-Moon, 2009: 2). Although Bellamy suggests that the three pillars are 'non-sequential' in so far as 'one does not need to apply pillars one and two before moving to pillar three'

(Bellamy, 2015: 45; see also Thakur, 2017: 299),[7] the international community's responsibility to react with military force (which has become the standard interpretation of pillar 3 (Pattison, 2018; Hehir, 2019)) only bites and is permissible when states fail to provide pillar 1, and when other less harmful options have been tried (pillar 2). In other words, while RtoP's substantive pillars overall may not be sequential, the different actors' responsibility to react by force *is* sequential. This much was clear from the Secretary-General's 2012 report on the issue. This report 'clarified the relationship between the three pillars, reiterating their mutual interdependence such that efforts under the first two pillars should reduce the need to exercise the third' (Bellamy, 2015: 50; Ki-Moon, 2012: 5).[8]

My own view is that the metaphor of pillars would be much clearer if it prioritized the same kind of entity/thing in each pillar and not – as Ban Ki-moon's rendition does – give priority to actors in the first two pillars, but to actions in the last pillar. This is all the more important considering that state actors under pillar 1 too can use all necessary means to react against atrocity crimes.

I have more to say about RtoP below, for now; however, it is necessary to examine whether the duty to act on atrocity crimes specified in RtoP by the UNSC is overriding or conditional. Put differently, can the duty to act on, for example, genocide be overridden by concerns of our three factors: (1) costs to the intervener (in, e.g., lives lost); (2) cost to stability/order; and (3) actual financial costs? Let me be clear, I am concerned here with the *moral duty* only. The fact that veto rights have not been removed in RtoP situations from

---

[7] In more detail, Bellamy argues that: 'Conceptually, the three pillars of RtoP are so intertwined as to make sequencing impossible in practice. States are supported in their efforts to fulfil the first pillar by both pillar two and those elements of the third pillar which relate to assisting "states under stress" before they reach the point of "manifest failure". It makes little sense to deny the obvious overlaps between the two injunctions. Equally, it makes little sense to argue that international society should withhold support from states (pillar two) until they face difficulty achieving their first pillar responsibilities. Nor does it make any sense to argue that pillar two activities should cease when "timely and decisive response" is needed or that international society's first response to state-based mass killing should be to furnish the perpetrators with assistance (pillar II)' (Bellamy, 2015: 53).

[8] Moreover, as Welsh points out the ICISS three responsibilities apply to more than one pillar. Notably, the responsibility to prevent applies to both pillars 2 and 3 (Welsh, 2016: 988).

the UNSC means that the legal duty to act is conditional (though see Trahan, 2022, 2020). In short, we must ask whether the moral duty of RtoP is overriding? In the first instance, it is important to recognize that there can be a disconnect between what morality and what the law requires. As Jeff McMahan explains: 'the law cannot simply restate the requirements of morality' (McMahan, 2008: 33). In essence, morality is much more demanding than law. Law 'has to be formulated to take account of the likely effects of its promulgation, institutionalization, and enforcement' (ibid: 33). Moreover, '[t]here are forms of seriously wrongful action that resist effective regulation by the law' (ibid: 33). McMahan exemplifies this by stating that while a pregnant woman commits a serious moral wrong against her foetus when she consumes alcohol, tobacco, or drugs, it is impossible to legislate against this behaviour without infringing the woman's right to privacy. Moreover, postnatal prosecution would perversely incentivize abortion (ibid: 33).[9]

---

[9] This difference between morality and the law can also be found with regard to the laws of war. Famously, McMahan holds that the legal principle of the moral equality of combatants which grants soldiers 'the same rights, immunities, and liabilities irrespective of whether their war is just' is – from a moral point of view – wrong (ibid: 21). Instead, he argues that '[t]he correct criterion of liability to attack [is the] moral responsibility for an unjust threat' (ibid: 21–22). In other words, 'morality forbids unjust combatants to attack just combatants' (ibid: 36).

The difference between the morality of war and the law of war is acutely apparent when we consider that the law permits unjust combatants to attack just combatants; this is the moral equality of combatants. According to McMahan, the law here rightly does not track morality, at least in part because of the epistemic uncertainty on the part of warriors over whether the cause of the war is just, but also because all combatants will claim to believe that their cause is just and simply assume the same rights as bona fide just combatants (ibid: 28). In short, while the morality of war is not neutral on the justice of combatants, epistemic constraints mean that the laws of war must be neutral on this issue. Importantly, for McMahan the morality of war cannot be rendered less demanding to fit with the law, for the morality of war – unlike the law – is not created by people, but immutable and simply discovered by people. This, McMahan calls 'the "deep" morality of war' (2004: 730). Another way of putting all this is that for McMahan law and morality fulfil different functions; the former seeks to prevent harm, while the latter protects individual rights (McMahan, 2009: 107).

In summary, the chasm between what the morality of war seems to require and that which the laws of war can meaningfully demand suggests that it is futile to translate moral principles into law. Be these moral principles governing war or securitization.

Of course, in the UNSC-RtoP case, the law would ideally track morality, but even if this is not the case, we can still ask whether morality permits inaction. I think it does not. Let me explain. We know from Chapters 2–4 that an overriding duty to securitize (this is relevant because RtoP can be ensured through securitizing action; see below) rests in either a social contract (in states) or a mutual defence clause (most notably in NATO). In the absence of a mutual defence clause, the suggestion that the UNSC's duty to act on atrocity crimes (when others have failed, etc.) is overriding must rest on a contractual situation between the UN and the people (the ultimate members of the UN). Pivotal to my argument that the UN/UNSC has an overriding duty to secure people against atrocity crimes is that there is a fundamental difference between the UN stepping in and another state stepping in, because as *signatories* to the UN Charter, member states stand in a different relationship to the UN/UNSC than they do to most other actors. Thus, although the members of the UN are states, the UN was founded to serve the people. Precisely, 'to save succeeding generations from the scourge of war, [...] to reaffirm faith in fundamental human rights, in the dignity and worth of the human person, in the equal rights of men and women [...]' (UN Charter, 2019). In other words, while states are the immediate members of the UN, people everywhere are the ultimate members. Viewed like this, we can see that the relationship between the UN and individuals is in fact contractual. Of course, individual persons have not agreed to this in person, but 'we' have accepted that 'our' states sign the Charter on our behalf (recall Chapter 1, Section 1.2, for that). In short, the UNSC's moral duty to meet the RtoP is overriding.[10]

In Chapter 4, Section 4.2, I argued that NATO's mutual defence clause that focuses on armed attack is lacking power in the twenty-first century, with many threats no longer taking the form of 'traditional' armed attacks. I showed how my theory of mandatory securitization can make Article 5 fit for the twenty-first century. In a similar vein, in

---

[10] The law scholar Jennifer Trahan argues that the UNSC has an overriding legal duty to act on atrocity crimes. Among other things, she argues that: 'The prohibition of genocide, crimes against humanity, and war crimes are all recognized as peremptory norms protected at the level of *jus cogens*. Because the U.N. is bound to respect *jus cogens*, its principal peace and security organ, the Security Council, is similarly constrained' (Trahan, 2022: 113); concretely, this means that veto use in such cases is unlawful.

the remainder of this chapter I wish to suggest that morally mandatory securitization can usefully refocus RtoP, so that inaction is avoided, while making it more applicable for the security threats we face. To make this argument, we must begin with a critical look at RtoP.

At risk of oversimplification, criticism of RtoP refers to three main issues:[11] (1) problems associated with armed military intervention, (2) inaction, and (3) its limited scope. The first is most evident in the context of Libya in 2011, which is widely seen as a test case for RtoP. Although the relevant resolutions[12] make no mention of RtoP duties on behalf of the international community, the Libyan intervention is generally considered the first-time military force (without consent by those subject to the intervention) was authorized citing RtoP. The resolution was passed with abstentions from among others, China, and Russia. Although NATO insists Operation Unified Protector was a success (Rasmussen, 2016), the intervention has done damage to RtoP as it seemingly proofs that all military interventions are made not on the grounds of protecting civilians but to further the intervener's interests.[13] Thus, many suspect that the real motive for intervention was

---

[11] This is from the point of view of western academia. As Thomas Peak has pointed out to me. There are also concerns about colonialism which are not limited to armed intervention, for instance. One line of attack is that the proponents of R2P mis-identify the causes of atrocity crimes. Where the focus is placed on 'good governance' and IHL/IHRL, this omits the fact that atrocity is caused by *practices* of the international community such as arms sales from the West to various tyrants, the ill-effects of sanctions regimes, and targeted assassinations, etc.

[12] '[R]esolution 1973 of 17 March 2011 authorized UN Member states to "take all necessary measures ... to protect civilians and civilian populated areas" in Libya' (Doyle, 2016: 679).

[13] The following extract from Welsh (2019: 60) catalogues this well. '[...] contestation over the appropriateness of the military dimension of RtoP's third pillar has continued to surface in the annual dialogues, with individual states explicitly referencing post-intervention chaos in Libya as a reason for reassessing RtoP's coercive dimension. Differences of views on both the conditions for the use of force and its management by the UN Security Council also constituted one of the leading factors in the inability of the General Assembly to adopt a substantive new resolution on RtoP in late 2015. [...] The formal debate on RtoP in the General Assembly during the summer of 2018 reinforces this picture of contestation over the third pillar, as Member States clashed over the issue of military intervention to halt atrocity crimes. The Russian spokesperson represented the furthest end of the spectrum, declaring that while RtoP had "powerful humanitarian potential", it had become associated with "illegal military interference, regime change, State destruction

regime change. While this is not the place to discuss this, it is noteworthy that the House of Common's Foreign Affairs Committee report found that 'The UK's intervention in Libya was reactive and did not comprise action in pursuit of a strategic objective. This meant that a limited intervention to protect civilians drifted into a policy of regime change by military means' (House of Commons, 2016–17: 18). This is important, because this change or drift of mandate has left RtoP wounded (Doyle, 2016: 685). It has given fuel to those states and voices that are weary of the loss of sovereignty in the face of RtoP. Ramesh Thakur points out that 'the policy of most Asian governments, including China as one of the UNSC five permanent members (P5), is to endorse the first and second [pillar] but not the third' (Thakur, 2017: 306; see also Hehir, 2019: 70, 107; Bloomfield, 2017: 33). Postcolonial scholars as well as some representatives from the Global South consider RtoP a new form of colonialism (Mahdavi, 2015: 11–12; cf. Bloomfield, 2017: 33). Frazer Egerton holds against this that 'most non-Western governments support R2P' (Egerton, 2012: 81). He also argued that many of those who do not support it 'reject it as placing unwanted limits on the exercise of their own power', which he sees a 'reason in itself to support R2P' (Egerton, 2012: 83).

The second problem is that of inaction. Many proponents criticize RtoP as approved by the World Summit as 'R2P-lite'. The term was coined by Thomas Weiss who means by this that RtoP was adopted 'without specifying the criteria governing the use of force and insisting upon Security Council approval' (Weiss, 2006: 750).[14] Without criteria designating when force should be used, 'it will always be politics all the way down' (Wheeler and Dunne, 2012: 99). In the light of this, some proponents of RtoP have called for UNSC reform, for non-use

---

and economic disaster". Iran also raised concerns over the way RtoP had paved the way for "interventionist policies", while Pakistan claimed that what was needed was a "surge in diplomacy, not war". The Government of India attempted a more constructive path, by reaffirming its commitment to the norm and welcoming the broad consensus on the first and second pillars, while at the same time acknowledging the need to address the "legally complex and politically challenging issues" which were connected to Pillar III. "The quest for a more just global order", declared its Ambassador Syed Akbaruddin, "should not take place in a manner that will undermine international order itself"'.

[14] Welsh, however, points out that by tying R2P to the UNSC the World Summit Document remedies a lacuna in the ICISS report which is not specific on who has a responsibility to react (Welsh, 2012: 109).

of the veto or even for moving RtoP decisions to the GA (cf. ICISS, 2001). Some consider what ought to happen when the UNSC fails to act. Toni Erskine (2016; 173, 178), for example, has suggested that when the international community (UNSC) fails to deliver on RtoP, the RtoP in all its guises falls to relevant proximate regional actors (e.g., the AU, the EU); in cases where the latter are unable to act, RtoP falls to sufficiently capable sub-systemic actors with global reach (e.g., NATO, ad hoc coalitions).

In the light of the failure to act in Syria (a failure that was at least in part a result of Libya (Doyle, 2016: 685)), sceptical commentators have declared the death and moral bankruptcy of RtoP (Dunford and Neu, 2019). Proponents of RtoP, however, opine that since Libya 'the Security Council has proven *more willing* to refer to R2P in relation to specific situations' (Bellamy, 2016: 261, emphasis in original; see also Welsh, 2016: 994), thus suggesting that RtoP is alive and well. Aiden Hehir holds against this that 82 per cent of the 67 UNSC's invocation of RtoP since Libya refer to pillar 1 (i.e., 'the host state's RtoP', the remaining 18 per cent to pillar 2 and none to pillar 3 (Hehir, 2019: 135)). This leads Hehir to conclude:

[T]he increase in Security Council Resolutions which mention R2P is not just *not* a positive development, it can be interpreted, in fact, as a negative one. Employing R2P language in the way the Security Council has to date, enables the P5 to deny responsibility and thus legitimise inaction, while *appearing* to be engaged with a particular issue. (2019: 137, emphases in original)

The third problem with RtoP is to do with its scope. RtoP is 'lite' also in the sense that it focuses only on atrocity crimes. Lloyd Axworthy (2016), for one, argues for the expansion of RtoP duties to other threats (notably human insecurity), specifically infectious diseases (he uses the example of Ebola), and environmental disasters (see also Glanville and Pattison, 2021). Like many writers supporting reform of RtoP, he makes his case by drawing on the visionary ICISS's report which, as we have seen above, envisaged RtoP protection for a wider range of threats.

But not all proponents of RtoP agree with widening the applicability criteria for RtoP. Joanna Harrington warns that expansion to other threats (she writes about natural disasters, and her view on infectious disease is unclear) 'risk draining the R2P concept of its vitality and strength, while also lending an air of unreality to the principle's practical aspirations' (Harrington, 2012: 141; see also Evans, 2009, Luck, 2009; Weiss and Thakur, 2010: 331). In her view, the restriction of RtoP to the four atrocity crimes is legitimate also because '[a]ll four agreed triggers are identifiable crimes under international law' while no such provisions exist for natural disasters (ibid: 142). RtoP during natural disasters only applies when there is also a risk of mass atrocity crimes (ibid: 147; see also Malone, 2009).[15]

To summarize, we can see that while RtoP has become established, albeit perhaps only as a – in Hehir's terminology – 'hollow norm', that is, one that 'is inherently malleable, can be affirmed without cost, and regulated by those it seeks to constrain [...]' (Hehir, 2019: 77), it remains unclear and/or contested. Specifically, what should define RtoP, and especially its third pillar? Who should act? And how should compliance with RtoP commitments be achieved? (cf. Welsh, 2013). In what follows, I shall argue that my theory of mandatory securitization can refocus RtoP, in the process addressing at least some of these problems and shortcomings.

5.5 Mandatory Securitization and Responsibility to Protect

We have seen that some proponents argue that RtoP should be restricted to atrocity crimes while others argue in favour of a broader spectrum of threats including natural disasters and health crises. Importantly, those that argue in favour of the former do so *not* because they are unconvinced by the real existence and severity of, for example, agent-lacking threats, but rather because they fear dilution of the concept and ultimately that states will go back on the hard-won 2005 commitment to RtoP. The sticking point regards broadening RtoP clearly is the third pillar which allows for the use of military force (i.e., war) as a last resort.[16]

---

[15] See also Gallagher, A., Raffle, E., and Maulana, Z. (2020). Failing to fulfil the responsibility to protect: The war on drugs as crimes against humanity in the Philippines. *The Pacific Review*, *33*(2), 247–277, who link Duerte's war on drugs to RtoP.

[16] Welsh (2019: 60) observes: 'while UN Member States all agree that the protection of populations from atrocity crimes is both a national and international responsibility, and that prevention is at the core of this responsibility, their discourse reveals differences over both the weight that should be placed on coercive measures and the processes that should regulate any collective use of military force'.

This is evident from the fact that most states have not merely accepted the realities of, for example, climate disasters, but that they – with the Paris agreement – signed up to *prevent* further disasters and complete climate catastrophe. Likewise, the ICISS' responsibility to *rebuild* is though contested, often practised. Notably, many states are engaged in humanitarian relief efforts after environmental disasters and health crises. Moreover, as explained above, those states that resist RtoP object to the third pillar (i.e., going to war for reasons of other-defence), and not to the fact that states' sovereignty is conditional or that other states ought to assist states in *preventing* atrocity crimes. If this is so, why broaden with mandatory securitization the realm of RtoP-type operations to encompass, for example, environmental threats?

My answer to this question is complex. In the first instance, it is important to notice that much of the scepticism regarding RtoP's third pillar is that this pillar's responsibility to react is often, and mistakenly, equated with humanitarian war[17] (cf. Pattison, 2018: 5; Hehir, 2019). The equation is however both wrong and unfortunate. As James Pattison has argued, 'the reactive (and direct preventative) part of RtoP should be seen as mostly about sanctions, embargoes, naming and shaming, denying membership, civilian (and UN) peacekeeping, positive incentives, and ICC actions rather than humanitarian intervention' (Pattison, 2018: 225).[18] A major advantage of mandatory securitization is that it reintroduces this important nuance; hence, it encompasses actions and measures that *prevent* further insecurity, armed conflict and war, as well as *reactive* measures including the use of (small-scale) military force.[19] Put differently, *mandatory securitization straddles the artificially constructed boundary between the responsibility to prevent and the responsibility to react.*[20] To fully

---

[17] By state actors not by scholars.

[18] Though Pattison's alternatives to war include political measures as well as securitizing ones, the response he has in mind is likely to always be at least a partial securitization because 'the measures will often work best when combined' (Pattison, 2018: 213).

[19] Some RtoP prevention measures, notably 'military surveillance, [provision of] defensive support to potential victims' (Woocher, 2012: 29), but most obviously sanctions are best understood as security action, thus as expressions of securitization.

[20] As Woocher explains, although the boundary between the two responsibilities is frequently invoked there is little clarity what counts as what '[...] the line between a direct R2P prevention strategy and an R2P reaction strategy could become blurry' (ibid: 29).

comprehend the importance of this finding for the broadening of scope of RtoP, recall firstly that *only* the responsibility to react is considered problematic.[21] Secondly, given that all states believe in the responsibility to prevent, the concept of mandatory securitization is more likely to convince reluctant policymakers of its rightfulness and the necessity to act than RtoP alone.

Second, mandatory securitization offers with 'must cause' a much clearer threshold than that offered by 'conscious shocking atrocity crimes'. But why should must cause – irrespective of the nature of the threat and *not* conscious shocking atrocity crimes – be the threshold for the responsibility to prevent/react by extraordinary, including forcible, means?[22] One reason why broadening the traditional just cause for RtoP is that atrocity crimes are relatively rare ('fewer than two episodes of mass killing began each year since 1990' (Woocher, 2012: 28)), while natural disasters and health emergencies occur frequently (6873 between 1994 and 2013 (CRED, 2015: 7)). With an average of 68.000 deaths per year and a total of 1,35 million for the years between 1994 and 2015, natural and health disasters also claim more lives than genocide (ibid: 7). This is not to diminish the horror and seriousness of atrocity crimes in any way, but rather to show that other threats also incur huge human costs. If this is so, I cannot see why there is an overriding moral duty to protect people from atrocity crimes but no corresponding moral obligation to protect people from more common and more deadly threats. Indeed, I cannot see how the UNSC can claim moral authority unless it acts on its moral and, indeed legal, duty to provide peace and security. In the long run, if the UNSC fails to act on these kinds of security threats it risks becoming irrelevant.[23] Hence,

---

[21] Please note, however, that in practice the boundaries between prevention and reaction are not clear cut. In some quarters, there is deep disagreement on how to interpret 'prevent', a disagreement which extends into the practices of the UN, for instance, the UN Office on Genocide Prevention and the Responsibility to Protect. For instance, Egypt (which is sometimes considered a non-western R2P 'champion') has explicitly rejected the UN frameworks for genocide prevention and 'hate speech' due to their 'political' and intrusive nature. I am grateful to Thomas Peak for this insight.

[22] I speak of the responsibility to react by forcible/extraordinary measures because in my theory relevant would-be securitizing actors have a duty of politicization prior to securitization, and politicization is a form of prevention/reaction.

[23] Certain that the veto power of the P5 would inhibit action, Buchanan and Keohane, for example, envisage a role for democratic coalitions in carrying out preventative intervention (Buchanan, 2018: 279).

broadening the domain from atrocity crimes to must cause does *not* run the risk of endangering the UNSC; on the contrary, it ensures the continuous existence and relevance of the UNSC.

It should also be noted that the inclusion of other types of threat does not mean that the UNSC must act in relevant ways on all manner of small-scale threats. It is important to remember that the UNSC must establish the existence of must cause anew and independently from other actors (cf. Chapter 2, Section 2.4). The principle of macroproportionality ensures that the scale of the threat for securitization (mandatory or simply permissible) where the UN is concerned is greater (i.e., more people are directly or indirectly objectively existentially threatened) than in cases of self-securitization by, for example, states, because the consequences of securitization across borders on stability and global security are expected to be more severe than those of self-securitization (cf. Chapter 2, Section 2.4). The collateral damage on peace and security caused by UN involvement render securitization disproportionate in cases where only a small number of people are objectively existentially threatened (cf. Pattison, 2010: 23). Such limiters are advantageous also for practical reasons, after all the UNSC cannot act on all possible instances of insecurity;[24] moreover, it ensures that the UNSC does not become over-interventionist frequently interfering into the affairs of sovereign states.

Another advantage of mandatory securitization is that it can account for threats that have not yet occurred (e.g., some new and previously unknown infectious disease, feminist-, climate-, or distinct identity-based terrorism, or threats caused by malfunctioning artificial intelligence,[25] etc.). In a word, must cause is future proof.

Finally, mandatory securitization and especially *must cause* provide a shift in language away from 'responsibility' towards explicit duties. Although responsibility implies obligation (cf. Chapter 2, Section 2.4; see also Welsh, 2019), many actors are likely to associate responsibility with outcome and moral responsibility. Consequently, while they might very well accept that they are responsible for protecting those they have (intentionally or carelessly) endangered, they might

---

[24] I think we must accept that there will always be, in Miller's terminology, protection gaps (2009).

[25] On the possibility of this, listen to HARDtalk interview with Stuart Russell, Monday, 14 October 2019, www.bbc.co.uk/programmes/w3csy98d

find it much harder to grasp why they should be *responsible* for acting on threats which they have not created or that do not affect them.
Although mandatory securitization is based on remedial responsibility, the language of must cause, mandatoriness, and duties is preferable because it is less ambiguous.

Before concluding, I want to make one thing crystal clear. I am not
a justice warrior who advocates the overthrowing of – in an English
school sense pluralist – institutions of territoriality, sovereignty, and
self-determination in the name of justice. At the same time, however,
I do believe that the international community has a responsibility
towards those that are objectively existentially threatened and that
do not have a protector. How can these two seemingly conflicting
impulses be reconciled into a coherent theory? The answer I think
rests with the all-important principle of proportionality. Like just war
theories, Just Securitization Theory (JST) is informed by two kinds of
proportionality. Macro-proportionality features in the just initiation
of securitization. It specifies that the expected good gained from securitization must be greater than the expected harm from securitization.
Second, micro-proportionality is a principle informing just conduct
in securitization. It specifies that, where possible, out of a range of
options the least harmful option must be chosen. And that if an option
is more harmful to the just referent object than the initial threat it
seeks to prevent, securitization must be abandoned. The corollary of
this is that we must accept that it is simply not possible to save all vulnerable people using all possible means all the time (cf. Miller, 2009).

Let me explain the role of proportionality on the example of the Uyghur
Muslims' fate in contemporary China.[26] Ostensibly to supress terrorism, Uyghur Muslims resident in Xinjiang providence are being detained
in vast so-called re-education centres. Evidence suggests that especially
female inmates are objectively existentially threatened in these camps
(Hill et al., 2021), raising the possibilty that securitization is morally permissible. For the sake of argument, let us assume that the responsibility
for the protection of the Uyghurs lies with the international community
because all other actors' pro tanto obligation to securitize is legitimately
overridden. Let us further assume that must cause is satisfied and that

---

[26] It is unclear when Uighurs were first detained. Satellite images show a camp in
2018 in a place barren just three years earlier in 2015 (see here: www.bbc.co
.uk/news/resources/idt-sh/China_hidden_camps).

the UNSC is morally required to securitize to protect the Uyghur. But what does this concretely mean? Importantly, does it mean that the UNSC is at this point morally required to order the invasion of China and free Uyghur Muslim? Lest anyone should think differently, the answer is most definitely no. Here is why. We know that a key element in just securitization is macro-proportionality. Macro-proportionality demands *ex ante* judgements of securitization's overall proportionality. Unlike with war, which inevitably involves foreseeably killing people and destroying stuff with kinetic force, gauging proportionality is exceedingly difficult with securitization, because of its shape-shifting nature.[27] This said, securitization could in principle mean dispatching a coalition of the willing to China, freeing the Uighurs interred in detention camps, and providing them with security against a Chinese army.[28] Notwithstanding the fact that we are at this point in the muddy waters separating securitization from armed humanitarian intervention, it should be clear that this kind of securitization does not satisfy macro-proportionality, because it can reasonably be expected to cause more harm than good. Most likely it would lead to war. The same is not straightforwardly true of other securitization measures. Arguably, macro-proportionality is satisfied if securitization were to take the form of remote concerted coercive action against China, including targeted sanctions, exclusion from the Olympic Games, and temporary expulsion from other international bodies. These and other security measures are subject to micro-proportionality (i.e., do they address the threat, are they the least harmful option, etc.) considerations.

This example shows that mandatory securitization is in no way an attempt to facilitate wide-ranging armed interventions. Often, unless direct securitizing intervention has the consent of affected parties, other-securitization is likely to refer to remote securitizing measures only. One aim of mandatory securitization is to prevent security threats from getting worse, thus preventing war.

---

[27] To be sure, when calls for securitization are made, they usually do not amount to 'we must securitize *simpliciter*' that is to say without any idea what securitization would involve. Instead, they are likely to include a tentative breakdown stating what securitization would mean (e.g., in COVID-19 we must have lockdown, we must close the borders, etc.). Should securitization shape-shift once under way macro-proportionality must be reassessed.

[28] This is for purposes of argument, and the same would obviously not gain approval in the UNSC.

5.6 Conclusion

This chapter has argued that the international community in the form of the UNSC has an important role to play in mandatory securitization. When other actors have failed to securitize or when there is no protector, the UNSC has residual responsibility for mandatory securitization. I have suggested that the relationship between the UNSC and the people is contractual, insofar as the UN is the guarantor of security to the people, not to member states. Based on this, its duty to securitize is overriding, provided conditions are met. I have also argued that emergency politics, and especially mandatory securitization, has rather a lot to do with the existing norm of the RtoP. After all, this norm requires states and other actors to protect populations from atrocity crime, if necessary, with resort to extraordinary measures, at its most extreme, military force. While RtoP has been an important milestone, I have shown that must cause and mandatory securitization can overcome some RtoP's shortfalls, including its narrow focus on atrocity crimes only. Most importantly, mandatory securitization decisively moves RtoP away from armed humanitarian intervention (war) towards securitizing action.

As briefly mentioned in Section 5.4, RtoP includes besides the responsibility to prevent/react by extraordinary means a set of additional responsibilities, namely (1) the responsibility to rebuild, (2) the responsibility while protecting, and (3) the responsibility to prevent without recourse to extraordinary measures. It is important to notice that these additional responsibilities are accounted for also within JST on which mandatory securitization builds. In other words, a shift from atrocity crimes to must cause and from RtoP to just and mandatory securitization does not jeopardize the greater structure that is RtoP. In more detail, the responsibility to rebuild features heavily in JST's third criterion for just desecuritization, which specifies that desecuritizing actors must not simply undo securitization but rather they must put in place context-specific restorative measures to *prevent* re-securitization (Floyd, 2019a: 199–204). While the exact nature of restorative measures is issue-specific, they refer to *rebuilding* relations damaged by securitization, including between the threatener and the securitizing actor/referent object, but also between the securitizing actor and innocent bystanders.

Just conduct in securitization (cf. Introduction) aims to ensure that executors of securitization 'during protecting' behave responsibly. Notably, just conduct in securitization places limits on what executors are permitted to do, including, for example, when they are permitted to use lethal force.

Finally, the responsibility to prevent or act using ordinary measures is a part of this book's framework for mandatory securitization. Most obviously, the duty to securitize derives from a duty to secure, which can be accomplished using ordinary political measures. Furthermore, the theory is suffused with an explicit commitment to prevent securitization. Not only does just desecuritization include an explicit commitment to prevent re-securitization, but also the threshold for just securitization and mandatory securitization is set high. After all, JST is not a moral crusade; instead, its aim is to reduce the number and adverse impact of securitizations in the world.

Moving on, I have suggested that within RtoP different actors' responsibility to react with force *is* sequential in accordance with the three pillars. This is useful for my purposes here, after all a pillar structure regarding mandatory securitization allows me to state clearly who must act when relevant actors fail in their duty of self-securitization. This said, however, it must be noted that because securitization is permissible before it is obligatory, actors, for example, NATO (a pillar 2 actor), can securitize against issues affecting a pillar 1 actor, before the affected actor does so. In short, the duty to other-securitize is sequential, but the permissibility to securitize against a threat to another is not.

It is now possible to summarize the research argument so far thus:

Pillar 1: Just states that have satisfied must cause[29] have an overriding duty of self-securitization. In the same situation, unjust states have an overriding duty to secure morally valuable referent objects within their territory, but they are not permitted to defend – by means of securitization – their unjust regime. When states fail to act on objective existential threats or when they pose an unjust threat to just referent objects, relevant non-state actors have a pro tanto obligation to act to secure people within the state, including when they have satisfied must cause, via securitization. These obligations extend to group insiders and outsiders.

States are the primary duty-bearers for mandatory other-politicization and – when they have satisfied must cause – mandatory other-securitization, in cases where they are morally or outcome responsible for the threat that gives rise to the need for politicization/securitization. And they can be

---

[29] Must cause = just cause, right intention, macro-proportionality, *and* last resort (see Chapter 1 for a detailed explanation and justification).

primary duty-bearers when they have relevant ties of security friendship with the entity in danger. Powerful or especially skilled states can also be designated primary duty-bearers for other-politicization and other-securitization based on capacity.

Pillar 2: When just sub-systemic collective security actors have satisfied must cause, they are morally obligated to self-securitize. In just collective defence organizations – provided member states seek assistance – this duty is overriding. Unjust collective security actors have a duty to secure morally valuable referent objects within their territory, including – when they have satisfied must cause – with securitization.

On the grounds of friendship and ties of community collectives also bear foremost responsibility for dealing with an unjust threat emanating from a rogue member state to the collective, or – if requested by the member state – to one of its members. Collectives are the primary duty-bearers for mandatory other-politicization and other-securitization when they are morally or outcome responsible for the insecurity. They can also be primary duty-bearers when they have relevant ties of friendship with another state or actor. In cases where individual states and collectives have comparable ties of friendship, the capacity to help trumps, rendering the collective – often – the primary duty-bearer for mandatory other-securitization.

Sub-systemic and systemic-level non-state actors are likely to have a duty to politicize and – when they have satisfied must cause – securitize, only when they are morally or outcome responsible for the threat. The exception would be cases where they are the most capable actor.

Pillar 3: When just referent objects have no other protector (e.g., a weak or 'friendless' persecuted just non-state actor), then the UNSC is the designated primary duty-bearer for mandatory politicization and – if they have satisfied must cause – securitization. Moreover, the UNSC is the secondary, or even tertiary duty-bearer for mandatory politicization and securitization where other duty-bearers have failed to act (including because their obligation to securitize is overridden for legitimate reasons, notably by the risk of death, disease, and disability; the risk of instability and insecurity as well as by prohibitive financial costs). The UNSC's duty to secure and/or securitize is overriding; based on the contractual relation, the UN charter creates between the people and the UN/UNSC.

This pillar structure retains much of RtoP's pillar structure while being much clearer on who has what kind of duties, when, and why. Assigned agency is important to foster the political will of relevant actors to abide by these moral norms (Keating, 2012). Pattison for one has argued that: 'Unless an agent is identified as the primary agent of protection [...] the duty to protect will remain an imperfect one – it is a duty that cannot be morally demanded of any particular state' (Pattison cited in Keating, 2012: 119). Put differently, when the grounds for assigned duties such as other-securitization are unclear, specific states and other actors cannot be expected to act. Indeed, they might simply pass the buck.

My framework is aware of the connection between political will and agency. Not only does it set out all possible actors that are, in principle, obligated to securitize, but it also identifies and ranks sequentially the triggers that render specific actors' primary duty-bearers for other-securitization. This should go some way towards convincing reluctant states of the value of mandatory securitization. Moreover, my framework ensures that securitizing intervention without consent cannot happen if states genuinely if somewhat imperfectly address an objective existential threat to a just referent object (cf. Chapter 2, Section 2.7).

Burden sharing for other-securitization is paramount for another reason. Recall that the veto is simultaneously important for the existence of the UNSC and at the same time obstructive to its efficacy. While UNSC reform away from the veto remains a pipe dream, by sharing the burden for the duty to secure and to securitize among a range of actors (not only states but also security friends hence regional actors and sub-global institutions), the importance of the veto is significantly reduced, because the UNSC is the primary duty-bearer for other-securitization in only a small number of cases.

The political will for intervention (here in a broad sense) also depends on whether the intervener is considered legitimate, either under international law or because they have UNSC authorization (Keating, 2012: 120). At first sight, this seems hard to reconcile with JST. Recall that in my framework the legitimate authority of the securitizing actor is irrelevant to the justice of securitization (Floyd, 2019a, Chapter 5), while UNSC authorization can come after the event (cf. Chapter 4, Section 4.6). And yet, it seems obvious that the perceived legitimacy of a theory or a norm is important to its success. Of course, theories such as mandatory securitization cannot enjoy legitimacy in the ordinary sense, whereby legitimacy is a property of institutions and their right to rule (Buchanan, 2018: 285). But other forms of legitimacy exist. Ronald Janse (2006) notes that NATO's unlawful intervention into Kosovo has widened, if not created, the gulf between legitimacy as legality (i.e., the situation when legitimacy is coterminous with the right to rule (i.e., political authority)) (Peter, 2017) and legitimacy as morally justifiable (cf. Roff, 2013: 35). It is easy to see that moral legitimacy is key to the success of new standards of behaviour (here mandatory securitization). Ultimately, it means that scholars, interested activists, and others can work to convince practitioners, who in turn influence decision-makers, of the moral legitimacy of just and mandatory securitization.

Perhaps the biggest single contribution scholars can make it to systematically engage with just and mandatory securitization. I should stress that I do not see my work on this as the final word on the subject; instead, I am keen to build a subfield of just securitization studies in which scholars try to discover what morality prescribes regarding securitization. The just war tradition shows that if a sufficiently large number of people address the ethics of emergency politics in a particular way, then this can and will transpire into the real world. Together, we can educate practitioners on what matters ethically and how things need to change.

Conclusion

In the summer of 2019, the well-known realist International Relations scholar Stephen Walt briefly pondered the idea of armed environmental intervention. In an article written for *Foreign Policy*, he imagined a futuristic hypothetical whereby the United States, backed by a coalition of the willing yet without a United Nations Security Council (UNSC) resolution, threatens a naval embargo and military strikes on critical infrastructure to stop Brazil's deforestation of the Amazon rainforest. Aware of the consequences of such a course of action, he argued: 'In a world of sovereign states, each is going to do what it must to protect its interests. If the actions of some states are imperilling the future of all the rest, the possibility of serious confrontations and possibly serious conflict is going to increase. That doesn't make the use of force inevitable, but more sustained, energetic, and imaginative efforts will be needed to prevent it' (Walt, 2019). The theory of mandatory securitization advanced in this book offers precisely such an imaginative and sustained effort. Securitization includes a range of powerful alternatives to large-scale armed military intervention, for short war, including sanctions, expulsion, and limited military strikes. The aim of the theory of mandatory securitization is not simply to ensure that something is done about insecurity in a justified way, but also that the occurrence of war is reduced. Thus, if just causes are addressed early through politicization and where necessary through mandatory securitization, humanitarian or environmental wars are less likely to be necessary. In the Brazil deforestation example, for instance, the coalition of the willing led by the United States could commence with political measures to stop Brazil's conduct, including positive incentives (trade), investment, and diplomacy. If these fail, and assuming the coalition is the primary duty-bearer for other-securitization, the coalition must securitize, for example, by issuing economic and diplomatic sanctions, perhaps even some targeted military strikes, showing power and resolve. Only if this fails, could armed environmental intervention be contemplated, provided of course all other criteria of just war are satisfied.

This example shows that just and mandatory securitization alter the relationship between securitization and war. One of the reasons why securitization has a negative reputation among securitization scholars is that – especially in the military sector – it can be a precursor to war. The Copenhagen School has argued as follows:

> Typically, the agent will override such rules, because by depicting a threat the securitizing agent often says someone cannot be dealt with in the normal way. In the extreme case – war – we do not have to discuss with the other party; we try to eliminate them. This self-based violation of rules is the security act, and the fear that the other party will not let us survive as a subject is the foundational motivation for that act. (Buzan et al., 1998: 26)

Mandatory securitization shows that an alternative reality is possible. If enacted, the proposed concept of *mandatory securitization* would ensure that suitable actors are more likely to act appropriately on relevant insecurities, while timely action would reduce the possibility and/ or need for war.

Although Walt's hypothetical plays out in the future (2025), the possibility of this kind of environmental war is hardly farfetched. In 2019, the word climate emergency, which is to say, 'a situation in which urgent action is required to reduce or halt climate change and avoid potentially irreversible environmental damage resulting from it' (BBC, 2019), was the word of the year. That year saw, *inter alia*, the United Kingdom, Ireland, and Canada all declare a climate emergency. Even if it is the case that the securitization against climate change is morally permissible, it is unclear whether these and other states have a moral obligation to utilize exceptional emergency measures to address the climate threat. The theory of mandatory securitization advanced in this book enables scholars, practitioners, and other interested parties to conclusively answer this question. In addition, the theory of mandatory securitization enables interested parties to answer the question whether entities other than states can have a moral obligation to securitize against climate change. (Note here that the European Union too declared a climate emergency in 2019.) It also answers the question whether states and other actors have such obligations only to themselves and to those they have a duty of care for, or to outsiders as well. Whether unjust securitizing actors can have an obligation to securitize?

And, how compliance with such obligations can be achieved? The theory developed in this book can answer these questions, not only with regards to the climate threat but also to all other conceivable threat scenarios, including hitherto unknown threats.

In brief, the theory of mandatory securitization holds that the moral duty to securitize depends – in addition to the principles of Just Securitization Theory (JST) that specifies when securitization is morally permissible – on the satisfaction of what I have in this book called the *must cause*.[1] I have argued that must cause is satisfied when a would-be securitizing actor has tried plausible less harmful alternatives to the threat and when politicization has failed to satisfy the just cause. In other words, must cause rests on concrete and sufficient evidence that other less harmful options do *not* work.

I have shown that alongside states and non-state actors, sub-systemic- and systemic-level actors too can have a moral duty to securitize. The only entity that does not have such a duty is individual persons, because no one can have a duty to compromise their own flourishing to enable or ensure someone else's flourishing.

The duty to securitize insiders is not equally strong or pronounced for all actors. For example, I have shown that states and collective defence organizations have a contractual obligation and consequently an overriding duty of mandatory securitization towards their populations and just member states. Collective security institutions at the sub-systemic level, in turn, merely have a conditional duty to securitize their member states. The difference is that in the latter case the duty of mandatory securitization can (quite legitimately) be overridden, notably due to (1) the risk of death, disease, and disability, (2) the risk of instability or insecurity for the securitizing actor (at large), or (3) prohibitive financial costs.

Beyond the obligation to securitize just insiders (what I have called here self-securitization), relevant just and unjust prospective securitizing actors also have an obligation to – if necessary – secure needy and sufficiently insecure outsiders ('others'). This is based on the premise of the equal moral worth of persons that is central to practically all secular morality. The duty of other-securitization, as indeed the duty

---

[1] To be sure, must cause is more stringent than criterion 5 of JST and supersedes the same.

of self-securitization, rests on a prior duty of politicization. This duty to secure using ordinary political measures morphs into a specific duty to securitize only once less harmful measures have demonstrably failed to satisfy just cause. Indeed, at that point must cause is satisfied.

Given that a multitude of actors (e.g., a specific state, a regional organization, or even the UNSC) can have the obligation to act on the same threat, it was important to identify the primary designated duty-bearer for other-securitization. Doing this also minimizes the risk that responsible actors pass the buck and hence eschew their remedial responsibilities. By drawing on David Miller's (2007) work on remedial responsibility coupled with insights from common-sense morality, I argued for a ranking of triggers of remedial responsibility ranging from moral/outcome responsibility to relevant ties of community/friendship to capacity. Ties of community and security friendship are probably the most innovative trigger I propose, after all the literature on global justice places duties most often based on either culpability or on capacity (cf. Brock, 2017), largely – of course – because cosmopolitans deny the existence of special duties. The importance of community and ties of friendship has important knock-on effects; most notably, it reduces the need for North Atlantic Treaty Organization (NATO) to act as the world's policeman while it also reduces the onus of mandatory securitization placed on the UNSC.

Overall, the heavily theoretical argument advanced in this book has the following practical implications for global security governance:

- It makes NATO's Article 5 fit for the security landscape of the twenty-first century.
- It shifts RtoP conclusively away from armed humanitarian intervention.
- It makes RtoP applicable to a wider, more acute, range of threats.
- It reduces the conditions leading to war.
- By shifting responsibility for relevant actions away from the most capable to the nearest and most trusted actors, it (a) ensures timely action and (b) reduces dominance-based grievances.

While my work on just securitization now comprises two monographs, it is still only a starting point for a much-needed debate. Many global ethics scholars will object to the communitarian view professed in this book, simply because most of such scholars (be they concerned with justice or – as here – security) are cosmopolitans. The mere moral cosmopolitanism embraced in this project, however, might be able to speak to those without an interest in global ethics, precisely because they reject cosmopolitan assumptions. In any case, my hope is that my project will encourage others to engage with this subject, including to bring the just war tradition to bear on securitization. But there is also room for the reverse. Over the course of this book, we have seen that mandatory securitization complements and takes inspiration from research on armed humanitarian intervention – war. With regard to mandatory other-securitization, it is helpful to view securitization, alongside politicization as part of the less harmful alternatives to war. In other words, there is a strong case for the relevance of just and mandatory securitization for the just war community. Moreover, just securitization is relevant for just war scholars interested in the ethics of unarmed conflict (Gross and Meisels, 2017). With the rise of cyber space, the prevalence of such conflicts is only going to go up. Beyond that, the argument in Chapter 1 on must cause could be used to revisit debates on whether and when armed humanitarian intervention is obligatory (cf. Chapter 1). Notably, in such cases, is not the failure of securitization the pivotal component of last resort?

As any research argument, this book answers some questions and opens many others. At various points of the analysis (e.g., Sections 1.6 and 2.7), I have discussed issues of coherence between JST (Floyd, 2019a) and mandatory securitization. I am certain that there are many more areas than I can see that question the compatibility between the 'two' theories. Questions for future research are likely to include: can unjust securitization ever be required? How can we judge securitization that was unjust but that renders the right outcome? Do we need a law against unjust securitization? What is the relationship between mandatory securitization and just desecuritization, especially where securitization was out of line with the principles of just conduct in securitization?

Although I have a keen interest in seeing mandatory securitization realized for the benefit of all, I want to end this book on a cautionary note. It is important to understand that while mandatory securitization has multiple benefits for the insecure, securitization, or better satisfaction of must cause is ultimately a failure. It is a failure because, for the most part, insecurity is caused by actions and/or omissions that are well known to cause conflict and insecurity. In my view, three drivers in particular stand out. In no particular order, these are: (1)

short-termism/self-interest; (2) underdevelopment; and (3) the politics of identity. Let us consider each one briefly.

My first category refers to a range of phenomena including nuclear proliferation, NATO's eastern enlargement, and climate inaction. Some scholars (notably some neo-realist scholars in International Relations such as Kenneth Waltz and John Mearsheimer) maintain that nuclear weapons are ultimately weapons of peace (see Krieger and Roth, 2007). Not only will they never be used, but also they deter the temptation of conventional war between adversaries (Waltz, in Sagan and Waltz, 2010). Contra this, some analysts hold that the risk of accidental usage, the danger posed by rogue leaders as well as terrorism means that nuclear proliferation is ultimately more of a problem than a solution (Sagan in Sagan and Waltz, 2010). I, for one, struggle to believe that anyone either felt safe, or was actually safe, when the ever-infantile Donald Trump and the equally challenged North Korean Leader Kim Jong-Un bragged about who had the biggest button back in 2018. Part of the solution to nuclear proliferation from rogue states (North Korea and Iran) is to curtail vertical proliferation (i.e., the stockpiling and development of nuclear weapons by existing nuclear weapon states). How else can we convince other aspiring nuclear weapons' states to refrain from proliferation? Non-proliferation is hardly radical, after all the Nuclear Non-Proliferation Treaty's commits signatory states to the same.[2] As so often then in world politics we know what is necessary to address the problem, missing is simply the political will.[3]

For a different example, neo-realists blame the West for the renewed tensions between Russia and the West (Mearsheimer, 2014) pointing to NATO's Eastern Enlargement as a promise broken to Russia (on whether this is true, see the debate between Kramer and Itzkowitz Shifrinson, 2017). They consider Russia's reaction predictable and even natural (Mearsheimer, 2014: 10). Liberals in turn blame Russia for the current

---

[2] Article VI of the Nuclear Non-Proliferation Treaty holds that: 'Each of the Parties to the Treaty undertakes to pursue negotiations in good faith on effective measures relating to cessation of the nuclear arms race at an early date and to nuclear disarmament, and on a treaty on general and complete disarmament under strict and effective international control'. The Treaty is available to view here: www.iaea.org/sites/default/files/publications/documents/infcircs/1970/infcirc140.pdf

[3] The Global Zero campaign offers a strategy how this can be achieved (see here www.globalzero.org/).

instability. They point out that by spreading democracy NATO (and European Union) enlargement has brought stability to many Eastern countries that incidentally have a right of self-determination including the ability to choose who or what they join. Moreover, they stress that membership of NATO was once open to Russia. Additionally, Russia is considered the belligerent given their unlawful actions in Ukraine. More can be said on either side, but I think that the blame game is ultimately not fruitful. Or perhaps better, both sides – the West and Russia – can be blamed for their unwillingness to understand the other side's reactions and emotions before acting. Arguably such understanding could be achieved if actors put themselves in the shoes of their opponent.

Moving on, world leaders' unwillingness to act on climate change has been a feature of international politics for more than twenty years. Since the 2007 Intergovernmental Panel on Climate Change report, it is common knowledge what will happen if climate change is not addressed, and yet little is done, mainly because world leaders put their short-term goals (e.g., re-election) first. These examples show that agent-intended and many agent-caused threats could be reduced if states thought more carefully about just how their behaviour and omissions will affect others.

The second great cause of insecurity is underdevelopment. Not only do the majority of armed conflicts occur in the developing world[4] but also poor states are comparatively less able to adapt to climate change and provide healthcare or education, all of which are vital components of human well-being and security. The reasons for underdevelopment are complex and individually different. Without a doubt, the structure of the global economy plays a role, so does – at times – the colonial past,[5] as well as widespread corruption (Collier, 2007). As with climate change, we (i.e., the people of the world) know what needs to be done to combat the problem.[6] Countless studies show that strong

---

[4] For details, see the Uppsala Conflict Data Program, for example, here www.pcr.uu.se/digitalAssets/667/c_667494-l_1-k_armed-conflict-by-region--1946-2018.pdf.

[5] See Tusalem, R. F. (2016). The colonial foundations of state fragility and failure. *Polity*, 48(4), 445–495, for an insightful analysis of state failure and the legacies of different colonial powers.

[6] On why the securitization of underdevelopment is not the answer, see, for example, Abrahamsen, R. (2005). Blair's Africa: The politics of securitization and fear. *Alternatives*, 30(1), 55–80.

institutions (i.e., good governance) are the key to combating under-development; that foreign aid money needs to enable needy people to help themselves; that money needs to reach the right people; and that education and gender equality are paramount. And yet not enough is being done. In an opinion piece by the organizer of the 2020 Annual Munich Security Conference, Wolfgang Ischinger (together with the German minister for International Development Gerd Müller) sums this up well. They argue: 'since 2014 global defence expenditure has risen some 8 per cent: 1600 billion US dollars can be juxtaposed with not quite 160 billon dollars for international development and humanitarian aid' (Müller and Ischinger, 2020, my translation). As before with climate change if the political will was there, things could markedly improve.

While the development–security nexus is well established and the statistical facts speak volumes, it has become controversial to invoke this nexus. After all, many believe that speaking of underdevelopment as a security threat is to socially construct as dangerous enemy others (migrants or terrorists) and to (further) legitimate surveillance and controlling of populations allegedly for their own benefit, but really for the benefit of the rich West (see, e.g., P. Owens, 2012). Likewise, the human security agenda, the UN Millennium Development Goals, and indeed the entire link between development and security have been interpreted as a form of neocolonialism (see, e.g., various in Chandler and Hynek, 2011; Duffield, 2007; Abosede Durokifa and Ijooma, 2018; P. Owens, 2012).

The post-colonial charge against universalism is fuelled by the rise of identity politics and vice versa. 'Identity politics is when people of a particular race, ethnicity, gender, or religion form alliances and organize politically to defend their group's interests. The feminist movement, the civil rights movement, and the gay liberation movement are all examples of this kind of political organizing' (Maquire, 2016). Some scholars hold that speaking on behalf of the (subaltern) referent object is a form of silencing (Bertrand, 2018). If we speak for other (races, classes, castes, etc., of) people and assume them to be insecure, we not only 'homogenise and essentialise the securitized [but also, we run the] risk of superimposing [our] own voice and agenda onto them' (Bertrand, 2018: 290). Moreover, this silencing itself is a form of neocolonialism whereby supressed 'brown' people are saved by white people (ibid: 291).

At the heart of critiques such as this one is the idea that any form of speaking for someone else is impossible and undesirable not only because there are no universal moral values but also because only in-groups of specific identities can speak for that group. What proponents of this ideology fail to see, however, is that identity politics is fast becoming the third biggest source of insecurity. Deep down everyone knows this, after all proponents of left-wing identity politics are concerned about the rise of right-wing identity politics because of its effects on out-groups (Fukuyama, 2018). For most people, the link between right-wing extremism and insecurity/conflict is clear. What they do not see is that the effect of left-wing identity politics too leads to conflict and societal insecurity, that is, the situation 'when communities of whatever kind define a development or potentiality as a threat to their survival as a community' (Wæver, 2008: 582). As evidence of this, consider that at university campuses across the United States 'woke' students have engaged in physical violence, vandalism and intimidation against invited speakers or staff they considered racists, bigoted, homophobic, transphobic, etc. (Lukianoff and Haidt, 2019: chapter 4). Because such acts were considered acts of 'self-defence' that in turn were justified on the grounds of (perceived) existential threats,[7] we can see that the politics of identity, be it left-wing, breeds insecurity and conflict. As people identify with ever smaller groups and overtly against the views of other groups, any rise of an opposing group will inevitably be interpreted as a threat to one's own identity. In short, conflict and insecurity are pre-programmed. The only way out of this insecurity trap is to embrace a common human identity (c.f. Lukianoff and Haidt, 2019).

My just securitization project is committed to reducing the occurrence and harmfulness of securitization. This is achieved in various ways, notably by setting the threshold for just securitization high and the one for mandatory securitization even higher; by specifying strict rules for just conduct during securitization; and by making just desecuritization partly about the prevention of re-securitization. The main premise of the just securitization research is that while securitization is not an unequivocal good, it can sometimes be morally permissible to securitize; indeed, it is sometimes morally required. Given the

---

[7] Lukianoff and Haidt cite original quotes from students in which they express that hate speech denies 'the right of black people to exist' (2019: 89).

general aim of reducing the occurrence of securitization, mandatory securitization is implicitly based on the understanding that the occasions that give rise of the need for securitization must be reduced. The sources of insecurity briefly examined above show that insecurity is largely caused by people's actions and omissions. In other words, it is down to people, and perhaps especially leaders, whether they make the world more secure. Steven Pinker (2011) has shown that progress, including towards greater security (as a state of being), is possible; the question is whether this is what people really want. None of this means, however, that scholars like me cannot call for change; indeed, if we know what is wrong and how things could be improved, we have a moral duty to improve the world in the ways we can. In my own case, this takes the form of theory development.

References

Abbas, T. (2019). 'Implementing "Prevent" in countering violent extremism in the UK: A left-realist critique', *Critical Social Policy*, 39(3), 396–412.

Abosede Durokifa, A. and Ijeoma, E. C. (2018). 'Neo-colonialism and Millennium Development Goals (MDGs) in Africa: A blend of an old wine in a new bottle', *African Journal of Science, Technology, Innovation and Development*, 10(3), 355–366.

Acharya, A. (2014). *Constructing a security community in Southeast Asia: ASEAN and the problem of regional order*. London: Routledge.

Adler, E. and Barnett, M. (1998). 'Security communities in theoretical perspective' In Emmanuel Adler and Michael Barnett (eds.) *Security communities*, Cambridge: Cambridge University Press, pp. 3–28.

African Union. (2000). 'Constitutive Act of the African Union', available at: au.int/sites/default/files/pages/34873-file-constitutiveact_en.pdf [accessed 22/05/2022].

Altman, A. and Wellman, C. H. (2009). *A liberal theory of international justice*. Oxford: Oxford University Press.

Amnesty International. (2017). *Dangerously disproportionate: The ever-expanding national security state in Europe*. London: Amnesty International.

Amnesty International. (2018). 'France: "Dehumanising" counter-terror measures being used to unjustly punish people – New report', available at: www.amnesty.org.uk/press-releases/france-dehumanising-counter-terror-measures-being-used-unjustly-punish-people-new [accessed 31/03/2022].

Annan, K. (1999). 'Secretary-General presents his annual report to general assembly' 20 September 1999, available at: www.un.org/press/en/1999/19990920.sgsm7136.html [accessed 19/06/2023].

Annan, K. (2000). 'We the peoples: The role of the United Nations in the 21st century, United Nations', available at: digitallibrary.un.org/record/413745?ln=en [accessed 19/06/2023].

Annan, K. (2005). In larger freedom: Towards development, security and human rights for all, available at: www.un.org/en/ga/search/view_doc.asp?symbol=A/59/2005 [accessed 25/09/2019].

Aradau, C. (2004). 'Security and the democratic scene: Desecuritization and emancipation', *Journal of International Relations and Development*, 7(4), 388–413.

Audard, C. (2007). *John Rawls*. Stocksfield: Acumen.

Aust, A. (2010). *Handbook of international law*. Cambridge: Cambridge University Press.

Axworthy, L. (2016). 'Resetting the narrative on peace and security: R2P in the next ten years' In Alex J. Bellamy and Tim Dunne (eds.) *The Oxford handbook of the responsibility to protect*, Oxford: Oxford University Press, pp. 968–983.

Axworthy, L. and Rock, A. (2012). 'Making R2P work: Now and in the future' In W. Andy Knight and Frazer Egerton (eds.) *The Routledge handbook of the responsibility to protect*, London: Routledge, pp. 181–193.

Bain, W. (2014). 'The pluralist-solidarist debate in the English school' In Cornelia Navari and Daniel M. Green (eds.) *Guide to the English school in international studies*, Chichester: John Wiley & Sons. pp. 159–169.

Balzacq, T. (2011). 'A theory of securitization: Origins, core assumptions, and variants' In Thierry Balzacq (ed.) *Securitization theory: How security problems emerge and dissolve*, London: Routledge, pp. 1–30.

Baylis, J., Smith, S., and Owens, P. (Eds.). (2020). *The globalization of world politics: An introduction to international relations*. Oxford: Oxford University Press.

BBC. (2019). 'Climate emergency is Oxford dictionary's word of the year 2019', available at: www.bbc.co.uk/newsround/50499514 [accessed 11/07/2023].

Beauchamp, T. (2019). 'The principle of beneficence in applied ethics' In Edward N. Zalta (ed.) *The Stanford encyclopedia of philosophy* (Spring 2019 Edition), plato.stanford.edu/archives/spr2019/entries/principle-beneficence/.

Beitz, C. R. (2009). *The idea of human rights*. Oxford: Oxford University Press.

Belk, R. and Noyes, M. (2012). *On the use of offensive cyber capabilities a policy analysis on offensive US cyber policy*. Harvard Kennedy School, available at: citeseerx.ist.psu.edu/viewdoc/download?doi=10.1.1.297.1370&rep=rep1&type=pdf [accessed 18/02/2019].

Bellamy, A. J. (2018). 'The responsibility to protect' In Paul D. Williams and Matt McDonald (eds.) *Security studies: An introduction*, Abingdon: Routledge, pp. 235–249.

Bellamy, A. J. (2015). 'The three pillars of the responsibility to protect', *Pensamiento propio*, 41(20), 35–64.

Bellamy, A. J. (2016). 'UN security council' In Alex J. Bellamy and Tim Dunne (eds.) *The Oxford handbook of the responsibility to protect*, Oxford: Oxford University Press, pp. 249–268.

Bellamy, A. J. and Williams P. D. (2012). 'On the limits of moral hazard: The "responsibility to protect", armed conflict and mass atrocities', *European Journal of International Relations*, 18(3), 539–571.

Berenskoetter, F. (2014). 'Friendship, security and power', available at eprints.soas.ac.uk/17941/1/berenskoetter-friendship-security-and-power.pdf [accessed 17/10/2019].

Bertrand, S. (2018). 'Can the subaltern securitize? Postcolonial perspectives on securitization theory and its critics', *European Journal of International Security*, 3(3), 281–299.

Betts, A. and Collier, P. (2017). *Refuge: Transforming a broken refugee system*. London: Penguin, UK.

Betts, A. and Collier, P. (2018). 'How Europe can reform its migration policy, foreign affairs', available at: www.foreignaffairs.com/articles/europe/2018-10-05/how-europe-can-reform-its-migration-policy [accessed 20/02/2019].

Biggar, N. (2020). *What's wrong with rights?* Oxford: Oxford University Press.

Blackburn, S. (2005). *Oxford: Dictionary of philosophy*, second edition, Oxford: Oxford University Press.

Bloomfield, A. (2017). 'Resisting the responsibility to protect' In Alan Bloomfield and Shirley V. Scott (eds.) *Norm antipreneurs and the politics of resistance to global normative change*, Abingdon: Routledge, pp. 20–38.

Booth, K. (1991). 'Security and emancipation', *Review of International Studies*, 17(4), 313–326.

Booth, K. (2007). *Theory of world security*. Cambridge: Cambridge University Press.

Boucher, D. (1998). *Political theories of international relations*. Oxford: Oxford University Press.

Bourbeau, P. and Vuori, J. A. (2015). 'Security, resilience and desecuritization: Multidirectional moves and dynamics', *Critical Studies on Security*, 3(3), 253–268.

Breen-Smyth, M. (2014). 'Theorising the "suspect community": Counterterrorism, security practices and the public imagination', *Critical Studies on Terrorism*, 7(2), 223–240.

Brock, G. (2008). 'Taxation and global justice: Closing the gap between theory and practice', *Journal of Social Philosophy*, 39(2), 161–184.

Brock, G. (2009). *Global justice: A cosmopolitan account*. Oxford: Oxford University Press.

Brock, G. (2017). 'Global justice' In Edward N. Zalta (ed.) *The Stanford encyclopedia of philosophy* (Spring 2017 Edition), plato.stanford.edu/archives/spr2017/entries/justice-global/

Brown, C. R. (1998). 'Common-Sense Ethics', doi:10.4324/9780415249126-L011-1. Routledge Encyclopaedia of Philosophy, Taylor and Francis, www.rep.routledge.com/articles/thematic/common-sense-ethics/v-1.

Browning, C. S. and McDonald, M. (2013). 'The future of critical security studies: Ethics and the politics of security', *European Journal of International Relations*, 19(2), 235–255.

Brunstetter, D. and Braun, M. (2013). 'From jus ad bellum to jus ad vim: Recalibrating our understanding of the moral use of force', *Ethics & International Affairs*, 27(1), 87–106.

Brunstetter, D. (2021). *Just and unjust uses of limited force: A moral argument with contemporary illustrations.* Oxford: Oxford University Press.

Buchanan, A. (2018). *Institutionalizing the just war.* Oxford: Oxford University Press.

Buckley, E. (2006). Invoking Article 5, *NATO Review*, summer 2006.

Burke, A. (2020). 'Review of the morality of security: A theory of just securitization'. By Rita Floyd. Cambridge: Cambridge University Press, 2019. 258p. $99.00 cloth. Perspectives on Politics, September 2020 | Vol. 18/ No. 3, 1009-10.

Burke, A., Lee-Koo, K., and M. McDonald (2014). *Ethics and global security: A cosmopolitan approach.* Abingdon: Routledge.

Buzan, B. (2004). *From international to world society?: English school theory and the social structure of globalisation.* Cambridge: Cambridge University Press.

Buzan, B., Wæver, O., and J. de Wilde. (1998). *Security: A new framework for analysis.* Boulder, CO: Lynne Rienner Publishers.

Cabinet Office. (2010). *A strong Britain in an age of uncertainty: The national security strategy* (Vol. 7953). London: The Stationery Office.

Cambridge Online Dictionary. (2019). 'Mandatory', dictionary.cambridge.org/dictionary/english/mandatory [accessed 19/07/2019].

Caney, S. (2005). *Justice beyond borders: A global political theory.* Oxford: Oxford University Press.

Caney, S. (2010). 'Cosmopolitan justice, responsibility, and global climate change'. In Stephen M. Gardiner, Simon Caney, Dale Jamieson, and Henry Shue (eds.) *Climate ethics: Essential readings.* Oxford: Oxford University Press, pp. 122–145.

Castree, N., Kitchin, R., and Rogers, A. (2013). *A dictionary of human geography.* Oxford: Oxford University Press.

Cater, C. and Malone, D. M. (2016). 'The genesis of R2P: Kofi Anna's intervention dilemma' In Alex J. Bellamy and Tim Dunne (eds.) *The Oxford handbook of the responsibility to protect*, Oxford: Oxford University Press, pp. 114–132.

Centre for Research on the Epidemiology of Disasters (CRED). (2015). 'The Human Cost of Natural Disasters', available at reliefweb.int/report/world/human-cost-natural-disasters-2015-global-perspective [accessed 22/06/2021].

Chalk, F., Dallaire, R., and Matthews, K. (2012). 'The responsibility to react' In W. Andy Knight and Frazer Egerton (eds.) *The Routledge handbook of the responsibility to protect*, London: Routledge, pp. 36–49.

Chandler, D. and Hynek, N. (Eds.). (2011). *Critical perspectives on human security: Rethinking emancipation and power in international relations.* London: Routledge.

Chertoff, M. and Rasmussen, A. F. (2019). 'The Unhackable Election: What it takes to defend democracy'. *Foreign Affairs*, January/February 2019, pp. 156–164.

Chesterman, S. (2001). *Just war or just peace? Humanitarian intervention and international law.* Oxford: Oxford University Press.

Chigwedere, P., Seage, G. R. 3rd, Gruskin, S., Lee, T. H., and Essex, M. (2008). 'Estimating the lost benefits of antiretroviral drug use in South Africa'. *Journal of Acquired Immune Deficiency Syndromes* 49(4), 410–415. doi: 10.1097/qai.0b013e31818a6cd5. PMID: 19186354.

Cholbi, M. (2017). 'Suicide' In Edward N. Zalta (ed.) *The Stanford encyclopedia of philosophy* (Fall 2017 Edition), plato.stanford.edu/archives/fall2017/entries/suicide/.

Clarke, M. (2011). 'Curious Victory for NATO in Libya', *London: Royal United Services Institute (RUSI) available here* rusi.org/commentary/curious-victory-nato-libya [accessed 08/04/2019].

Cochran, M. (2014). 'Normative theory in the English school' In Cornelia Navari and Daniel M. Green (eds.) *Guide to the English school in international studies*, Chichester: John Wiley & Sons, pp. 205–221.

Cohen, R. (2012). 'From sovereign responsibility to R2P' In W. Andy Knight and Frazer Egerton (eds.) *The Routledge handbook of the responsibility to protect*, London: Routledge, pp. 7–2.

Collier, P. (2007). *The bottom billion: Why the poorest countries are failing and what can be done about it.* Oxford University Press.

Conca, K. and Dabelko, G. D. (Eds.). (2002). *Environmental peacemaking.* Washington, DC: Woodrow Wilson Center Press.

Corera, G. (2019). 'NATO: Cyber-attack on One Nation Is an Attack on All', 27 August 2019 BBC news website available at: www.bbc.co.uk/news/technology-49488614 [accessed 26/02/2021].

Corry, O. (2012). 'Securitisation and "riskification": Second-order security and the politics of climate change', *Millennium*, 40(2), 235–258.

Côté, A. (2016). 'Agents without agency: Assessing the role of the audience in securitization theory', *Security Dialogue*, 47(6), 541–558.

Coticchia, F. and Davidson, J. W. (2019). *Italian foreign policy during Matteo Renzi's government: A domestically focused outsider and the world*. Lanham: Rowman & Littlefield.

Council on Foreign Relations. (2018). 'The UN Security Council', available here www.cfr.org/backgrounder/un-security-council [accessed 25/07/2019].

Delmas, C. (2018). *A duty to resist: When disobedience should be uncivil*. Oxford: Oxford University Press.

Deutsche Welle. (2017). 'NATO: Russia Targeted German Army with Fake News Campaign', available at www.dw.com/en/nato-russia-targeted-german-army-with-fake-news-campaign/a-37591978 [accessed 07/10/2019].

Dey, A., Heinemann, C., and Unger, C. (2017). 'Das Rätsel um die Kosten des G20-Gipfels' *Hamburger Abendblatt* available www.abendblatt.de/hamburg/g20/article211016533/Das-Raetsel-um-die-Kosten.html [accessed 05/04/2019].

Dill, J. (2016). 'Forcible alternatives to war' In Ohlin, Jens David (ed.) *Theoretical boundaries of armed conflict and human rights*. ASIL Studies in International Legal Theory, New York, USA: Cambridge University Press, pp. 289–314.

Dimari, G. and Papadakis, N. (2022). 'The securitization of the Covid-19 pandemic in Greece: A just or unjust securitization?', *Quality & Quantity* doi.org/10.1007/s11135-022-01341-9

Dobos, N. and Coady, C. A. J. (2014). 'All or nothing: Are there any "merely permissible" armed humanitarian interventions?' In Don E. Scheid (eds.) *The ethics of armed humanitarian intervention*, Cambridge: Cambridge University Press, pp 78–94.

Doherty, K. (2014). 'What an Ebola Curfew Looks Like', *The Guardian*, 15 December 2014 available www.theguardian.com/cities/2014/dec/15/ebola-curfew-sierra-leone-freetown-photographs [accessed 25/02/2019].

Donnelly, J. (2003). *Universal human rights in theory & practice*, 2nd edition, Ithaca: Cornell University Press.

Doyal, L. and Gough, I. (1991). *A theory of human needs*, Basingstoke: Macmillan.

Doyle, M. (2016). 'R2P before and after Libya' In Alex J. Bellamy and Tim Dunne (eds.) *The Oxford handbook of the responsibility to protect*, Oxford: Oxford University Press, pp. 673–690.

Duffield, M. (2007). *Development, security and unending war: Governing the world of peoples*. Cambridge: Polity.

Dunford, R. and Neu, M. (2019). *Just war and the responsibility to protect: A critique*. London: Zed Books.

Dunn Cavelty, M. (2010). 'Cyber-threats' In Myriam Dunn Cavelty and Victor Mauer (eds.) *The Routledge handbook of security studies*, Abingdon: Routledge, pp. 180–189.

Dyzenhaus, D. (2010). 'The "organic law" of Ex Parte Milligan' In Austin Sarat (eds.) *Sovereignty, emergency, legality*, Cambridge: Cambridge University Press, pp. 16–56.

Dworkin, G. (2020). 'Paternalism' In Edward N. Zalta (ed.) *The Stanford encyclopedia of philosophy* (Fall 2020 Edition), plato.stanford.edu/archives/fall2020/entries/paternalism/.

Eckersley, R. (2007). 'Ecological intervention: Prospects and limits', *Ethics & International Affairs*, 21(3), 293–316.

Egerton, F. (2012). 'What is right with R2P?' In W. Andy Knight and Frazer Egerton (eds.) *The Routledge handbook of the responsibility to protect*, London: Routledge, pp. 77–84.

Erskine, T. (2003). 'Introduction: Making sense of "responsibility" in international relations – key questions and concepts'. In *Can institutions have responsibilities? collective moral agency and international relations*. London: Palgrave Macmillan UK, pp. 1–16.

Erskine, T. (2016). 'Moral agents of protection and supplementary responsibilities to protect' In Alex J. Bellamy and Tim Dunne (eds.) *The Oxford handbook of the responsibility to protect*, Oxford: Oxford University Press, pp. 167–185.

ESCR. (2019). 'Non-State Actors', available at www.escr-net.org/resources/non-state-actors [accessed 12/11/2019].

EUCOM. (2018). 'House Armed Services Committee Hearing On Security Challenges In Europe', 16 March, available at www.eucom.mil/transcript/36275/test [accessed 7/11/2023].

EUR-Lex. (2023). 'Mutual Defence Clause', available at eur-lex.europa.eu/EN/legal-content/glossary/mutual-defence-clause.html [accessed 11/7/23].

EUROPA. (2019). 'The EU in Brief: Goals and Values' available at europa.eu/european-union/about-eu/eu-in-brief_en [accessed 22/07/2019].

European Centre for Disease Prevention and Control. (2019). 'Factsheet about Dengue Fever' available at ecdc.europa.eu/en/dengue-fever/facts/factsheet [accessed 25/02/2019].

European Commission. (2016). Directorate-General for Communication, Juncker, J., *State of the Union* 2016, Publications Office of the European Union, 2016, data.europa.eu/doi/10.2775/968989

European Union. (2016). 'A Global Strategy for the European Union's Foreign And Security Policy-Shared Vision, Common Action: A Stronger Europe'.

European Union External Action Service. (2016). 'European Neighbor-
hood Policy (ENP)' available at eeas.europa.eu/diplomatic-network/
european-neighbourhood-policy-enp/330/european-neighbourhood-
policy-enp_en

Evangelista, M. (2008). *Law, ethics, and the war on terror.* Cambridge:
Polity.

Evans, G. (2009). 'The responsibility to protect in environmental emergencies', *Proceedings of the Annual Meeting (American Society of International Law)*, 103, 27–32.

Evans, G. and Newnham, J. (1998). *The Penguin dictionary of international
relations.* London: Penguin Group USA.

Fabre, C. (2007). 'Mandatory rescue killings', *The Journal of Political Philosophy*, 15(4), 363–384.

Fabre, C. (2012). *Cosmopolitan war.* Oxford: Oxford University Press.

Falkner, R. (2016). 'The Paris Agreement and the new logic of international
climate politics', *International Affairs*, 92(5), 1107–1125.

Feinberg, J. (1961). 'Supererogation and rules', *Ethics*, 71(4), 276–288.

Fierke, K. M. (2007). *Critical approaches to international security.* Cambridge: Polity.

Finlay, C. J. (2015). *Terrorism and the right to resist: A theory of just revolutionary war.* Cambridge: Cambridge University Press, 2015.

Flinch Midtgaard, S. (2021). 'Paternalism, Oxford Research Encyclopaedia
of Politics', doi.org/10.1093/acrefore/9780190228637.013.201

Floyd, J. (2017a). *Is political philosophy impossible?: Thoughts and behaviour in normative political theory.* Cambridge: Cambridge University
Press.

Floyd, J. (2017b). 'Rawls methodological blueprint', *European Journal of
Political Theory*, 16(3), 367–381.

Floyd, R. (2010). *Security and the environment: Securitization theory and
US environmental security policy.* Cambridge: Cambridge University
Press.

Floyd, R. (2011). 'Why we need needs-based justifications of human rights',
Journal of International Political Theory, 7(1), 103–115.

Floyd, R. (2016a). 'Extraordinary or ordinary emergency measures: What,
and who, defines the "success" of securitisation?', *Cambridge Review of
International Affairs*, 29(2), 677–694.

Floyd, R. (2016b). 'The promises of just securitization theories' In Jonna
Nyman and Anthony Burke (eds.) *Ethical security studies: A new research
agenda*, London: Routledge, pp. 75–88.

Floyd, R. (2018). 'Parallels with the hate speech debate: The pros and cons
of criminalising harmful securitising requests', *Review of International
Studies*, 44(1), 43–63.

Floyd, R. (2019a) *The morality of security: A theory of just securitization.* Cambridge: Cambridge University Press.

Floyd, R. (2019b). 'Collective securitization in the EU: Normative dimensions', *West European Politics*, 42(2), 391–412.

Floyd, R. (2019c). 'States, last resort, and the obligation to securitize', *Polity*, 51(2), 378–394.

Floyd, R. (2019d). 'Evidence of securitisation in the economic sector of security in Europe? Russia's economic blackmail of Ukraine and the EU's conditional bailout of Cyprus', *European Security*, 28(2), 173–192, DOI: 10.1080/09662839.2019.1604509

Floyd, R. (2021). 'Securitisation and the function of functional actors', *Critical Studies on Security*, 9(2), 81–97, DOI: 10.1080/21624887.2020.1827590

Floyd, R. (2022). 'The morality of security: A reply to critics and where to from here', *European Journal of International Security*, 7(2), 275–282.

Foreign Affairs Council. (2014). 'Council Condemns the Illegal Referendum in Crimea', 17 March available at www.consilium.europa.eu/en/meetings/fac/2014/03/17/ [accessed 05/06/2020].

Fox, C. (2019). 'What's special about the insult of paternalism?', *Law and Philosophy*, 38(3), 313–334.

Frederick, D. (2015). 'Pro tanto obligations and Ceteris-Paribus rules', *Journal of Moral Philosophy*, 1, 255–266.

Friend, C. (2004). 'Social Contract Theory' *Internet Encyclopaedia of Philosophy* available at www.iep.utm.edu/soc-cont/ [accessed 06/03/2019].

Fritz, O., Christen, E., Sinabell, F., and Hinz, J. (2017). 'Russia's and the EU's sanctions. Economic and trade effects, compliance and the way forward'. *WIFO Studies*.

Frowe, H. (2011). *The ethics of war and peace: An introduction*, Abingdon: Routledge.

Frowe, H. (2014a). *Defensive killing*. Oxford: Oxford University Press.

Frowe, H. (2014b). 'Judging armed humanitarian intervention' In Don E. Scheid (eds.) *The ethics of armed humanitarian intervention*, Cambridge: Cambridge University Press, pp. 95–112.

Frowe, H. (2016). *The ethics of war and peace*, second edition, Abingdon: Routledge.

Frowe, H. (2018). 'Lesser-evil justifications for harming: Why we're required to turn the trolley', *The Philosophical Quarterly*, 68(272), 460–480.

Fukuyama, F. (2018). 'Against identity politics: The new tribalism and the crisis of democracy', *Foreign Affairs*, 97, 90.

Gardner, J. (2001). 'The mysterious case of the reasonable person', *The University of Toronto Law Journal*, 51, 273.

Gardner, J., (2015). 'The many faces of the reasonable person', *Law Quarterly Review*, 131(1), 563–584.

Gauthier, D. P. (1969). *The logic of Leviathan: The moral and political theory of Thomas Hobbes*. Oxford: Oxford University Press.

Glanville, L. (2013). *Sovereignty and the responsibility to protect*. Chicago: University of Chicago Press.

Glanville, L. (2014). 'Is just intervention morally obligatory?' In Caron E. Gentry and Amy E. Eckert (eds.) *The future of just war*, Athens: University of Georgia Press, pp. 48–61.

Glanville, L. (2021). *Sharing responsibility: The history and future of protection from atrocities*. Chicago: University of Chicago Press.

Glanville, L. and Pattison, J. (2021). 'Where to protect? Prioritization and the responsibility to protect', *Ethics & International Affairs*, 35(2), 213–225.

Goodin, R. E. (1988). 'What is so special about our fellow countrymen?', *Ethics*, 98(4), 663–686.

Graham, G. (2008). *Ethics and international relations*, second edition, Oxford: Blackwell Publishing.

Griffin, J. (2008). *On human rights*. Oxford: Oxford University Press.

Grigore, N. (2019). 'On why there is a problem of supererogation', *Philosophia*, 47(4), 1141–1163.

Gross, M. and Meisels, T. (Eds.) (2017). *Soft war: The ethics of unarmed conflict*. Cambridge: Cambridge University Press.

Halbfinger, D. M. (2020). 'Virus Soars Among Ultra-Orthodox Jews as Many Flout Israel's Rules' *New York Times*, 30 May 2020.

Hansen, L. (2012). 'Reconstructing desecuritization: The normative-political in the Copenhagen School and directions for how to apply it', *Review of International Studies*, 38(03), 525–546.

Hansen, L. (2020). 'Are "core" feminist critiques of securitization theory racist? A reply to Alison Howell and Melanie Richter-Montpetit', *Security Dialogue*, 51(4), 378–385.

Hansen, L., & Nissenbaum, H. (2009). 'Digital disaster, cyber security, and the Copenhagen School', *International studies quarterly*, 53(4), 1155–1175.

Harms, W. and Juncker, P. (2019). 'Wie regeln andere EU-Länder die Grundsicherung?' Taggesschau, 6.03.2019

Harrington. J. (2012). 'R2P and natural disasters' In W. Andy Knight and Frazer Egerton (eds.) *The Routledge handbook of the responsibility to protect*, London: Routledge, pp. 141–150.

Haworth, L. (1955). 'Common sense morality', *Ethics*, 65(4), 250–260.

Hehir, A. (2017). '"Utopian in the right sense": The responsibility to protect and the logical necessity of reform', *Ethics & International Affairs*, 31(3), 335–355.

Hehir, A. (2019). *Hollow norms and the responsibility to protect*. London: Palgrave.

Hehir, A. and Lang, A. (2015). 'The impact of the security council on the efficacy of the international criminal court and the responsibility to protect', *Criminal Law Forum, 26*, 153–179.

Herington, J. (2013). 'The concept of security: Uncertainty, Evidence and Value', PhD diss., Australian National University.

Herington, J. (2015). 'Philosophy: The concepts of security, fear, liberty, and the state' In Philippe Bourbeau (ed.) *Security: Dialogue across disciplines*, Cambridge: Cambridge University Press, pp. 22–44.

Heyd, D. (2019). 'Supererogation' In Edward N. Zalta (ed.) *The Stanford encyclopedia of philosophy* (Winter 2019 Edition), plato.stanford.edu/archives/win2019/entries/supererogation/.

Hill, M., Campanale D. and Joel G. (2021). '"Their goal is to destroy everyone": Uighur camp detainees allege systematic rape', *BBC News* 02, February 2021.

HM Government. (2015). 'National Security Strategy and Strategic Defence and Security Review 2015: A Secure and Prosperous United Kingdom'. www.un.org/press/en/1999/19990920.sgsm7136.html [accessed 24/06/2019].

Hobbes, T. (2002). 'The Project Gutenberg eBook of Leviathan', available at www.gutenberg.org/files/3207/3207-h/3207-h.htm

Hoogensen Gjørv, G. (2012). 'Security by any other name: Negative security, positive security, and a multi-actor security approach', *Review of International Studies, 38*(4), 835–859.

House of Commons Foreign Affairs Committee. (2016–17). 'Libya: Examination of intervention and collapse and the UK's future policy options Third Report of Session 2016–17', London: House of Commons.

Howell, A., & Richter-Montpetit, M. (2020). 'Is securitization theory racist? Civilizationism, methodological whiteness, and antiblack thought in the Copenhagen School'. *Security Dialogue, 51*(1), 3–22.

Hurrell, A. (2014). 'Order and justice' In Cornelia Navari and Daniel M. Green (eds.) *Guide to the English school in international studies*, Chichester: John Wiley & Sons, pp. 143–158, chapter 9.

Huysmans, J. (2011). 'What's in an act? On security speech acts and little security nothings', *Security Dialogue, 42*(4–5), 371–383.

ICISS. (2001). *The responsibility to protect: Report of the international commission on intervention and state sovereignty*. Ottawa: The International Development Research Centre.

IISS. (1992). 'The challenge of self-determination', *Strategic Survey, 93* 1992 – (1), 16–23.

Jackson, R. (2000). *The global covenant: Human conduct in a world of states*. Oxford: Oxford University Press.

Janse, R. (2006). 'The legitimacy of humanitarian interventions', *Leiden Journal of International Law, 19*(3), 669–692.

Jenkins, S. (2017). 'If we overreact to this attack on Paris then terrorism will "just never end"' *The Guardian*, 21 April 2017.

Jeske, D. (2014). 'Special obligations' In Edward N. Zalta (ed.) *The Stanford encyclopedia of philosophy* (Spring 2014 Edition), plato.stanford.edu/archives/spr2014/entries/special-obligations/.

Johansen, R. C. (2006). 'Proposal for a United Nations emergency peace service to prevent genocide and crimes against humanity' In Robert C. Johansen (ed.) *A United Nations emergency peace service: To prevent genocide and crimes against humanity*, New York: World Federalist Movement, pp. 23–42.

Kaldor, M. (2012). *New and old wars* 3rd edition, Cambridge: Polity.

Kasic, A. (2014). 'Australia's Border Control: The Anxiety of a Nation', Unpublished Master's Thesis available at: projekter.aau.dk/projekter/files/198384830/Thesis_Australia_s_Border_Control.pdf [accessed 24/07/2023].

Keating, T. (2012). 'Mobilising the troops: Generating the political will to act' In W. Andy Knight and Frazer Egerton (eds.) *The Routledge handbook of the responsibility to protect*, London: Routledge, pp. 115–125.

Kegley, C. W. and Wittkopf, E. R. (2001). *World politics: Trend and transformation*, 8th edition, Bedford/St.Martin's: Macmillan Press.

Ki-Moon, B. (2009). Implementing the responsibility to protect Report of the Secretary-General, A/63/677, 12 January 2009.

Ki-Moon, B. (2012). Responsibility to protect: Timely and decisive response, Report of the Secretary-General A/66/874–S/2012/578, 25 July 2012.

Kleine, K. (2015). 'Will R2P be ready when disaster strikes? - The rationale of the responsibility to protect in an environmental context', *The International Journal of Human Rights*, 19(8), 1176–1189.

Kramer, M. and Harlan, J. (2019). 'Parkland Shooting: Where Gun Control and School Safety Stand Today' *The New York Times*, 13 February 2019 available at www.nytimes.com/2019/02/13/us/parkland-shooting.html [accessed 29/07/2019].

Kramer, M. and Itzkowitz Shifrinson, J. R. (2017). 'Correspondence: NATO enlargement – Was there a promise?', *International Security*, 42(1) (Summer 2017), 189–192.

Krieger, D., Mendlovitz, S., and Pace, W. (2006). 'Introduction' In Robert C. Johansen (ed.) *A United Nations emergency peace service: To prevent genocide and crimes against humanity*, New York: World Federalist Movement, pp. 11–20.

Krieger, Z., &and Roth, A. I. (2007). 'Nuclear weapons in neo-realist theory', *International Studies Review*, 9(3), 369–384.

Ladenburg, T. (2007). 'Woodrow Wilson and the League of Nations, Digital History', available at www.digitalhistory.uh.edu/teachers/lesson_plans/pdfs/unit8_12.pdf

Lango, J. W. (2014). *The ethics of armed conflict: A cosmopolitan just war theory*. Edinburgh: Edinburgh University Press.

Lazar, N. C. (2009). *States of emergency in liberal democracies*. Cambridge: Cambridge University Press.

Lazar, S. (2012). 'Necessity in self-defense and war', *Philosophy & Public Affairs*, *40*(1), 3–44.

Linn, L. (2015). 'Ebola Diaries: From Denial and Fear to Action', available at www.who.int/features/2015/ebola-diaries-linn/en/ [accessed 11/02/2019].

Loader, I. (2022). 'Not just securitization: On the limits of limiting security practices', *European Journal of International Security*, 7, 252–256.

Luck, E. C. (2009). 'Environmental Emergencies and the Responsibility to Protect: A Bridge Too Far?', *Proceedings of the ASIL Annual Meeting* (Vol. 103, pp. 32–38). Cambridge: Cambridge University Press.

Lukianoff, G. and Haidt, J. (2019). *The coddling of the American mind: How good intentions and bad ideas are setting up a generation for failure*. London: Penguin Books.

Lyotard, J. F. (1984). *The postmodern condition: A report on knowledge*. Manchester: Manchester University Press.

Makahamadze, T. and Sibanda, F. (2021). 'Gratuitous benefit for the ZANU-PF government? Securitisation of COVID-19 and authoritarian politics in Zimbabwe', *African Security Review*, DOI: 10.1080/10246029.2021.1982739

Mahdavi, M. (2012). 'R2P in the Middle East and North Africa' In W. Andy Knight and Frazer Egerton (eds.) *The Routledge handbook of the responsibility to protect*, London: Routledge, pp. 257–275.

Mahdavi, M. (2015). 'A postcolonial critique of responsibility to protect the Middle East', *Perceptions*, *xx*(1), 7–36.

Malone, L. A. (2009). 'Green helmets: Eco-intervention in the twenty-first century', *Proceedings of the ASIL Annual Meeting*, *103*, 19–27.

Maquire, L. (2016). 'Identity Politics' Philosophy Talks' available at www.philosophytalk.org/blog/identity-politics [accessed 24/07/2023].

Mareš, M. (2011). 'Terrorism-free zone in East Central Europe? Strategic environment, risk tendencies, and causes of limited terrorist activities in the Visegrad Group countries', *Terrorism and Political Violence*, *23*(2), 233–253.

Martin, R. (2014). 'Overlapping consensus' In John Mandle and David Reidy (eds.) *The Cambridge Rawls Lexicon*, Cambridge: Cambridge University Press, pp. 588–594.

McClean, E. (2014). 'Hard evidence: Who uses veto in the UN Security Council most often – And for what?' *The Conversation*, 31 July 2014.

McDonald, M. (2012). *Security, the environment and emancipation: Contestation over environmental change*. Abingdon: Routledge.

McGuire, B. (2016). 'How Climate Change Triggers Earthquakes, Tsunamis and Volcanoes', *The Guardian*, 16 October, available at www.theguardian.com/

world/2016/oct/16/climate-change-triggers-earthquakes-tsunamis-volcanoes [accessed 24/07/2023].

McInnes, C. and Rushton, S. (2013). 'HIV/AIDS and securitization theory', *European Journal of International Relations*, *19*(1), 115–138.

McLaughlin, K. (2017). 'Jihadist Terrorists Have Long Had Spain in Their Sights – Here's Why' *The Conversation*, 18 August available at theconversation.com/jihadist-terrorists-have-long-had-spain-in-their-sights-heres-why-82703 [accessed 4/4/2019].

McMahan, J. (2004). 'The ethics of killing in war', *Ethics*, *114*(4), Symposium on Terrorism, War, and Justice (July 2004), 693–733.

McMahan, J. (2005). 'Just cause for war', *Ethics & International Affairs*, *19*(3), 1–21.

McMahan, J. (2006). 'The ethics of killing in war', *Philosophia*, *34*, 23–41.

McMahan, J. (2008). 'The morality of war and the law of war' In David Rodin and Henry Shue (eds.) *Just and unjust warriors: The moral and legal status of soldiers*, Oxford: Oxford University Press, pp. 19–43.

McMahan, J. (2009). *Killing in war*, Oxford: Oxford University Press.

McMahan, J. (2010). 'Humanitarian intervention, consent, and proportionality' In N. Ann Davis, Richard Keshen, and Jeff McMahan (eds.) *Ethics and humanity: themes from the philosophy of Jonathan Glover*, Oxford: Oxford University Press, pp. 45–73.

McMahan, J. (2018). 'Foreword' In Larry May (eds.) *The Cambridge handbook of the just war*, Cambridge: Cambridge University Press, pp. ix–xiii.

McSweeney, B. (1996). 'Identity and security: Buzan and the Copenhagen School', *Review of International Studies*, *22*(1), 81–93.

Mearsheimer, J. J. (2014). 'Why the Ukraine crisis is the West's fault: The liberal delusions that provoked Putin', *Foreign Affairs*, *93*, 77.

Medcalf, J. (2005). *NATO: A beginner's guide*. Oxford: Oneworld.

Meierding, E. (2013). 'Climate change and conflict: Avoiding small talk about the weather', *International Studies Review*, *15*(2), 185–203.

Memorandum on Security Assurances in Connection with Ukraine's Accession to the Treaty on the Non-Proliferation of Nuclear Weapons. (1994). 5 December; available at www.pircenter.org/media/content/files/12/13943175580.pdf [accessed 17/10/2019].

Miller, D. (2001). 'Distributing responsibilities', *The Journal of Political Philosophy*, *9*(4), 453–471.

Miller, D. (2007). *National responsibility and global justice*. Oxford: Oxford University Press.

Miller, D. (2009). 'The responsibility to protect human rights' In Lukas H. Meyer (ed.) *Legitimacy, justice and public international law*, Cambridge: Cambridge University Press, pp. 232–251.

Miller, D. (2016). *Strangers in our midst: The political philosophy of immigration*, Oxford: Oxford University Press.

Morello, C. (2017). 'U.S. Threatens Countries with Loss of Aid over U.N. Vote on Jerusalem', *The Washington Post*, 20 December 2017, available at: www.washingtonpost.com/world/national-security/us-threatens-countries-with-loss-of-aid-over-un-jerusalem-vote/2017/12/20/3ddacadc-e5bc-11e7-833f-155031558ff4_story.html?utm_term=.ea2e73e6b9b7 [accessed 26/02/2019].

Morris, J. and Wheeler, N. (2016). 'The responsibility not to veto: A responsibility too far?' In Alex J. Bellamy and Tim Dunne (eds.) *The Oxford handbook of the responsibility to protect*, Oxford: Oxford University Press, pp. 227–248.

Morkevicius, V. (2022). 'How do Russia's reasons for war stack up? An expert on "just war" explains', *The Conversation* Published: March 5, 2022, 1.39pm GMT

Mueller, J. E. (2006). *Overblown: How politicians and the terrorism industry inflate national security threats, and why we believe them.* New York City: Simon & Schuster.

Müller, G. and Ischinger, W. (2020). 'Entwicklung und Sicherheit gehören zusammen' *FAZ*, 14 February available at www.faz.net/aktuell/politik/sicherheitskonferenz/muenchner-sicherheitskonferenz-gastbeitrag-von-gerd-mueller-und-wolfgang-ischinger-16632571.html?GEPC=s5 [accessed 17.02.2020].

Mulgan, T. (2001). *The demands of consequentialism.* Oxford: Oxford University Press.

Nagel, T. (2005). 'The problem of global justice', *Philosophy & Public Affairs*, 33(2), 113–147.

NATO. (2021a). 'NATO 2030 Young Leaders' Recommendations and Conversation with the Secretary General', 4 Feb 2021, available at www.nato.int/cps/en/natohq/opinions_181209.htm?selectedLocale=en

NATO. (2021b). 'NATO in a Competitive World', 5 October, available at www.nato.int/cps/en/natohq/opinions_187140.htm

NATO. (1949/2019). 'The North Atlantic Treaty', 10 April 2019, available at www.nato.int/cps/en/natolive/official_texts_17120.htm [accessed 25/09/2019].

NATO. (2019). 'Relations with Sweden' available at www.nato.int/cps/en/natohq/topics_52535.htm[accessed 9/08/2021].

NATO. (2018). 'Resilience and Article 3' 25 June 18 available at www.nato.int/cps/en/natohq/topics_132722.htm [accessed 1/05/2019].

NATO. (2010). 'Strategic Concept "Active Engagement, Modern Defence"' available at www.nato.int/cps/en/natohq/topics_82705.htm [accessed 12/04/2023].

Neal, A. (2013). 'Legislative practices' In Mark B. Salter and Can E. Mutlu (eds.) *Research methods in critical security studies*, Abingdon: Routledge, pp. 125–128.

Neal, A. (2019). *Security as politics: Beyond the state of exception*. Edinburgh, Edinburgh University Press.

Neocleous, M. (2008). *Critique of security*. Edinburgh: Edinburgh University Press.

Nyman, J. (2018). *The energy security paradox: Rethinking energy (in) security in the United States and China*. Oxford: Oxford University Press.

Oberman, K. (2015). 'The myth of the optional war: Why states are required to wage the wars they are permitted to wage', *Philosophy & Public Affairs*, 43(4), 255–286.

O'Driscoll, C. and Lang, A. F. J. (2013). 'The just war tradition and the practice of political authority' In O'Driscoll, Cian, Lang, Antony F. Jr., and Williams, John. (eds.) *Just war: Authority, tradition, and practice*, Georgetown, Washington, DC: Georgetown University Press, pp. 1–16.

Official Journal of the European Union (2017). 'Commission Recommendation (EU) 2017/1584 of 13 September 2017 on coordinated response to large-scale cybersecurity incidents and crises', available at eur-lex.europa.eu/eli/reco/2017/1584/oj

O'Neill, K. (2009). *The environment and international relations*. Cambridge: Cambridge University Press.

Orend, B. (2006). *The morality of war*. Peterborough, Ontario: Broadview Press.

Orend, B. (2019). *War and political theory*. Cambridge: Polity.

Orford, A. (2012). 'Constituting order' In James Crawford and Martti Koskenniemi (eds.) *The Cambridge companion to international law*, Cambridge: Cambridge University Press, pp. 271–289.

Owens, D. (2015). 'On Duty', Philosophy Bites podcast, 2 September 2002, available at philosophybites.com/2015/09/david-owens-on-duty.html

Owens, P. (2012). 'Human security and the rise of the social', *Review of International Studies*, 38(3), 547–567.

Oxford Lib Guide. (2018). 'United Kingdom Law: Case la', available here ox.libguides.com/c.php?g=422832&p=2887381 [accessed 20/06/2019].

Panke, D. (2016). 'Living in an imperfect world? Incomplete contracting & the rational Design of International Organizations'. *Journal of International Organizations Studies*, 7(1), 25–38.

Panke, D. (2017). 'Regional actors in international security negotiations', *European Journal of Security Research*, 2, 5–21.

Parfit, D. (2011). *On what matters*, Vol 1. Oxford: Oxford University Press.

Parry, J. (2017a). 'Legitimate authority and the ethics of war: A map of the terrain', *Ethics & International Affairs*, 31(2), 169–189.

Parry, J. (2017b). 'Defensive harm, consent, and intervention', *Philosophy & Public Affairs, 45*(4), 356–396.

Parry, J. (2022). 'What's wrong with paternalism?' Jurisprudence Discussion Group, Oxford: Oxford University available at www.youtube.com/watch?v=IfLcAJbi6LA

Pattison, J. (2010). *Humanitarian intervention and the responsibility to protect: Who should intervene?.* Oxford: Oxford University Press.

Pattison, J. (2014). *The morality of private war.* Oxford: Oxford University Press.

Pattison, J. (2018). *The alternatives to war.* Oxford: Oxford University Press.

Pattison, J. (2022). 'Beyond imperfection: The demands of the international responsibility to protect', *Global Responsibility to Protect, 14,* 105–108.

Peeters, W., De Smet, A., Diependaele, L., Sterckx, S., McNeal, R. H., and De Smet, A. (2015). *Climate change and individual responsibility: Agency, moral disengagement and the motivational gap.* Basingstoke: Palgrave McMillan.

Peter, F. (2017). 'Political legitimacy' In Edward N. Zalta (ed.) *The Stanford encyclopedia of philosophy*, plato.stanford.edu/archives/sum2017/entries/legitimacy/

Peters, A. (2009). 'Treaty Making Powers' Max Planck Encyclopaedia of Public International Law [MPEPIL], Oxford; Oxford Public International Law available at: opil.ouplaw.com/view/10.1093/law:epil/9780199231690/law-9780199231690-e1494

Philipsen, L. (2020). 'Performative securitization: From conditions of success to conditions of possibility', *Journal of International Relations and Development, 23*(1), 139–163.

Pinker, S. (2011). *The better angels of our nature.* New York, NY: Viking.

Pogge, T. (2007). *John Rawls: His life and theory of justice.* Oxford: Oxford University Press.

Pogge, T. W. (2001). 'Eradicating systemic poverty: Brief for a global resources dividend', *Journal of Human Development, 2*(1), 59–77.

Polko, P. and Ratajczak, S. (2021). 'Vaccination as a matter of security and security management in European Union', *European Research Studies Journal, 24*(Special 4), 446–456.

Pouliot, V. (2010). *International security in practice: The politics of NATO-Russia diplomacy.* Cambridge: Cambridge University Press.

Rachels, J. (1986). *The elements of moral philosophy.* New York: McGraw-Hill/Random.

Rafanelli, L. M. (2021). *Promoting justice across borders: The ethics of reform intervention.* Oxford: Oxford University Press.

Rasmussen, A. (2016). 'Crisis in Libya: Who's to blame?' | UpFront, available here www.youtube.com/watch?v=AZHB28DnXYU [accessed 9/11/23].

Rasmussen, A. (2019). 'NATO Boss: Libya Still a "Model Intervention" available at: www.aljazeera.com/programmes/upfront/2016/10/nato-boss-libya-model-intervention-161022075802390.html [accessed 23/09/2019].

Rawls, J. (1996). *Political liberalism*. Cambridge, MA: Harvard University Press.

Rawls, J. (1997). 'The idea of public reason revisited', *The University of Chicago Law Review*, Summer, 64(3), 765–807.

Rawls, J. (2001). *The law of peoples*. Cambridge: Harvard University Press.

Raz, J. (1986). *The morality of freedom*. Oxford: Clarendon Press.

Ripstein, A. (1998). *Equality, responsibility, and the law*. Cambridge: Cambridge University Press.

Risse, M. (2012). *On global justice*. Princeton: Princeton University Press.

Roberts, A. and Kingsbury, B. (1993). 'Introduction: The UN's roles in international society since 1945' In Adam Roberts and Benedict Kingsbury (eds.) *United Nations, divided world: The UN's roles in international relations*, Oxford: Clarendon Press, pp. 1–62.

Rodin, D. (2002). *War & self-defense*. Oxford: Oxford University Press.

Roff, H. M. (2013). *Global justice, Kant and the responsibility to protect*. London: Routledge.

Rotaru, V. (2020). 'Silencing the contestant. Legitimizing Crimea's annexation by mimicking the West', *European Security*, 1, 96–118.

Rotberg, R. I. (2004). 'The failure and collapse of nation-states: Breakdown, prevention, and repair' In Robert Rotberg (ed.) *When states fail: Causes and consequences*, Princeton: Princeton University Press, pp. 1–49.

Runciman, D. (2003). 'Moral responsibility and the problem of representing the state' In Toni Erskine (ed.) *Can institutions have responsibilities?*, London: Palgrave Macmillan, pp. 41–50.

Sagan, S. D. and Waltz, K. N. (2010). 'Is nuclear zero the best option?', *The National Interest*, (109), 88–96.

Sarat, A. (2010). 'Introduction: Towards new conceptions of the relationship of law and sovereignty under conditions of emergency' In Austin Sarat (ed.) *Sovereignty, emergency, legality*, Cambridge: Cambridge University Press, pp. 1–15.

Scheid, D. E. (2014). 'Introduction to armed humanitarian intervention' In Don E. Scheid (ed.) *The ethics of armed humanitarian intervention*, Cambridge: Cambridge University Press, pp. 3–25.

Schimmelfennig, F. (2001). 'The community trap: Liberal norms, rhetorical action, and the Eastern enlargement of the European Union', *International Organization*, 55(1), 47–80.

Scott, L. (2020). 'International history in the twentieth century' In John Baylis, Steve Smith, and Patricia Owens (eds.) *The globalisation of world politics*, Oxford: Oxford University Press, pp. 54–69.

Selby, J., Daoust, G., and Hoffman, C. (2022). *Divided environments: An international political ecology of climate change, water and security.* Cambridge: Cambridge University Press.

Shea, J. (2019). 'NATO at 70: An Opportunity to Recalibrate' *Nato Review* 5.04.2019, available here: www.nato.int/docu/review/2019/Also-in-2019/nato-at-70-an-opportunity-to-recalibrate/EN/index.htm [accessed 25/07/2019].

Shue, H. (2018). 'Last resort and proportionality' In Seth Lazar and Helen Frowe (eds). *The Oxford handbook of the ethics of war*, Oxford: Oxford University Press, pp. 260–276.

Singer, P. (1972). 'Famine, affluence, and morality', *Philosophy & Public Affairs*, *1*(3), 229–243.

Singer, P. (2013). 'The Why and How of Effective Altruism' TED Talk available here www.ted.com/talks/peter_singer_the_why_and_how_of_effective_altruism [accessed 08/04/2019].

Smith, D. (2018). 'Trump Grants Troops Guarding Border Authority to Use "Lethal Force" – Report' *The Guardian*, 21 November 2018, available at: www.theguardian.com/us-news/2018/nov/21/trump-us-mexico-border-troops-decision-memorandum-force-report [accessed 18/02/2019].

Soanes, C. (2000). *The compact English dictionary*. Oxford: Oxford University Press.

Sorell, T. (2013). *Emergencies and politics: A sober Hobbesian approach.* Cambridge: Cambridge University Press.

Sperling, J. and Webber, M. (2017). 'NATO and the Ukraine crisis: Collective securitisation', *European Journal of International Security*, *2*(1), 19–46.

Sperling, J. and Webber, M. (2019). 'The European Union: Security governance and collective securitisation', *West European Politics*, *42*(2), 228–260.

Statman, D. (2008). 'On the success condition for legitimate self-defense', *Ethics*, *118*(4), 659–686.

Steinberger, P. J. (2002). 'Hobbesian resistance', *American Journal of Political Science*, *46*(4), 856–865.

Stoltenberg, J. (2020). 'Remarks on Launching #NATO2030 – Strengthening the Alliance in an Increasingly Competitive World', 8 June 2020, available at www.nato.int/cps/en/natohq/opinions_176197.htm

Stritzel, H. (2007). 'Towards a theory of securitization: Copenhagen and beyond', *European Journal of International Relations*, *13*(3), 357–383.

Tesón, F. R. (2014). 'The moral basis of armed humanitarian intervention' In Don E. Scheid (eds.) *The ethics of armed humanitarian intervention*, Cambridge: Cambridge University Press, pp. 61–77.

Tesón, F. R., and Van der Vossen, B. (2017). *Debating humanitarian intervention: Should we try to save strangers?*. Oxford: Oxford University Press.

Thakur, R. (2017). *The United Nations, peace and security: From collective security to the responsibility to protect*, second edition, Cambridge: Cambridge University Press.

The General Secretariat of the Council (GSC). (2020). 'EU at the UN General Assembly' available at www.consilium.europa.eu/en/policies/unga/ [accessed 4/02/20].

Thumfart, J. (2022). 'The (Il)Legitimacy of cybersecurity. An application of just securitization theory to cybersecurity based on the principle of subsidiarity (November 17, 2022)', *Applied Cybersecurity & Internet Governance*, 1(1), 97–120.

Topgyal, T. (2016). 'The Tibetan self-immolations as counter-securitization: Towards an inter-unit theory of securitization', *Asian Security*, 12(3), 166–187.

Trahan, J. (2020). *Existing legal limits to security council veto power in the face of atrocity crimes*. Cambridge: Cambridge University Press.

Trahan, J. (2022). 'Why the veto power is not unlimited: A response to critiques of, and questions about, existing legal limits to the veto power in the face of atrocity crimes', *Case Western Reserve Journal of International Law*, *54*, 109 (2022). Available at: scholarlycommons.law.case.edu/jil/vol54/iss1/9

Trump, D. J. (2017). *National security strategy of the United States of America*. Executive Office of The President Washington DC Washington United States.

UN. (2005). 'Vienna Convention on the Law of Treaties 1969' available at legal.un.org/ilc/texts/instruments/english/conventions/1_1_1969.pdf [accessed 05/02/2020].

UN. (2019). 'UN Charter' (full text) available at www.un.org/en/sections/un-charter/un-charter-full-text/ [accessed 15/07/2019].

UNA. (2015). 'UN Security Council and the Responsibility to Protect: Voluntary Restraint of the Veto in Situations of Mass Atrocity Briefing by UNA – UK', October 2015, available at una.org.uk/sites/default/files/Veto%20R2P%20code%20of%20conduct%20briefing%20October%202015%20update_0.pdf [accessed 9/08/2021].

UN University. (2013). 'David Miller – Extent and Limits of Global Justice' available at: www.youtube.com/watch?v=8RkoKxuCUvU [accessed 25/09/2019].

UNFCCC. (2018). 'The Paris Agreement', 22 October 2018, available at unfccc.int/process-and-meetings/the-paris-agreement/the-paris-agreement [accessed 26/02/2019].

UNGA. (2005). 'Resolution Adopted by the General Assembly on 16 September 2005' available at www.un.org/en/development/desa/population/migration/generalassembly/docs/globalcompact/A_RES_60_1.pdf [accessed 25/06/2019].

Varden, H. (2011). 'Duties, positive and negative' In Chatterjee, Deen K. (ed.) *Encyclopedia of global justice*, Dordrecht: Springer, pp. 281–283.

Vuori, J. (2008). 'Illocutionary logic and strands of securitization: Applying the theory of securitization to the study of non-democratic political orders', *European Journal of International Relations*, 14, 65–99.

Wæver, O. (1989). 'Security, The Speech Act: Analysing the Politics of a Word' unpublished paper, presented at the Research Training Seminar, Sostrup Manor, revised Jerusalem/Tel Aviv 25–26 June 1989.

Wæver, O. (1995). 'Securitization and desecuritization' In Ronnie D. Lipschutz (ed.) *On security*, New York: Columbia University Press, pp. 46–86.

Wæver, O. (2003). 'Securitisation: Taking stock of a Research Programme in Security Studies', unpublished manuscript.

Wæver, O. (2008). 'The changing agenda of societal security' In Brauch H. G., et al., (eds.) *Globalization and environmental challenges*, Berlin, Heidelberg: Springer, pp. 581–593.

Wæver, O. (2011). 'Politics, security, theory', *Security Dialogue*, 42(4–5), 465–480.

Wæver, O. (2015). 'The theory act: Responsibility and exactitude as seen from securitization' *International Relations*, 29(1), 121–127.

Wæver, O. (2017). 'Afterword: The Arctic security constellation', *Politik*, 20(3). doi.org/10.7146/politik.v20i3.97157

Wæver, O. and Buzan, B. (2020). 'Racism and responsibility – The critical limits of deepfake methodology in security studies: A reply to Howell and Richter-Montpetit', *Security Dialogue*, 51(4), 386–394. doi: 10.1177/0967010620916153.

Walker, S. (2018). 'Hungary to Criminalise Migrant Helpers with "Stop Soros" Legislation', *The Guardian*, 29 May 2018, available at: www.theguardian.com/world/2018/may/29/hungary-criminalises-migrant-helpers-stop-george-soros-legislation [accessed 20/02/2019].

Wallander, C. A. (2018). 'NATO's enemies within: How democratic decline could destroy the alliance', *Foreign Affairs*, 97, 70.

Walt, S. (2019). 'Who Will Save the Amazon (and How)?' *Foreign Policy*, 5 August 2019, available at foreignpolicy.com/2019/08/05/who-will-invade-brazil-to-save-the-amazon/ [accessed 5/6/2020].

Walzer, M. (1990). 'The communitarian critique of liberalism'. *Political Theory*, 18(1), 6–23. www.jstor.org/stable/191477

Walzer, M. (2006 [1977]). *Just and unjust wars: A moral argument with historical illustrations*, fourth edition, New York: Basic Books.

Watts, J. (2016). 'Zika Virus Command Center leads Biggest Military Operation in Brazil's History' *The Guardian* 30 March 2016 www.theguardian.com/world/2016/mar/30/brazil-zika-war-virus-military-operation [accessed 25/02/2019].

Webber, M. (2009). 'Thinking NATO through Theoretically' Paper presented to the ECPR Joint Sessions, Lisbon 14–19 April 2009-04-08 Workshop 24: 'Theorizing NATO'

Weber, M. (1946). *Politics as Vocation* available at polisci2.ucsd.edu/foundation/documents/03Weber1918.pdf [accessed 7/03/2019].

Weinberg, J. (2011). 'Is government supererogation possible?', *Pacific Philosophical Quarterly*, 92, 263–281.

Weiss, T. G. (2006). 'R2P after 9/11 and the World Summit', *Wisconsin, International Law Journal*, 24, 741.

Weiss, T. G. (2016). *What's wrong with the United Nations and how to fix it*, 3rd edition, Cambridge: Polity.

Weiss, T. G. and Thakur, R. (2010). *Global governance and the UN: A unfinished journey*. Bloomington and Indianapolis: Indiana University Press.

Wellman, C. H. and Cole, P. (2011). *Debating the ethics of immigration: Is there a right to exclude?*. Oxford: Oxford University Press.

Welsh, J. (2012). 'Who should act? Collective responsibility and the responsibility to protect' In W. Andy Knight and Frazer Egerton (eds.) *The Routledge handbook of the responsibility to protect*, London: Routledge, pp. 103–114.

Welsh, J. (2013). 'The Evolution of the Responsibility to Protect: Securing Individuals in a World of States' Centre for International Governance Innovation available at: www.youtube.com/watch?v=P3WJZND3z8M [accessed 07/10/2019]

Welsh, J. (2016). 'R2P's next ten years: Deepening and extending the consensus' In Alex J. Bellamy and Tim Dunne (eds.) *The Oxford handbook of the responsibility to protect*, Oxford: Oxford University Press, pp. 984–999.

Welsh, J. M. (2019). 'Norm robustness and the responsibility to protect', *Journal of Global Security Studies*, 4(1), 53–72.

Wenar, L. (2021). 'John Rawls' In Edward N. Zalta (ed.) *The Stanford encyclopaedia of philosophy* (Summer 2021 Edition), plato.stanford.edu/archives/sum2021/entries/rawls/.

West, D. M. (2016). 'Internet Shutdowns Cost Countries $2.4 Billion Last Year, Center for Technology Innovation at Brookings', available at www.brookings.edu/wp-content/uploads/2016/10/intenet-shutdowns-v-3.pdf [accessed 18/02/2019].

Wheeler, N. J. (2018). *Trusting enemies*. Oxford: Oxford University Press.

Wheeler, N. and Dunne, T. (2012). 'Operationalising protective intervention: Alternative models of authorisation' In W. Andy Knight and Frazer

Egerton (eds.) *The Routledge handbook of the responsibility to protect*, London: Routledge, pp. 87–102.

Wheeler, N. J. and T. Dunne. (1998). 'Good international citizenship: A third way for British foreign policy', *International Affairs*, 74(4), 847–870.

WHO. (2012). 'Global Strategy for Dengue Prevention and Control 2012–2020' available at: afro.who.int/sites/default/files/2017-06/9789241504034_eng.pdf [accessed 25/02/2019].

WHO. (2017). 'Vector Borne Diseases, 31 October 2017', available at: www.who.int/news-room/fact-sheets/detail/vector-borne-diseases [accessed 20/02/2019].

WHO. (2018). 'Dengue: A Mosquito-Borne Disease' available at: www.who.int/bangladesh/news/detail/28-05-2018-dengue-a-mosquito-borne-disease [accessed 10/04/2023].

WHO. (2023). DROUGHT available at: [accessed 10/04/2023].

Whyte, C. and Mazanec, B. (2018). *Understanding cyber warfare: Politics, policy and strategy*. London: Routledge.

Williams, G. L. and Jones, B. J. (2001). 'Collective security or collective defence?' In Geoffrey Lee Williams and Barkley Jared Jones (eds.) *NATO and the transatlantic alliance in the 21st century*, London: Palgrave Macmillan, pp. 87–96.

Williams, J. (2015). *Ethics, diversity & world politics*. Oxford: Oxford University Press.

Wolfendale, J. (2017). 'Defining war' In Michael L. Gross and Tamar Meisels (eds.) *Soft war: The ethics of unarmed conflict*, Cambridge: Cambridge University Press, pp. 16–32.

Wolfendale, J. (2022). White supremacy as an existential threat: A response to Rita Floyd's The morality of security: A theory of just securitization, *European Journal of International Security*, 7(2), May 2022, 248–282. DOI: doi.org/10.1017/eis.2022.3.

Woollard, F. (2015). *Doing & allowing harm*. Oxford: Oxford University Press.

Woollard, F. (2016). 'Doing and allowing', *Oxford Bibliographies*, 1. DOI: 10.1093/obo/9780195396577-0304

Woocher, L. (2012). 'The responsibility to prevent' In W. Andy Knight and Frazer Egerton (eds.) *The Routledge handbook of the responsibility to protect*, London: Routledge, pp. 22–35.

Young, S. P. (2006). 'Rawlsian reasonableness: A problematic presumption?', *Canadian Journal of Political Science*, 39(1), 159–180.

Zedner, L. (2009). *Security*. Abingdon: Routledge.

Zimmerman, M. J. (2010). 'Responsibility: Act and omission' In John Skorupski (ed.) *The Routledge companion to ethics*, London: Routledge, pp. 607–616.

Index